W9-CXX-817

CYPRUS: A PLACE OF ARMS

CYPRUS
A PLACE OF ARMS

POWER POLITICS AND ETHNIC CONFLICT IN THE EASTERN MEDITERRANEAN

ROBERT STEPHENS

FREDERICK A. PRAEGER, *Publishers*
New York · Washington · London

FREDERICK A. PRAEGER, *Publishers*
111 Fourth Avenue, New York 3, N.Y., U.S.A.
77–79 Charlotte Street, London W.1, England

Published in the United States of America in 1966
by Frederick A. Praeger, Inc., Publishers

Library of Congress Catalog Card Number: 66–12987

PRINTED IN GREAT BRITAIN

FOR MY MOTHER

CONTENTS

MAPS

(*Maps drawn by Richard Leadbetter of the* Observer)

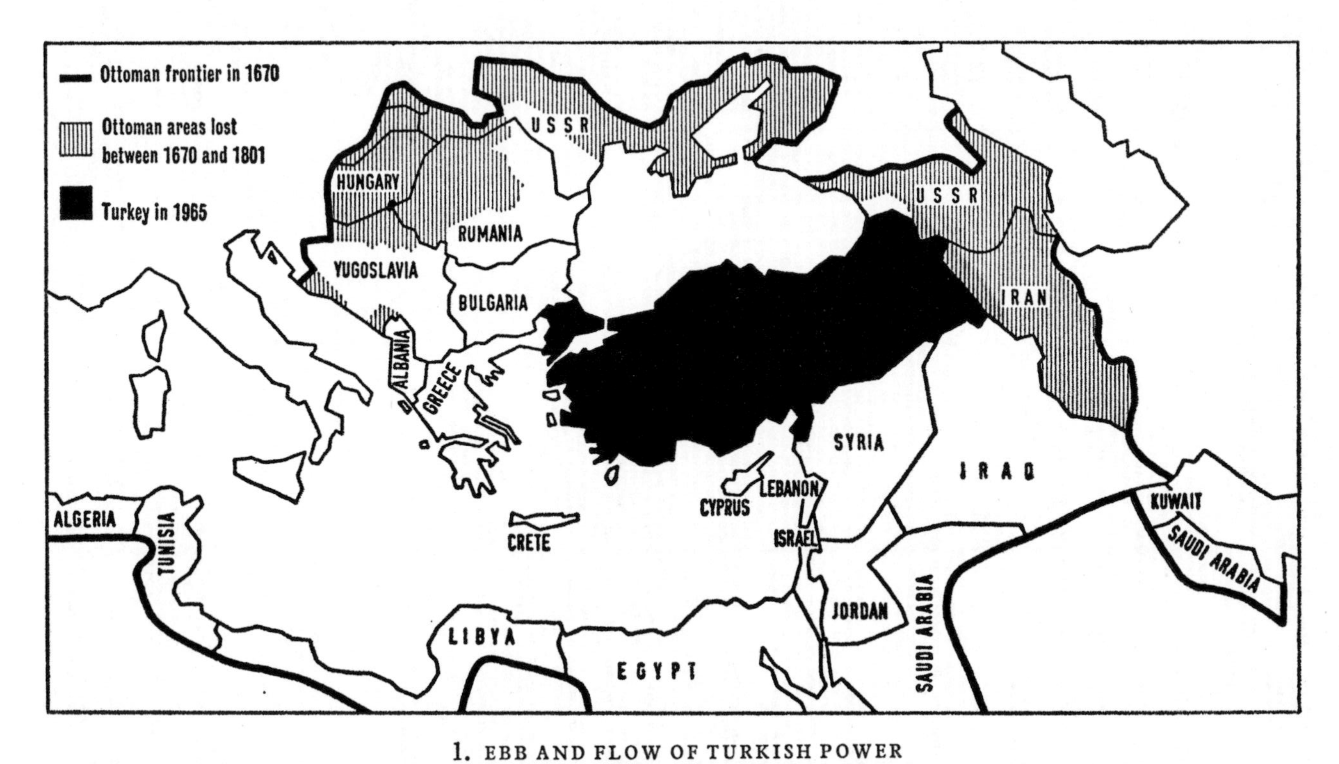

1. EBB AND FLOW OF TURKISH POWER

The boundaries of the Ottoman Empire and the Turkish Republic superimposed on the political map of 1965

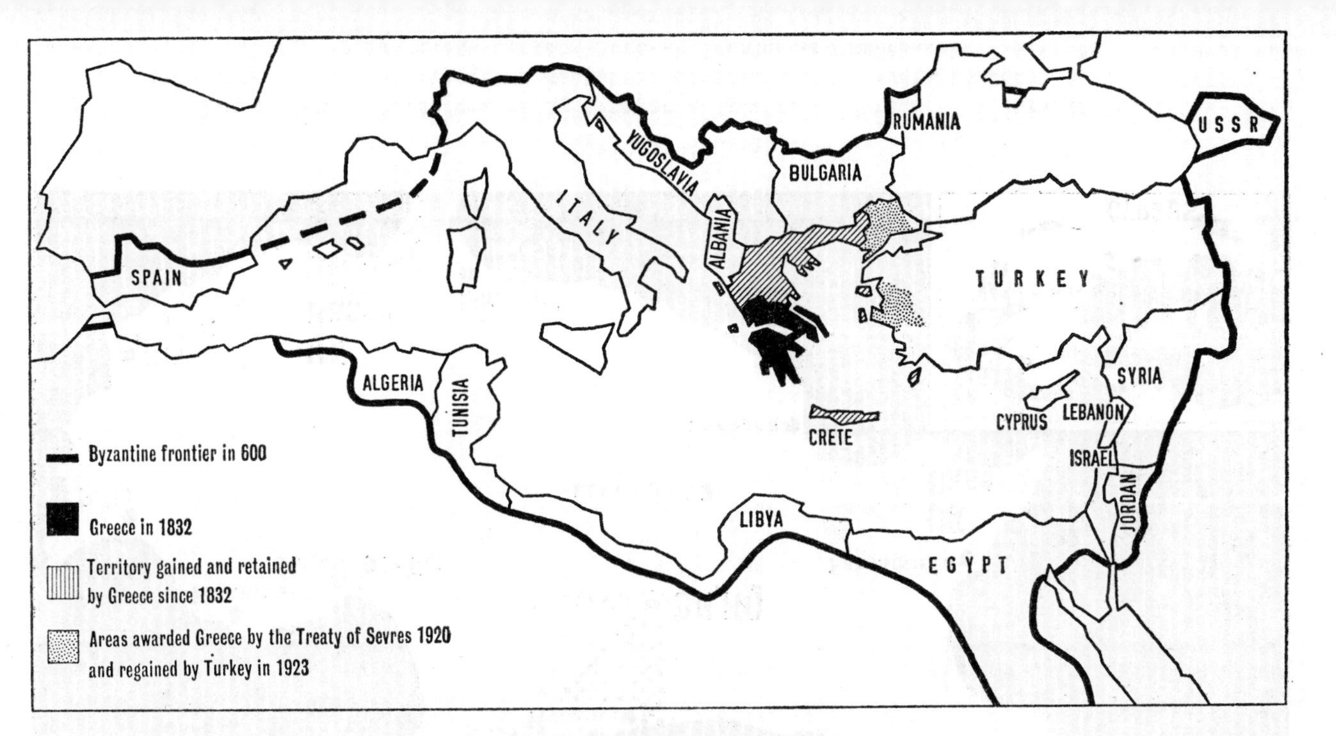

2. GREEK DECLINE AND REVIVAL

The boundaries of the Byzantine Empire and the Greek Kingdom superimposed on the political map of 1965

3. CYPRUS IN 1965

The chequered area represents the approximate location of the main Turkish enclave.
Other places with substantial sectors under Turkish control include
Famagusta, Larnaca, Limassol, Louroujina and Kokkina

Introduction

CYPRUS is an ancient and beautiful Mediterranean island, smaller than Sicily and Sardinia and with a population of little more than half a million. Why did it become a world problem threatening war and arousing deep national emotions like those once stirred by Ireland or Alsace-Lorraine? Every party to the Cyprus dispute has a different, heart-felt answer. But there are some obvious reasons which even the heart cannot deny: Cyprus is not only divided by race, language and religion but also lies in a sensitive area of international politics near the strategic and cultural meeting-point of Europe and the Middle East.

In the island itself, 80 per cent of the people speak Greek and are Greek Orthodox Christians by religion. About 18 per cent are Turkish-speaking Moslems. The present dispute between them is the latest—and perhaps the last—episode in a long and often bloody struggle between Greek Christians and Turkish Moslems in the Near East, which began in the Middle Ages with the gradual conquest of the Greek-speaking Byzantine empire by the Turks. It was revived and intensified in the last century when the Greeks began to win back their independence, first in mainland Greece and then in the Greek-speaking islands.

For the Greek Cypriots, Greece is their motherland and their protector from Turkish domination, although it is five hundred miles away. For the Turkish Cypriots, their motherland and their protector against Greek domination is mainland Turkey, only forty miles distant, which, as the heartland of the Ottoman empire, ruled Cyprus for three centuries. But the problem spreads wider. Greece and Turkey are members of NATO and Britain keeps two military bases in Cyprus to support her Middle East commitments. This makes the future of the island and the balance of power in the area of intense interest to America, Russia, Britain and many other states in Europe and the Middle East.

The reasons which led Britain to gain control of Cyprus from Turkey in 1878 were primarily strategic, reinforced by political ambitions in the Middle East. The same reasons impelled her to oppose the Greek

Cypriot demand for enosis, or union with Greece, when under the leadership of Archbishop Makarios this demand flared up into open rebellion after the second world war. Turkey also opposed enosis and proposed instead partition of the island, which the Greeks rejected. Turkey argued that only her physical control of part of the island would properly protect the Turkish minority and ensure Turkey's own security. In 1959, after nearly five years of terrorism and guerrilla warfare against British rule—led by the Greek Cypriot organisation, EOKA, under Colonel, now General, Grivas—a compromise settlement was reached in the Treaties of Zürich and London. Cyprus became an independent republic within the Commonwealth. Both enosis and partition were ruled out and Britain kept her sovereignty over two small areas to be used for military bases. There were elaborate constitutional safeguards for the Turkish community. Turkish troops, together with Greek troops, were stationed in the island and a treaty of guarantee gave Britain, Greece and Turkey certain rights to intervene in Cyprus if the agreements were broken.

The constitution, however, proved unworkable in practice, largely because of continued suspicions and fears for the future on the part of both Greek and Turkish Cypriots. In December 1963, President Makarios proposed a revision of the constitution, but Turkey declared this unacceptable. The growing tension led to widespread communal fighting just before Christmas of that year. Turkey threatened to intervene and so did Greece. Britain then stepped in as policeman and peace-maker. But Britain could not solve the problem either alone or with the help of America and NATO, so it went to the United Nations. A UN force, including British troops, took over the peace-keeping in Cyprus and a UN mediator was appointed to help produce a political settlement. In January 1966, when this book was completed, the UN force was still keeping an uneasy peace in the island, and a political solution was not yet in sight.

Such are the bare outlines of a problem of which a great historian of the Near East, Dr William Miller, observed, in his *History of the Greek People* more than forty years ago: 'Strategic reasons may delay, but history will doubtless record, the inevitable solution of this question'.[1]

Naturally, I hope that this book will enable the background of the current Cyprus dispute to be better understood. If, as I also hope, the dispute has been settled before the book appears, its matter may still be of interest as a small contribution to the history of the problem and as a study of a kind of situation that is likely to recur in other parts of the world. Although to most of the world Cyprus is still probably known chiefly for the rebellion and civil war which have brought it into the newspaper headlines and on to the television screens during the past ten years, this period is only a decade in the life of a country whose recorded history stretches back nearly four thousand years.

Much has already been written about the EOKA rebellion against the British and it is still too early for a more thorough history of it than the journalistic accounts and memoirs, many of them excellent and revealing in their fields, which have already appeared. Nor is it my intention merely to try to present a short digest of the history of Cyprus as a whole. For those interested in the often fascinating details of Cypriot vicissitudes from the New Stone Age to Archbishop Makarios—especially its most colourful period as a Crusader outpost under the Lusignan kings—there are already numerous works available, including the monumental four-volume *History of Cyprus* by Sir George Hill; the one-volume *Cyprus in History* by the Greek Cypriot historian, Doros Alastos; and the short, delightful and entertaining *Cyprus* by Sir Harry Luke.

Although I have included in this book an outline of the general history of Cyprus and some account of the EOKA rebellion, my main purpose, as the subtitle suggests, has been to try to relate the present problems of Cyprus to the broader framework of Near Eastern and world politics and, particularly, to the modern history in the Near East of the peoples now most closely concerned: the Greeks, the Turks and the British. I have therefore concentrated selectively on three elements whose confluence and interaction has formed the background of the Cyprus problem today and whose meaning and importance are perhaps still not fully understood in Western countries: the rise of Greek nationalism and the Hellenic idea; the collapse of the Ottoman empire and the creation of modern Turkish nationalism; and the rise and decline of British imperial power in the Middle East. These three elements began to act upon one another at the beginning of the nineteenth century and I have touched upon the history of earlier times only in so far as it is needed to explain this interaction, particularly the manner in which Cyprus has now emerged as the climax, or perhaps rather the epilogue, to the secular conflict between Greek and Turk, and as part of the last as well as the first chapter of Britain's career as a Near Eastern imperial power.

If Cyprus is now caught in the climax of old historic processes, it may also be the starting point of new ones. A small problem in itself, it reflects great issues. Linked with the fate of three famous imperial races, the Greeks, the Turks and the British, it illuminates some of the problems created when old empires give way to new nations: the fate of minorities, the stability of new states and the viability of small ones, the ability of the United Nations to replace either a single imperial power or such an alliance as the nineteenth-century Concert of Powers in dealing with problems of national minorities and international security.

The scheme of the book is therefore as follows: Chapter 1 gives some description of the island and its people and their history up to the Turkish conquest in the sixteenth century. This is followed by chapters on the Ottoman empire, including its impact on Cyprus, and on the Greek national movement which led to the independence of modern Greece. Chapter 4 brings the British nearer to the centre of the stage with the Congress of Berlin, the Cyprus Convention of 1878 which gave Britain control of the island, and the new Near Eastern policy inspired by Disraeli which lay behind it. Chapter 5 describes the development of the Turkish revolution, and the relations of Greece, Turkey and the great powers in dealing with Crete and the Balkan Wars. In Chapter 6 an attempt is made to show how the simultaneous collapse of the European great power system and the rise of both Greek expansionism and Turkish nationalism led to a climax of disaster for almost all concerned: the first world war, which brought about the fall of the Ottoman empire, the Greek defeat and withdrawal in Anatolia, and, for the victorious British and French, the dubious compensation of imperial gains in the Middle East as against their enormous war losses in Europe.

Chapter 7 describes the situation between the wars after the settlement between Greece, Turkey and the Allies at the Treaty of Lausanne; Cyprus is transformed into a British crown colony and a renewed agitation of the Greek Cypriots for union with Greece leads to a mild revolt, the burning of Government House and a long suppression of constitutional liberties. Britain's Middle East power seems at its peak and Greece and Turkey are busy at home with reconstruction, reform and the struggle between dictatorship and democracy.

The second world war and its aftermath up to 1950, and their effect on relations between Cyprus, Greece, Turkey, Britain and other great powers form the theme of Chapter 8. It covers briefly the Greek civil war, the rise of parliamentary democracy in Turkey, the failure of the attempt to introduce a new constitution into Cyprus and the revival of the Enosis campaign; the attempted entry into the Middle East arena of Soviet Russia through pressure on Greece, Turkey and Iran, and the counter-intervention of the United States with the proclamation of the Truman Doctrine. Chapters 9, 10 and 11 cover the period from 1950 to 1958 during which the Cyprus question becomes an international issue with the launching of the EOKA rebellion and Greece's decision to take the matter to the United Nations. Britain, forced to withdraw from Egypt and other parts of the Middle East and repulsed at Suez, fights to hold sovereignty over Cyprus for military and political reasons, but begins talks with Greece and Turkey. The period of more serious negotiation, following a British decision that sovereignty is not needed over the whole island but only over a base, and leading to the Zürich and London agreements in 1959, is described in Chapter 12. The condition of the new Cyprus Republic and the gradual breakdown of its constitution, coinciding with important political changes in both Greece and Turkey are dealt with in Chapter 13, which also describes the effect of the changing international political climate, the easing of the cold war and the adherence of Cyprus to the policy of non-alignment and the Afro-Asian bloc of nations. Chapter 14 gives an account of the 'Christmas crisis' at the end of 1963, the outbreak of communal fighting in Cyprus with the threat of Turkish intervention, the British intervention as peace-keepers and mediators, the unsuccessful attempts to find a settlement through the London conference, through NATO or direct American diplomacy, and the taking of the problem to the United Nations.

Chapter 15 deals with the United Nations' efforts to keep the peace with an international force in Cyprus and to find a political settlement through both the United Nations and other diplomatic channels. Chapters 16 and 17 comment on some of the proposed solutions for Cyprus, sum up some of the lessons of the past and look for pointers to the future in terms of Greco-Turkish relations, Britain's policy in the Middle East and the role of the United Nations as keeper of the peace and protector of minorities.

This book does not claim to be a work of original scholarship: it is rather more in the nature of a political essay. Consequently, I have drawn heavily for information on the works of others, especially up to the period of the second world war when my own personal acquaintance began with Cyprus, Greece, Turkey and other countries of the Middle

East. For the later period also, I am naturally indebted to other writers but have been helped, especially in matters of interpretation, by personal knowledge as a working journalist, both 'in the field' and as a result of covering diplomatic conferences relating to some of the places, people and events described.

I am deeply grateful to all those ministers, political leaders, military men, officials, journalists and others, in Cyprus, Greece, Turkey and Britain who kindly gave me their time to talk about the subject of this book. They included Archbishop Makarios and Dr Fazil Küchük and other Greek and Turkish members of the Cyprus government; ex-president Inönü and Mr Bayulken, director-general of the Turkish Ministry of Foreign Affairs; Mr Costopoulos, former Greek foreign minister, and three of his predecessors in that office, Mr Stefanopoulos, Mr Theotokis, and Mr Averoff (to whom I am particularly indebted); Mr George Cavounides, director-general of Information for the Greek government, whose help both in arranging interviews and in providing the benefit of his own long political experience was invaluable; the late General Thimayya, commander of the United Nations force in Cyprus until his untimely death in December 1965; Mr Duncan Sandys, PC, MP, former secretary for Commonwealth Relations and minister of Defence; Sir Arthur Clark, former British high commissioner in Cyprus; Mr Leslie Finer, Mr Kenneth Mackenzie and Mr David Hotham, correspondents for the *Observer* and other journals in Athens, Nicosia and Ankara respectively; and Mr Papademos of the Cyprus High Commission in London.

I am especially grateful to Miss Elizabeth Monroe, who read the typescript and made many valuable suggestions; to Mr John Silverlight of the *Observer* for his careful reading of the typescript; and to Mr John Dickie of the *Daily Mail* for helpful comments on the later chapters.

This book could not have been written but for the *Observer* in whose service I have travelled to the countries it deals with, and which generously gave me time off in which to write it.

At the end of the book will be found a list of the principal books, documents and other sources on which I have drawn, together with suggestions for further reading for those who are interested in following up some aspects in greater detail. But I should like to acknowledge here my particular indebtedness to the three books on the history of Cyprus already mentioned, and also to *The Ottoman Empire and its Successors* and *A History of the Greek People* by Dr William Miller; C. M. Woodhouse's brilliant *Greek War of Independence*; Professor Edward S.

Forster's *A Short History of Modern Greece*; A. Pallis's *Greece's Anatolian Venture and After*; Professor Arnold Toynbee's *The Western Question in Greece and Turkey*; Professor Bernard Lewis's masterly *Emergence of Modern Turkey*; my old friend Geoffrey Lewis's lively *Turkey*; Lord Kinross's authoritative biography of *Ataturk*; J. A. R. Marriott's *The Eastern Question*; and Charles Foley's vivid account of the rebellion and civil war in Cyprus in *Island in Revolt* and *Legacy of Strife*.

CHAPTER ONE

The Imperial Sanctuary

CYPRUS is the legendary birthplace of Venus, but during its history of nearly four thousand years it has often seemed more like the seat of Mars. 'The rosy realm of Venus, the romantic Kingdom of the Crusades', was how Disraeli described the island in a letter to his sister during a visit there in 1831. But forty-seven years later, in the Convention he made in 1878 with Sultan Abdul Hamid of Turkey, Disraeli described Cyprus more accurately as a 'place of arms' which Britain must control in order to defend the creaking empire of her ally, the sultan, against the ambitions of Russia.

Yet, although the island has often suffered from the sword, the Cypriots themselves are not a warlike people. Compared with other Mediterranean islanders, such as the Cretans or Sicilians, they had for long a reputation for being mild and docile, albeit stubborn. They have produced saints, philosophers and growers of wine rather than soldiers and statesmen. There is a legend that we owe champagne to vines brought home to France by a Crusader count from Cyprus. Zeno, the founder of the Stoic school of philosophy, might still fairly claim to be the island's most famous citizen.

Certainly, some of its foreign rulers made their mark as warriors. Such a one was the Lusignan monarch, Peter I: an indefatigable Crusader who was received in state by Edward III of England and dined by the Lord Mayor of London in 1362. After ten years of battle with the Moslems, during which time he sacked Alexandria and slaughtered twenty thousand men, women and children, Peter died in his bed —but not peacefully. His jealous wife, Eleanor, to whom he was notoriously unfaithful, egged on some of his barons to kill him as he lay with one of his mistresses. They cut off his head, and a knight, Jacques de Nores, 'proceeded to cut off those organs that had contributed to Peter's undoing'.[1]

But, until Archbishop Makarios and General Grivas in our day, the only native Cypriots who can be said to have made international reputations in politics or war were the Byzantine empress, Theodora, and the Ottoman statesman, Mohammed Kiamil Pasha. Theodora was the daughter of a Cypriot keeper of the bears in the Constantinople theatre. In turn actress, prostitute and courtesan, she rose through her native wit and varied talents to rule the Byzantine empire with Justinian I. Mohammed Kiamil Pasha, a Turkish Cypriot of humble origin, served in the Ottoman civil service and became four times grand vizir of the Ottoman empire at the end of the nineteenth century. In 1913, after the Young Turk revolution, he returned, aged eighty-two, to Cyprus where he died.

Greek Cypriot historians, it is true, would add the name of Helena Palæologus, a Greek imperial princess, whose marriage in 1441 to John, the Lusignan King of Cyprus, is said to have inspired the Greek Cypriots with hopes of reunion with Byzantium and the end of Latin rule. These hopes were somewhat belated since Constantinople fell to the Turks only twelve years later and the Byzantine empire was extinguished. For Western historians, Helena's chief claim to notice was the violent temper which is alleged to have led her to bite off the nose of her husband's mistress, Marietta of Patras. She appears, nevertheless, to have been regarded by the Greeks in Cyprus as a symbol of national revival because she achieved the re-establishment of Greek as an official language, together with French, of the Lusignan administration.

The history of Cyprus has been interwoven with the rise and fall of neighbouring empires, with great movements of peoples and religions; but, at least until recently, the Cypriots themselves have been more usually the victims than the makers of history. Nor has Cyprus itself ever been of decisive strategic importance or one of the great battlefields of the world, like the plains of Flanders or Cilicia.

The fact that the island is only forty miles from what is now the Turkish mainland—whose mountains are visible from the island on a clear day—and sixty miles from Syria might suggest that its possession is vital in any struggle for power or control of communications in the Levant. And for more than three thousand years Cyprus has indeed been an object of strife between the contending powers of the Near East: Egypt and the empires of Asia Minor and Greece as well as their challengers from outside. Sometimes the challenge was from the East, such as that of the Persians; but more often it came from the West. Even so, the strategic rule of Cyprus has on the whole been marginal. Throughout most of Near Eastern history, the main movements of armies and civilisations have been on the mainland of Asia Minor and the Levant. Cyprus has sometimes been an imperial outpost or redoubt, but it has more usually been a sanctuary or last ditch of a declining empire rather than the springboard for new conquests. This was true of the Crusaders, of the Venetians and is now true of the British.

Although Cyprus itself has been conquered many times, it has more often been the object of plundering raids and temporary domination than of permanent settlement. It has proved more useful as a place for loot and trade and as a cultural frontier than as a military bastion. If the island has remained on the margin of the great Near Eastern empires, this is not for lack of physical attractions, or because of a puny size or unhealthy climate. Cyprus is one hundred and forty miles long from Paphos in the south-west to Cape Saint Andreas in the north-east tip of the Karpass Peninsula which sticks out in a long panhandle towards the Turkish coast. The island measures sixty miles across from Cape Kormokiki in the north to Cape Gata in the south. Its area of 3,572 square miles is divided into roughly half mountain and half plain. Between the two mountain chains, the long, narrow and craggy Kyrenia range running up to three thousand feet in the north, and the heavily forested Troodos massif in the south-west, lies the great plain of the Mesaoria. The climate is typically Mediterranean, with the plain very hot and dry in summer and snow on the higher mountains in winter. The landscape is both grand and gentle: bold eroded mountains, deep valleys, pine forests, with the lower slopes terraced by vineyards, olive groves and gardens, and the plain covered with grain-fields, vegetables and orchards. It is today further adorned with an immense variety of historical monuments, a few classical remains but, more especially, spectacular medieval castles and monasteries, Gothic churches and Venetian fortresses.

The capital, Nicosia, lies on the northern edge of the plain. The other main towns of Famagusta, Limassol, Larnaca, Paphos and Kyrenia are all on the coast. Nicosia and Famagusta both have magnificent stone fortress walls built by Venetian engineers round the old quarters of the towns. Eighty-two years of British influence have helped to impart an air of genteel tidiness to the suburbs outside the Venetian walls, giving the capital sometimes the air of some small market or garrison town in the Home Counties—say Camberley or Colchester. But a modern visitor can still feel here and there the atmosphere which is special to Cyprus and other parts of the Near East where the cultures of West and East, of Orthodox Greek, Moslem Turk or Arab and Catholic Crusader have met and mingled. This atmosphere has been well described by Sir Harry Luke, who first saw Nicosia in 1908, before much of its suburbanisation had taken place:

> The peculiar charm possessed by the remnants of the Latin East, that East which knew the rule of Crusading lords and the magnificence of Frankish merchant princes, is of a rare and subtle kind, the offspring of oriental nature and medieval Western art. It lies, if the attempt to define so elusive a thing may be allowed, in Gothic architecture blending with Saracenic beneath a Mediterranean sky, in the courts of ruined castles overgrown with deep green cypresses, in date-palms rearing their stately crowns above some abbey's traceried cloisters, in emblazoned flamboyant mansions of golden sandstone warmed and illumined, as they could never be in the West, by the glow of an eastern sun.[2]

Cyprus has more than once been lucky in the literacy of its foreign administrators and officials, from Cicero to Sir Harry Luke, Sir Ronald Storrs and, last of all, Lawrence Durrell, whose book *Bitter Lemons* is an inspired evocation of the physical beauty of the island, the spirit of its people and their modern political tragedy. It is, however, sad to think that from the presence in Cyprus of Arthur Rimbaud in 1878 and 1880 not a line of poetry was born. He had put poetry behind him and, aged twenty-four, was working for £6 a month as a contractor's foreman building a summer cottage in the mountains for the newly installed British high commissioner.

The first written records of Cyprus go back nearly fifteen hundred years before Cicero and 3,500 before Durrell. The island's first identifiable settlers were New Stone Age men who probably came there from the mainland of Asia Minor, early in the fourth millennium BC. They were followed by Bronze Age settlers, and the copper industry—with which the name of Cyprus is associated and which still flourishes there—was well established before 2100 BC, at about the same time as the first appearance of writing in the form of linear inscriptions. The island was probably in contact with the Egyptian and Babylonian empires and with the Minoan civilisation which spread from Crete. The payment of tribute by Cyprus to the Egyptian Thothmes III provides the island's first entry in the record of written history in about 1500 BC.

Greek colonisation of the island appears to have begun from about 1400 BC, towards the end of the Mycenaean age. The Phoenicians followed three centuries later with trading posts, and for about twelve hundred years Cyprus was a series of small independent kingdoms, mostly Greek but some Phoenician, paying tribute at various times to the neighbouring empires of Egypt, Assyria and Persia. The predominance of Greeks in the island is indicated by the cylinder, dated 673 BC, which shows the kings of Cyprus, nine Greeks and one Phoenician, offering homage to Esarhaddon, the Assyrian emperor. In the inter-imperial struggles in which Cyprus became involved, the Phoenician elements in the island usually sided with the mainland Phoenicians and the Persians, while the Greeks, centred on the great trading city of Salamis, tended to sympathise with the other Greek states. The Cypriot Greeks joined in the unsuccessful revolt of the Ionian Greeks against Persia but, in the later Greco-Persian struggles, Athenian naval power operating five hundred miles from its base was never sufficient to establish effective control of Cyprus—a fact not without significance for Athens today.

One of the Greek Cypriot leaders, Euagoras, tried to profit from the confused three-cornered struggle between Persia, Athens and Sparta at the beginning of the fourth century by attempting to bring all of Cyprus under his control. He introduced the Greek alphabet and coinage, but failed to hold his conquests against the Persians.[3] It was left to Alexander the Great to bring a temporary unity to Cyprus. However, its real unification was not achieved until the Ptolemies took over the island in 294 BC in the fight for the succession to Alexander's empire. The Ptolemies, with their headquarters in Egypt, abolished the local kingships in Cyprus and set up the first of the imperial bureaucracies that were to rule the island—except for the three hundred years of the medieval independent Lusignan kings—until 1960.

During this time, from 300 BC until 1960, Cyprus was under seven sets of rulers: the Ptolemies, the Romans, the Byzantines, the Lusignans, the Venetians, the Turks and the British. Though it has never been totally Greek in population, its Greek-speaking majority has always considered itself as forming a part of the Hellenic world, whether that world was open or submerged. However, the nature of the Hellenic world itself underwent many changes. The failure to appreciate the nature of these changes, and the consequent meaning of Hellenism to a modern Greek or Greek Cypriot, is one of the more common causes of misunderstanding among many Westerners who still think of Greece only in terms of classical Athens and Sparta when considering problems such as Cyprus.

Alexander the Great and his successors created a Hellenistic empire which spread Greek culture far beyond the bounds of the classical

Greek states and their maritime colonies. At the same time the nature of Greek culture and political organisation changed with the influence of Oriental religions and Oriental political traditions of imperial absolutism and bureaucracy, such as those of Egypt and Persia. This Hellenistic world was dominated politically by Roman conquest but culturally it absorbed Roman influences into itself. The resultant Greco-Roman culture was fused into a new Hellenistic empire with the spread of Christianity, the transfer of the Roman imperial capital to Constantinople and the subsequent breach between the Byzantine rulers and the collapsing Roman empire of the West. The political break with the West was deepened by the Great Schism in AD 1054 between the Orthodox Church in the East and the Western Catholic Church in Rome. The main doctrinal reason for the schism was a dispute over the nature of the Trinity. The Eastern Church believed the Holy Ghost proceeds from the Father alone, while the Western Church asserted that the Holy Ghost proceeds from both Father and Son. The schism strengthened the identification of Hellenism with religion and with the Orthodox Church, as much as with the Greek language. It also intensified the challenge to the Byzantine empire from Western Europe. This challenge had developed from the raids of the Normans to the more organised assaults of the Latin and Frankish Crusaders. The depredations of the Crusaders on their way to fight the Saracens in the Holy Land culminated, during the Fourth Crusade, in the sack and seizure of Constantinople and the temporary establishment of a Latin empire.

Hellenism had already fought off a series of attacks from the Slavs, the Serbs and the Bulgars, which might have swamped its Greek language, and repeated invasions from the Moslem Arabs and later the Seljuk Turks which threatened to destroy its Christian religion. Under the Latins, Hellenism was submerged politically, culturally and ecclesiastically. It recovered politically within a small area round Constantinople after the Latin empire until it was subjugated by the Ottoman Turks. Under the Ottomans the political power of Hellenism was broken completely for three and a half centuries, but culturally it was able to survive in a modified form and was even able to revive its own Orthodox Church which suffered less from the more tolerant Moslem Turks than from the vindictive heresy-hunting Latin Christians. Hellenism was reborn as a political power with the revolution in 1821 which created modern Greece. But 'modern Greece is politically, and especially in foreign policies, far more the child of the Byzantine Empire than she is the grandchild of the little classical Republics'.[4] Therefore, to argue against enosis on the grounds that 'Cyprus has never been ruled from mainland Greece' is not only untrue but irrelevant. For the point is that the Greek Cypriots feel they share, with the Greeks of the mainland and the other islands, an Hellenic world whose political centre at the moment is Athens but which has also at different times been Alexandria and Constantinople. Under the Ottoman empire the political centre of Hellenism was the Orthodox Church. During the past one hundred and fifty years the ideas of Western nationalism brought Hellenism into a new phase in which a sense of Hellenic identity demanded not only a common language, culture and religion but also incorporation in a single national state.

From the Roman annexation of Cyprus in 58 BC until the end of Byzantine rule in the twelfth century, the island was part of a single empire which itself changed in character in two profound ways: language and religion. The first Roman conquest was, like that of earlier invasions, more of a looting raid than an endeavour to attain permanent acquisition of the island. Under the Ptolemies, Cyprus had become prosperous and cultured. The main centre of Greek culture in the island, Salamis, is estimated to have had 120,000 people—which is nearly twice as many as Nicosia today. The Romans had already established themselves on the Cilician mainland opposite Cyprus before Cato seized the island. The auction of the treasures of the last Ptolemy ruling on the island, who poisoned himself, raised 1,700,000 gold pounds to be sent back to Rome. Initially, Cyprus was a Roman province for eleven years, with Cicero as one of its governors. Julius Caesar then gave the island back to the Ptolemies, one of whom, Cleopatra, was his mistress. But after the defeat of Mark Antony in 31 BC and the death of Cleopatra, Cyprus became part of the Roman empire again. This time it was under a more solid and permanent imperial rule. The first Roman rulers, like the later Turkish governors, used provincial posts such as those of Cilicia and Cyprus to feather their own nests. Later, from Augustus onwards, the island began to prosper again under a provincial administration which embodied most of the system set up by the Ptolemies.

The great historical event of Roman Cyprus was the arrival of Christianity. In AD 45 Saint Paul and Saint Barnabas—the latter a native of the Cypriot city of Salamis—landed in the island. Although Paul was scourged and eventually Barnabas was martyred in his native city, they succeeded in converting the Roman proconsul, Sergius Paulus, who thus gained the distinction of becoming the world's first Christian ruler. By AD 313, when Constantine officially recognised

Christianity in the Edict of Milan, most of Cyprus had become Christian, and was represented by three bishops at the first Oecumenical Council of Nicaea in AD 321. Politically the island was still part of the Roman province of the East, with its capital at Antioch on the Syrian mainland. And so it continued to be when the Roman empire split into its Western and Eastern halves in AD 395. By then the island had already begun to pass into a new kind of Roman world. As the Western empire gradually collapsed under barbarian invasions, the Eastern Roman empire, centred on Constantinople, began independently to develop the new culture and political system which became known as Byzantine. At first the most significant characteristic of this new Eastern Roman empire was its fusion of Christian church with an imperial centralised state of an Oriental absolutist type. At the same time the empire was also increasingly permeated with Hellenic cultural influences. By the sixth century, when Byzantine power was at its height, Greek had already become the official language of the empire.

After the Persian destruction of Antioch in AD 540, Cyprus became a separate Byzantine province under a proconsul. Although Justinian threw back the Persians, a more dangerous enemy was on the way. From the middle of the seventh century the peace which Cyprus had enjoyed under Byzantine rule was shattered by a series of Arab raids and invasions. The tidal wave of Islam swept outwards from Arabia, to roll westward round the shores of the Mediterranean and up to central France, and eastward to India and the borders of China. For over three hundred years it battered at the frontiers of the Byzantine empire in Asia Minor and ebbed and flowed over Cyprus. It was the first, but not the decisive, stage in the struggle of Christian and Moslem in the Eastern Mediterranean. The Arabs made their first attack on Cyprus in about AD 647 after having conquered Syria, Palestine and Egypt. They were chiefly interested in plunder or tribute, and never stayed in control of the island for long. At times the island was a 'no man's land between two warring worlds',[5] and sometimes the Byzantines and the Arabs came to agreements to share the island's taxes.

The defeat of the Arabs in AD 965 by the Byzantine emperor, Nicephorus Phocas, gave Cyprus another two centuries of peace until the Western Crusaders brought a new element into the struggle between Christians and Moslems. It was an element which in the end was to prove far from welcome to the Orthodox Christians of the East. The Crusaders created the three-cornered pattern of struggle among the West, the Christian East and Islamic peoples which has since been characteristic of the history of Cyprus and the rest of the Eastern Mediterranean. In more recent times this struggle has been chiefly between Greeks, Turks and British. It is curious that, after the Greeks, the next of these three to make their mark in the history of Cyprus were not the Turks but the British (or, more correctly at that time, the English). If it be true, as has been said, that the British empire was acquired in a fit of absent-mindedness, then it may also be characteristic that the English first conquered Cyprus by accident and because of the weather.

At the close of the twelfth century the island was being ruled by a Byzantine rebel prince, Isaac Ducas Comnenus, who had been governing Cilicia. In 1184, he had seized the island for himself, proclaimed himself 'Holy Emperor' and defeated a Byzantine expedition sent to bring him to heel. But his conquest was short-lived. In 1191, Richard I of England set out on the Third Crusade to recover Jerusalem from Saladin. The English fleet, carrying in separate ships Richard and his bride-to-be, Princess Berengaria of Navarre, set sail from Sicily for Syria but was dispersed by a storm. The ship with Berengaria on board was blown towards Cyprus and took refuge at Limassol, where the Emperor Isaac's threatening behaviour forced it to put to sea again. But a romantic rescue was at hand. Richard's fleet came over the horizon. Soon Richard himself had landed, occupied Limassol, defeated Isaac in the battle of Tremousha, and married Berengaria in the chapel of the Limassol fortress where she was also crowned Queen of England. As Sir Harry Luke points out, Cyprus thus became the only British overseas territory to be the scene of a wedding of an English monarch and of an English coronation.[6] Richard, however, was impatient to get on with his Crusade, so he sold the island to the Knights Templars for one hundred thousand bezants. The Templars soon found they had made a bad bargain and within a year tried to sell it back to Richard on the same terms. He had already spent too much of the Templars' down payment, so he suggested handing Cyprus over to a French nobleman to whom Richard owed a favour. This was Guy de Lusignan of the House of Poitou and widower of Sybil, Queen of Jerusalem. Cyprus was to be compensation for the rights that Guy had lost in Palestine to Henry of Champagne, a nephew both of Richard and of the king of France.

So began the Lusignan dynasty. Eighteen sovereigns of this house ruled Cyprus as an independent Norman French kingdom for nearly three hundred years until they were overthrown by the Venetians in 1489. The first to gain the royal title was Aimery, who succeeded his brother Guy on the latter's death in 1194 and was given the royal crown by the Holy Roman Emperor, Henry VI. The crown of Jerusalem was added by marriage to that of Cyprus and, in 1393, there was also joined to it by inheritance the crown of Armenia, though by then the Armenian kingdom had shrunk to almost nothing. These titles passed, in the course of time, to the House of Savoy. For long they were titles without significant rights, but they were not formally extinguished until 1946, with the ending of the Italian monarchy.

Western historians have waxed lyrical over the glories of Lusignan Cyprus, when the island enjoyed 'the most brilliant years' of its history and when most of its beautiful churches and abbeys and formidable castles were built. A supply base and refuge for the Crusaders operating from their shrinking foothold in Syria, and a model medieval feudal state, it became—after the fall of Jerusalem in 1244 and of Acre in 1291—the last great outpost of Latin civilisation in the Levant. Its cities bulged with the wealth of a growing entrepôt trade in which the rising Italian maritime republics of Genoa and Venice took an increasing part. Famagusta in particular became legendary among medieval travellers for its luxury and the magnificence of its great merchants.

Greek Cypriot historians, however, sometimes tell a different tale. The Byzantine rule had been harsh, they admit, and Isaac had been a 'squalid tyrant', but the Franks brought something worse. The Cypriot monk, Neophytos, whose letter written in 1196 is the only Greek Cypriot document from the period, says that Cyprus was 'utterly despoiled' by Isaac and then looted by Richard. 'The wicked Englishman achieved nothing against his fellow-criminal Saladin, only this: that he sold our country to the Latins for 200,000 pounds of gold. Since then, great has been the wailing and unbearable has been the smoke which came from the north. . . .' From then on, says the modern Greek Cypriot historian, Doros Alastos, the history of Cyprus split into two: the history of the dominant nation and that of the Cypriot people.[7] The Byzantine rulers might have been brutal and greedy, but at least they were Orthodox in religion and spoke Greek. The new Latin rulers institutionalised serfdom among the Greek peasantry; they formed a Catholic French-speaking ruling class and a merchant class mostly of Italian-speaking foreigners. But worst of all they persecuted the Orthodox Church. A bull issued in 1260 by Pope Alexander made the Latin archbishop the supreme religious authority in the island. The Orthodox archbishopric was suppressed and Orthodox property and tithes seized. By then, after the Great Schism, the Crusading movement had become almost as much a struggle to crush Christian Byzantium as to recover the Holy Land from the Moslems.

Cyprus had been spared from the Crusader impact for a time because the first of the 'Frankish' armies went overland to Syria through the Balkans and Anatolia. But when the impact came it inflicted a particular indignity on the Orthodox Church in Cyprus. For the Church in Cyprus had been (and still is) autocephalous ever since its independence from the patriarchate of Antioch was recognised in 431 by the Council of Ephesus. This independence had been confirmed in 478 by Emperor Zeno, after the discovery of the tomb of Saint Barnabas, together with the copy of the Gospel of Saint Matthew which had been buried with the martyred saint. With an independence only less ancient than that of the four original Orthodox patriachates of Constantinople, Alexandria, Antioch and Jerusalem, the archbishop of Cyprus also enjoyed certain special privileges. He was permitted to wear a cope of imperial purple, to carry a sceptre instead of a pastoral staff and to sign his name in red ink. The proud, independent Church of Cyprus, like the peasantry, now became a source of foreign loot. Yet there was some compensation in the fact that more of the loot was now being spent in the island. 'For the first time in twelve centuries, the tribute gathered from the island was not sent to the treasure chests of Rome or Constantinople. For the most part it was left in the island, enriching the foreign nobles, knights and merchants who settled there, and who remained a caste separate from, and living on, the people.'[8]

The fall of the Crusader principalities in Syria increased the wealth of Cyprus as a trading centre, but this prosperity masked the island's comparative stagnation in agriculture and industry. It also increased the power and ambitions of the Italian trading republics in the island. First, Genoa seized Famagusta, imposed a crippling tribute and kept Lusignan princes as hostages. And finally, Venice, by a combination of diplomacy and force, ended the Lusignan rule and substituted her own in 1489.

The change brought little benefit to the Cypriots. On the contrary; the Venetians simply ran the island for the money they could get out of it and as a useful military strongpoint in their conflict with the rising Ottoman power in the Eastern Mediterranean. By then all Greek Cypriot hopes of ending Latin rule by a rescue expedition from a revived Byzantium had completely disappeared. When Venice gained control of Cyprus, the Turks had already been in Constantinople for thirty-six years, and were fully launched on that extraordinary career of conquest which was to swallow up two empires and many kingdoms in three continents. Nevertheless the Venetians ruled Cyprus for eighty-two years—exactly the same length of time as the British—before the Turks in 1571 launched their successful assault on what had become the last Christian outpost in the Moslem East. The siege of Famagusta, defended by the Venetian general, Marcantonio Bragadino, was a grisly epic. In four months' fighting against a small garrison, the Turks lost 80,000 men. When Bragadino finally surrendered, the Turkish general, Lala Mustafa, broke the surrender terms. The Venetian commander's nose and ears were cut off and then, after other humiliations, he was executed by being flayed alive. His skin was stuffed with straw and sent as a war trophy to Constantinople. (It was later recovered by Bragadino's children and is now preserved in Venice.)

The defeat of the Ottoman fleet by the papal alliance under Don John of Austria at the great naval battle of Lepanto failed to save the Venetian position in Cyprus and on March 7, 1573, Venice signed a peace which confirmed the Turkish sultan's possession of the island. From here on the history of Cyprus merges with that of the Ottoman empire as a whole; it forms part of the record of the Ottoman empire's relations with its Greek Orthodox subjects and with Western and other foreign powers. Now that the Turks have joined the story, it is time to say something more of their own spectacular history.

CHAPTER TWO

Old Greeks and New Turks

NATIONALISM LIKE COMMUNISM writes its own history. The Turks of today are a racial mixture such as one might expect to find in regions like Asia Minor and the Balkans that have been over-run and fought over by many different peoples. But at one time Turkish historians liked to claim that the Turks were the original settlers of Anatolia, like the Hittites. The more generally accepted idea is that the Turks were a nomadic people who began migrating south-westwards from Central Asia from about the sixth century AD onwards. They gradually penetrated into the Arab empires and adopted the new Arab religion of Islam. They served as soldiers under the caliphs, or as free-booting warriors on the borders of the vast Islamic realm which then stretched from Spain to China and from Ethiopia to the Caucasus. As the Arab empires weakened from within, the Turks began to stake out more ambitious claims for themselves, either through the assumption of key positions of command or through the seizure of territory.

The first organised Turkish bid for power on a large scale was made by the Seljuk Turks who captured Baghdad in 1055 and went on to attack the Byzantine empire in Asia Minor. Though Turks may often have fought Greeks in earlier campaigns of the Arab armies against the Byzantines, the battle of Manzikert in 1071 between the Seljuk and Byzantine armies marks the beginning of the great rivalry (also often a partnership) of Greek and Turk of which the Cyprus dispute is, nearly nine hundred years after, the latest mild flicker. At Manzikert the Byzantines were routed. Their empire had been weakened by a century of war with that of the Bulgars on their western flank while, at the same time, they were holding the Moslem raiders at bay in the south and east. The Seljuks held eastern and central Anatolia and raided as far as Nicaea, second city of the empire. In the areas of Anatolia occupied by them, they succeeded in converting the local Greek-speaking Christian peasants into Turkish-speaking Moslems. This process by which the Anatolians, having once been Hellenised, were Turkified by 'a barbarous nomadic people from the steppes' has been described by

Professor Toynbee as 'one of the puzzles of history'.[1] His answer to it is that the peasantry had already become alienated from the Byzantine feudal lords and priests who ruled them in conditions of increasing oppression and anarchy. Hence they were more ready to accept a change of masters: a phenomenon that was to recur in later Turkish conquests, including that of Cyprus.

The Turkish conquest of the Byzantine Greek empire was not a sudden overwhelming but a slow and gradual process. Nearly four centuries passed from the battle of Manzikert to the fall of Constantinople. By that time the van of the Turkish advance had been taken over from the Seljuks by the Ottoman Turks, of the House of Osman, whose founder, Ertogrul, brought them to the north-west corner of Asia Minor between Brusa and Nicaea. The Byzantines had held the Seljuks back for 200 years but had been dealt a shattering blow from the West by the Fourth Crusade and the rise of the Slavonic and Hungarian empires. The Fourth Crusade led, in 1204, to the establishment of the Latin empire in Constantinople under Baldwin, Count of Flanders. This Frankish rule in the mother-city of the Greek empire lasted fifty-seven years. Although the Greek emperor, Michael Palaeologus, recaptured Constantinople from the Latins in 1271, most of the former European territories of the Byzantine empire remained in the hands of the Franks and the Serbs. By the time the Ottomans arrived on the scene, the Greek empire had shrunk in Asia to a small area round Trebizond and the cities of Nicaea and Nicomedia, both of which the Ottomans soon took. In Europe, the empire still held Constantinople and Thrace but otherwise only the coast of Macedonia and the eastern Peloponnese. The rest of central and southern Greece was held by Frankish kings and princes who also ruled Cyprus and many of the Aegean Islands. Much of northern Greece was in the hands of the medieval Serbian empire of Stephen Dushan, who was pressing hard against the Greek empire.

It was to meet this Serbian threat that the Ottoman Turks first crossed the Hellespont and entered Europe. They came at the appeal of the Greek emperor, Cantacuzenos, who had sealed his alliance with the Turks by marrying his daughter, Theodora, to Orkhan, the Turkish leader. On the third of these expeditions against the Serbs, the Ottomans came to stay and began a rapid conquest of the Balkans. They crushed the Serbs and their Slav allies at the battle of Kossovo Polye (the Field of Blackbirds) in 1389 and again at Nicopolis seven years later. Serbia and Bulgaria disappeared as independent states for nearly 500 years.

It is a curious paradox that, while in its heyday the strength of Byzantium lay in Asia Minor, the Ottoman Turks began their first serious imperial expansion, not in Moslem Asia, but in Christian Europe. It was their European conquests, as allies of the Greek emperors, which gave them the momentum needed to complete their control of Asia Minor. It was not until a later stage that they extended this control to the Arab lands of Syria, Iraq, Egypt and Arabia and so became rulers of an empire most of whose subjects were Moslem and not Christian. Just as the Byzantine empire had already been greatly reduced and over-run by other invaders and conquerors, so the Arab countries had been devastated by the Mongols and earlier Turkish raiders. The fall of Constantinople to the Ottomans in 1453 has become for most Western-educated people a dramatic turning-point in their view of world history. Traditionally, it represents, for them, the cataclysmic destruction of an imperial centre of Western civilisation by barbarian Asian hordes. But by 1453 most of the Byzantine empire had already been lost, not in the first place to the Turks but to European 'barbarians' from the West. A large part of the struggle for the Byzantine heritage was less between Turks and Greeks and more between Turks and Serbs, Bulgars and Franks—with the Turks sometimes in alliance with the Greeks. Nor was it simply a struggle between Moslem and Christian, for the hatred between Orthodox and Latin Catholic Christian was often such that the Greeks would prefer a Moslem to a Latin as ally and even as master.

The Turkish conquest of Cyprus, for example, was not simply the belated mopping-up of a last outpost of Byzantium. It was part of a long campaign between the Ottoman Turks and Venice for control of the islands and commercial seaways of the Eastern Mediterranean and even of part of the Greek mainland. Cyprus fell to the Turks in 1571, but it was not until 1669 that they took Crete from the Venetians. In the Peloponnese, the southern part of Greece, the Venetians retained their hold until 1718. The Ionian Islands were never taken by the Turks wholly or for long, but remained under Venice's control until, after Napoleon's destruction of the Venetian Republic, they passed into French, then into British, and finally into Greek hands. While the full subjection of the Greek-speaking lands to Turkish rule took several centuries to complete—and in parts of mainland Greece the Turkish dominance lasted little more than a century—the Ottoman empire expanded in spectacular fashion into Europe and Asia during the fifteenth and sixteenth centuries. The limit of the Turks' expansion into Europe was marked by their defeat at the siege of Vienna in 1683, but the Ottoman empire continued to be a great power for another hundred years, and thereafter a major factor in international affairs up to the first world war. Its apogee was probably reached under Suleiman the Magnificent (1520–66). 'When Henry VIII ruled over about four million people, the subjects of the Sultan Suleiman numbered fifty million. These included not less than twenty distinct races. . . . The empire stretched from Buda to Basra, from the Caspian to the Western Mediterranean; and embraced many lands in Europe, Asia and Africa. . . . It was no vain boast of the Ottoman Sultan that he was the master of many kingdoms, the ruler of three continents and the lord of two seas.'[2] There had come into being a new world empire with its own distinctive civilisation and political institutions.

Historians differ about the specifically Turkish contribution to this civilisation except in its provision of the central military power; there is no disagreement on one thing—the quality both past and present of the Turks as fighting men. We have already mentioned the nationalist theory that the Turks were the original settlers of Anatolia; its corollary is that all subsequent cultural achievements of this region must also be credited to the Turks. At the other extreme is the view long current among European historians—and also often politically inspired by philhellenism—that the Turks remained essentially a race of warrior nomads who contributed nothing to the lands they over-ran but simply camped as conquerors among hostile subjects whom they plundered in order to live. Even Professor Toynbee (than whom no one has made more effort to remain objective in judging the inter-reaction of peoples and cultures) has suggested that the Turks became 'shepherds of men' instead of 'shepherds of cattle'; the relation of the Ottoman ruling institutions of the sultan and his slave household to the conquered peoples were 'a re-creation of the old nomadic pattern of the shepherd, his watchdogs and his cattle'.[3] But it is clear that, in the course of centuries of conflict and coexistence, the men who made the Ottoman empire must have been greatly influenced by the political organisation and cultures of the former empires with which they came into contact. It is also evident that with their military qualities went some of the characteristics still noted among the Turks today: dourness, pride, discipline, and a realistic appreciation of the role of power in government. What is chiefly in dispute is how much and at what stages the Ottomans borrowed elements of their political institutions from Byzantium or from Islam, the Arabs and Persians. It is beyond the scope or purpose of this book to give a detailed description of the

Ottoman system, but there are certain aspects which are worth noting briefly because of their particular relevance to the development of Turkish relations with the Greeks, with the European powers, and finally with Cyprus.

The central ruling institution of the empire in its prime was the sultan himself. An absolute monarch, he was served by an elaborate bureaucracy whose members, from the grand vizir downwards, were personal servants of his imperial household, and was supported by a specially recruited army of slaves. These Janissaries ('New Troops') supplemented the feudal levies of *sipahis*, or cavalry, from the *timars*, or military fiefs. Some of the main features of this system were similar to those of the Byzantines and some to the Arab and Persian empires. Others echoed a glorified tribal system familiar to nomadic peoples. But these institutions developed a special character under the Ottomans because of two peculiar facts. The Ottoman empire was first and foremost an Islamic state: at the same time it was ruling a multireligious as well as multiracial society, and its foreign relations were chiefly with non-Moslem states. This led to a number of complications in dealing with the Christian subjects of the sultan and the Christian European powers. Islamic doctrine, developed during the early Arab missionary conquests, divided the world into the Realm of Islam, in which lived Moslem believers, and the Realm of War, inhabited by non-Moslem unbelievers. It was the duty of Moslems to extend the first realm at the expense of the second. But unbelievers were divided into two classes: People of the Book (Christians, Jews and Zoroastrians, whose sacred writings had preceded the Koran), and the heathen rest. People of the Book who became subjects of the sultan were granted immunity from forcible conversion to Islam and allowed to practise their religion in exchange for payment of special taxes. But they were not allowed to bear arms; they had to wear distinctive dress and, although tolerated, were in other ways second-class citizens. For example, their evidence could not be accepted against that of a Moslem in a court of law, and Moslems found guilty of killing them were not punishable by death. In practice, virtually all the non-Moslem subjects of the Ottoman sultan were in this category and known as 'rayahs, (literally 'human cattle').

There were two further complications. The first arose from the fact that in theory, a freeborn Moslem or one of the People of the Book could not be enslaved. The recruitment of much of the ruling bureaucracy and of the standing army of this Islamic state had therefore to be made from non-Moslems who would first become slaves and then be converted to Islam. At first this was done from young prisoners of war, but later and until 1638 it was achieved by the *devşirme*, or 'collection' a levy every four years of one in five of boys from non-Moslem families. In practice, the *devşirme* was limited chiefly to Orthodox Christians—Greeks, Serbs, Bulgars—and excluded Armenians and Jews. The Janissaries were at first recruited solely by the *devşirme* from Christian boys who were then brought up as Moslems and celibates under military discipline. But in 1506 they were allowed to marry; thereafter they developed into a hereditary military caste. They became the Praetorian Guard of the empire and a source of great political power. Thus, while the *devşirme* was in one sense an inhuman burden on the Christians, it also opened up to them—at the price of conversion—a road to the highest posts in the state which were virtually denied to freeborn Moslems.

The second complication was the position inside the empire of foreign Christians, usually Latins (i.e. Catholics), who were not subjects of the sultan. If only for practical reasons of commerce, some way had to be found of regularising their position. This became even more necessary as Ottoman relations with the European powers ceased to be a state of perpetual war for the expansion of Islam and settled into the European balance-of-power pattern of diplomacy and alternating war and peace. So under what was described as the 'Capitulations' system, the Frankish merchant communities—especially the French who were the sultan's earliest European allies—were granted special privileges of limited self-government through their consuls. These communities corresponded roughly to the *millets*, or religious communities, by means of which the sultan's Christian and Jewish subjects were allowed to organise and administer their own personal affairs under the direction of the heads of their faith, who were in turn responsible to the imperial government. Something resembling the *millet* system and the capitulations had already existed in Constantinople under the Byzantines.

One of the first acts of Sultan Mehmed II on capturing Constantinople was to recognise and confirm the authority of the Orthodox patriarchate. The Ottomans by then would have been quite familiar with the workings of the political and religious machinery of what was left of the Greek empire. Most of the sultan's new subjects were Orthodox Christians and most of these were Greek-speaking. By the time of the Turkish conquest the population of Constantinople had probably fallen from about a million before the Latin conquest to less than a hundred thousand. But it was still a great city with the remnants of an imperial machinery in which the Greeks were the people who 'knew the ropes'. From the beginning, being themselves the ex-imperial race, the Greeks occupied a special position under the Turks. Among the rival Christians they were guaranteed supremacy over the hated Latins who were also associated by the Turks with hostile European powers. Through the *millet* system, the patriarchate became the intermediary between the sultan and a large number of his subjects. In Constantinople, the Phanariotes—the old Greek patrician families of the Phanar quarter—were influential in the administration, especially in relations with foreign powers and in foreign commerce. Until the eighteenth century they filled two of the highest official posts: the 'Dragoman [Interpreter] of the Porte', who became virtually a foreign minister, and the 'Dragoman of the Fleet', chief adviser to the *kapidan pasha*, the commander-in-chief of the Ottoman navy. Until 1821, they also provided the *hospodars*, or governors, of the autonomous Danubian principalities of Moldavia and Wallachia which eventually formed modern Rumania. Together with the Armenians and Jews, the Greeks furnished almost all of the commercial class and a large part of the professional class of the empire, as well as dominating its merchant marine.

In addition to some communal autonomy within their *millet*, the Greeks also enjoyed varying degrees of territorial autonomy. The whole pattern of rule within the empire was very varied, ranging from direct rule in some areas to nominal suzerainty in others. Among Greek-speaking territories, for example, the island of Samos and the community of Aivali on the Anatolian coast had, by the eighteenth century, officially recognised forms of self-government under Turkish suzerainty. In other areas the degree of self-government varied with the vigour or indolence of the local Turkish governor, or the astuteness and toughness of the local population. By the end of the eighteenth century, free-born Moslems had replaced Greeks or Christian converts in many high posts. But the degree to which traditional local government had been preserved in the Peloponnese and the Aegean Islands was to have an important bearing on the eventual recovery of Greek independence.

In Cyprus, the Turks were at first welcomed by the Greeks as the liberators who had delivered them from both the rapacious rule of the Venetians and the suppression of their church by the Latins. The Turks made two popular moves by restoring the supremacy of the Orthodox archbishop and by ending the system of serfdom among the peasants.

Cyprus was joined with four *sanjaks*, or administrative districts, of the nearby Anatolian mainland to form a new province of the Ottoman empire. War, famine and emigration had led to a decline in the Greek population of the island. The movement of emigration seems to have continued unhalted during the period of Turkish rule, varying in intensity with economic conditions. After the conquest, 20,000 Turks were established in Cyprus, either soldiers or settlers—both Moslem and Christian—who were forcibly transferred thither from the mainland, in line with the usual Ottoman method of consolidating new conquests by transfers of population.[4] The island had a Turkish governor, assisted by a military commander; a *mufti*, or Moslem religious leader; and a *qadhi*, or Moslem chief justice.

The sultan seems to have had three main objectives in Cyprus: to keep out the Venetians or any other threatening Western maritime power; to extract the maximum revenue from the island; and to do these two things without provoking a local revolt or economic decay and consequent emigration which would have killed the goose that laid the golden eggs. The Cypriots were promised just treatment without tyranny or provocation. But, as was to be the case throughout the later centuries of Ottoman history, such good intentions depended in practice on the ability or willingness of the local administration to fulfil them and on the degree of real authority being exercised from Constantinople. As the personal power of the sultans declined and the empire itself began to weaken, the system of provincial administration became more and more one of tax-farming on a large scale. Sometimes, if the exactions of the tax-gatherer became too unbearable and complaints could be got through to the Porte, the sultan's government in Constantinople, then a more determined sultan or grand vizir might intervene and recall or even execute an unpopular governor. This happened in Cyprus after the archbishop and bishops had been granted direct access to the Porte and made responsible for paying, assessing and collecting the tribute payable by the Christians in the island.

In fact, the honeymoon period after the defeat of the Venetians did not last long, and the Greek Cypriots were soon looking for new 'liberators'. There were various intrigues, with Venice, Spain and other Christian powers, and particularly with the duke of Savoy who had successfully taken over from Venice the claim to the royal crown of Cyprus. There were plots for conquest and for Greek revolt, together with proposals to buy Cyprus from the sultan. One of the oddest of these plans was to purchase the island for the French Protestant leader,

Henri, duc de Rohan, as an asylum for French and German Protestants in 1630. But this vision of a Huguenot Cyprus faded when its chief supporters died. Most of the schemes, like the unsuccessful attack on Famagusta in 1607 by a fleet financed by the grand duke of Tuscany and (in the words of the English ambassador to Venice, Sir Henry Wotton), 'principally adorned with English pirates',[5] were isolated hare-brained adventures. The Turkish conquest of Crete in 1669 helped to convince the Greek Cypriots that they had little to hope from any Western rescue expeditions. 'Cyprus was henceforward forgotten by the West except as a stage in Levantine commerce.'[6]

The European powers—principally the Italian republics, France and England—had already begun to build up again their trade relations in the Levant in the sixteenth century. The English Levant Company was set up in 1592, and the first two English consulates were established on Chios and in Aleppo. By 1636 there was a regular English consular officer operating in Cyprus under control from Aleppo, and in 1722 the English vice-consulship in the island became an independent post. One of the main commodities of the English Levant trade was cotton lint from Cyprus which helped to build the Lancashire textile industry.

As the prospects of Western help disappeared, the Greek Cypriot archbishops gave up foreign intrigues and began to concentrate instead on getting the best deal they could from the Turks for themselves and their community. They were not unsuccessful. Gradually, Greek influence in commerce, foreign relations and adminstration increased in Constantinople and in the empire as a whole, with the result that in Cyprus the archbishops and Greek notables were able to build a stronger position for themselves. By the eighteenth century their influence began to rival that of the Turkish governor himself, although even among the Turks the real power lay with the *aghas* (wealthy notables) of Nicosia who, except under an unusually strong and competent governor, were able to control most of the administration. During most of the century the island was an estate assigned to the grand vizir in Constantinople. Holders of this office sold the island at intervals to the highest bidder, who would thereupon be appointed *muhassil* or tax-collector. The *muhassil's* first objective was to show a profit on his investment by collecting taxes from the reluctant peasantry. This was also how the governor made his fortune and paid such administrators as he employed.

The archbishop was the intermediary between the governor and the Greek community, and, where he could, tempered the wind to the shorn lambs. At times, it appears, some archbishops also did a good bit of the shearing on their own account. When the extortions of a governor or a *muhassil* appeared too outrageous, the archbishop was able to complain direct to the Porte in Constantinople—unless physically prevented from doing so by the governor. Or there might be a minor revolt by either Greeks or Turks, or even by both together. There was a dramatic and ludicrous moment in 1764 when a particularly greedy governor, Chil Osman Agha, was killed and the treasury looted by a rioting mob. This governor had tried to wipe out all his critics at once by an ingenious device. A mission from the sultan had come to Nicosia to hold an enquiry into the taxes being demanded. The archbishop and a crowd of complainants had come to give evidence to the mission. The governor set his men to saw away the beams supporting the floor of the room in the Saray, his palace, where the enquiry was being held. But this unkindest cut of all was discovered in time and instead it was the governor who died.[7]

In 1785, Cyprus was transferred to the control of the *kapidan pasha* who appointed the governors. The latter worked closely with the archbishops and the dragoman of the Saray, who was the chief civilian authority of the Greek community. The growing power of the Greek leaders, helped by their relations with Greek officials holding high posts in Constantinople, was one of the causes of a revolt in 1804 by Turkish troops and civilians in Cyprus. The revolt was suppressed by an expedition of two thousand troops sent by the sultan and by the mediation of the European consuls in Cyprus. Three of the ringleaders were savagely executed by impalement and others sold into slavery.

Was it a coincidence or a consequence that the period, in the eighteenth century, when the archbishops' power and splendour were at their height was also the time when the people of Cyprus were in the most miserable state of want? Sir George Hill gives a judicious summing up: 'Though we need not always accept the foreigners' insinuations that the Archbishops were hand in glove with the Governors who oppressed the people, it must be admitted that they do not shine as protectors of the poor. . . . Inefficiency rather than corruption (although there may have been cases of the latter) is the fault that must be laid to the charge of the spiritual heads of the Church. The diplomacy which . . . they may have been driven to practise, could never be more than a temporary palliative of the ruthless exactions of the Governors. When it failed, recourse was had to flight from the island and appeal to the Porte. From such excursions, even if in some degree successful, the Archbishops would return heavily involved in debt, the burden of which, directly or indirectly, found its way to the shoulders of the rayahs.'[8]

By the end of the eighteenth century, Turkish power had begun to lose its grip not only in Cyprus but throughout the empire. The decline of the empire had begun to set in at the end of the sixteenth century, but had been postponed by the Thirty Years War which kept its European enemies busy fighting each other. Then there was a revival, in the second half of the seventeenth century, under a brilliant dynasty of grand vizirs: the Albanian family of Köprülü, the Cecils of the Ottoman empire. But during the eighteenth century the decline was resumed and was measured by a series of foreign treaties each marking a new defeat or concession. The low-water mark was the Treaty of Küchük Kaynarja in 1774 after an unsuccessful war against Russia. The sultan had to give up the Crimea (the empire's first loss of a Moslem-populated territory) and other lands; but, worst of all, he had to give to the Russian empress, Catherine II, what amounted to a virtual right of protectorate over his own Orthodox Christian subjects.

Many reasons have been given for the Ottoman decline. The most important appear to be connected with the decay in the empire's own governing institutions and with changes in the general world picture of power and trade, rather than with serious internal revolts by the subject peoples against Ottoman misgovernment. The first obvious weakening in the ruling institutions was in the personal quality of the sultans themselves. None of the sultans of the seventeenth and eighteenth centuries was of great distinction, until Selim III (1789–1807). This process of decay had been hastened by two factors. Mehmed the Conqueror (1451–81) had laid down the rule that the sultan should kill all his brothers when he ascended the throne. This cruel tradition was abandoned in favour of the detention of the brothers in pavilions secluded from the outside world. Then, in 1617, it was decreed that the succession to the sultanate should go to the eldest surviving male of the imperial family, rather than from father to son. The combination of these two factors meant that some later sultans came to the throne after having been weakened in mind and spirit by years of seclusion. Only one of these monarchs, however, showed uncontrovertible signs of madness: Sultan Ibrahim (1640–48) who 'once levied a special tax to pay for the import of sables from Russia so that he might cover the walls of his apartment with them, and was pleased to encase his beard in a network of diamonds'.[9] The weakness of the sultans led to the corruption of other organs of government: the grand vizir, the army, the bureaucracy, the religious hierarchy and the judiciary. Control from the centre over the provincial administrations was loosened.

Professor Bernard Lewis has stressed two other important factors arising out of the essentially Islamic character of Ottoman society. The first was that Ottoman society was 'geared to expansion'. The extension of the borders of Islam was its main life-purpose, so that once it had reached the limits of its expansion in the sixteenth century it began to lose its real motive force. The second factor was that, partly because of an attitude of self-sufficiency and superiority inherited from classical Islamic civilisation, fundamentally the Ottoman empire 'had remained or reverted to a medieval state' while modernising nation states were emerging in the sixteenth century.[10] Moreover, those classes of merchants, manufacturers and professional men who provided much of the driving force in the development of post-Renaissance Europe were, in the Ottoman empire, composed almost entirely of non-Moslems and foreigners who had no political standing. This represented an aspect of another inherent source of weakness: the sharp division between the rulers and ruled, between peasants and townspeople, and between Moslems and non-Moslems. 'By the sixteenth century the Moslems and the Christians of the Ottoman empire were alike separated by sectarian differences from their nearest co-religionists beyond its frontiers, with the result that a distant culture, embracing both, was able to arise within them. Nevertheless, the various races of which the subject populations were composed were not to be welded into a nation; and this largely for the reason that the ruling class, though to a great extent recruited from the Christian element, on the one hand represented the political domination of Islam and on the other was isolated by its constitution from all the ruled of whatever faith.'[11] Yet, in some respects, it was the very inefficiency of the Ottoman government that was its saving grace, since otherwise the effects of the corruption of its ruling class would have been far more onerous and grievous for the peoples it governed.

International economic changes also played their part in the Ottoman decline. Trade in the Eastern Mediterranean was depressed by the voyages of discovery of the nations on the Atlantic seaboard. These had the double effect of diverting the rich trade of the East from the Levantine landroute to the new searoute round Africa, and of opening up vast resources of gold and silver in the Americas. The influx of precious metals from across the Atlantic produced inflation in the Turkish silver currency. Falling revenues coincided with increasing costs in maintaining a large army and civil service.[12] Then there was the changing pattern of international power. The modern states system of Europe was taking shape, and Russia, expanding into Central Asia and attempting to westernise herself, was beginning to play a large part in the European system. Outside pressures on the Ottoman empire, especially from Russia and the Hapsburg empire, were increasing. To meet this pressure the Ottomans needed both allies and new methods. They needed first of all to learn the new military techniques that had been used successfully against them.

The Ottoman empire was never altogether cut off from contact with Western ideas, but for long its main borrowings from the West were in the military field. European renegades were often of help in instructing the Turks in the making of artillery and in improving ship design and navigation. During the eighteenth century, there were intermittent attempts at westernisation. These, again, mainly concerned the army, but they also led to the introduction of printing. For technical help the Porte looked to the country which had been its traditional ally in Europe—France. Under the French monarchy this help was on a modest scale. Paradoxically, it was the French Revolution, followed by the eruption of Napoleon into the Near East, which really helped this backward empire to move forward into the modern world. The impulse thus given to modernisation enabled the sultanate to survive for over another century. On the other hand, the political ideas which came in the baggage train of westernisation eventually led to the disappearance of both sultan and empire together. The French Revolution and its aftermath marked the beginning of what Arnold Toynbee has called the 'Western Question': the repercussions caused by the powerful impact of European civilisation on the civilisations of the Near and Middle East. The new ideas and techniques from the West began to affect not only the Ottoman administration but, even more so, its subject races. The Christians in the empire, in closer touch with the West through commerce, culture, religion and their knowledge of European languages, were more quickly stirred.

The new ideas had three main elements, which were often in conflict. There was, first, the idea of reform in the sense of technical modernisation; secondly, there was the idea of greater political freedom in the form of constitutional government and personal liberties; and, finally, there was the idea of nationality, of national freedom from foreign or imperial rule. The interplay of these ideas was to provide much of the conflict and confusion of the nineteenth and twentieth centuries in the political development of the Turks and Greeks. It affected their internal affairs, their relations with each other and eventually their dealings with other powers, especially Britain.

The first Ottoman reformers believed that efficiency and modernisation could be achieved only through a strengthening of the central autocratic power. This trend was bound to conflict with the movement towards decentralisation and autonomy for subject peoples inspired by the principle of nationality. It also ran counter to the later campaign for constitutional liberalism which aimed at reducing the absolutist power of the sultan. Thus throughout the nineteenth and early twentieth centuries there was within the Turkish reform movement a tragic struggle over internal, foreign and imperial policies. It was a clash between modernisers and constitutionalists; between centralisers and autonomists; between efficiency experts and liberty-lovers. This struggle continues within the new Turkish nation to this day and forms part of the background to the present Cyprus problem. Its main concern is now with the nature of Turkish democracy, for the problems of national autonomy have largely—though not entirely—disappeared with the disappearance of the Ottoman empire.

By the end of the eighteenth century the characteristics of the last period of the empire were already apparent: great power interference; the rise of nationalities; and attempts at domestic reform, which were sometimes genuine and sometimes diplomatic whitewash for the eyes of the European powers. The Turks, no longer the conquering warriors of Islam, were on the defensive on all fronts. They had lost a great power's capacity to take the initiative though they were still a force to be reckoned with. The possibility of a collapse of the Ottoman empire in Europe, whetting the appetites of other powers for the spoils, brought into being the 'Eastern Question' as a central issue in European diplomacy. Henceforward the Ottoman empire was to be saved more often by the rivalries of its enemies than by its own strength. In the end it was by a combination of both—when the 'Eastern' and 'Western' questions emerged in the explosive climax of the Greco-Turkish conflict after the first world war—that Turkey itself was saved and built.

CHAPTER THREE

Greek Independence and Turkish Reform

THE MODERN HISTORY of Cyprus, Greece and Turkey begins in the 1820s with a series of massacres. In March 1821, the Greek war of independence erupted with the slaughtering of Turkish villagers in the Peloponnese. Sultan Mahmud II's swift reprisals shocked Europe. On Good Friday, the Orthodox patriarch was hanged in his church robes by the gate of the patriarchal residence in Constantinople. The Greek 'Dragoman of the Porte' was also executed, and Greek Christians were massacred in other parts of the empire.

Five years later, Turks were massacring Turks. Sultan Mahmud, the Peter the Great of the Ottoman empire—urged on by the weakness of the Turkish army in the war against the Greeks and by the humiliation of having to call on the help of Mohammed Ali, the Albanian adventurer who was nominally his vassal in Egypt—had seized the chance of one more mutiny by the Janissaries to wipe out once and for all this troublesome Praetorian Guard which had been holding back urgently needed military reforms.

At first Cyprus was spared in Turkish reprisals against Greeks. It had not joined in the Greek revolt. But eventually the Porte reluctantly agreed to the urgings of its governor of the island who demanded a massacre to forestall an alleged plot for a Cypriot rebellion. On June 9, 1821, Archbishop Kyprianos was hanged from a mulberry tree in the square outside the Saray, the governor's palace in Nicosia. He and scores of other Greek notables had been summoned to the Saray ostensibly to hear a proclamation expressing the sultan's pleasure at their peaceful and loyal behaviour. His archdeacon was hanged from a plane tree opposite and three bishops were beheaded in the same square. According to one, possibly apocryphal, version, the Turks had first saddled the bishops and ridden them like horses, breaking their teeth as they thrust the bits into their mouths and pricking them with spurs to make them prance.

Brutal executions and massacres had happened before. What was new was their cause. In Cyprus, it is true, the main reason was probably the desire to pay off old scores and weaken the growing power of the archbishops which had roused local Turkish jealousies. But the Greek war of independence had introduced the explosive new idea of nationality, 'this fatal Western idea',[1] into a region which hitherto had known only empires, religious communities or non-territorial linguistic groups. As the first serious national movement in Europe or the Near East, the Greek rebellion ushered in a new phase in Eastern and European politics. For the first time a struggle had been launched, not only for control of territory or sovereignty, or for the recognition of identity through religion or language, but for that combination of land, language, culture and political sovereignty which is the characteristic of modern nationalism and is at the root of the Cyprus problem in its modern form.

Previously there could have been no 'enosis' movement because there would have been no 'Greece' for Cyprus to unite with. There were merely 'Greeks' living in different parts of the empire, identified by Greek language and Orthodox Christian religion—especially the latter. If the 'Greeks' identified themselves with any political organisation in the present, it was either local in character or the church, the Orthodox *millet*. In the past, their political consciousness linked them not so much with the states of classical Greece as with the Byzantine empire. For long the 'Greeks' had in fact called themselves 'Romaoi', or Romans, Byzantium having been originally the East Roman Empire. The Turks had taken over the Arab name for the Romans, referring to the Greeks in general as 'Rumi'. The Greek Orthodox community was referred to—as it still is among Moslems today—as the *milleti-Rum*. Moreover, for many centuries the term 'Rumi' or 'Greek' was used to refer to any Orthodox Christian, whether Greek, Bulgar or Serb.

If there was no such place as 'Greece' until the early nineteenth century, equally there was no such place as 'Turkey' until a century later, at least to the Turks themselves. The Turkish-speaking Moslems of the empire did not like to be called 'Turk', which was a term implying a primitive boorishness or worse—rather like calling a German a 'Hun' to his face. The 'Turks' were first and foremost Moslems. This differentiated them from Christians and people of other religions (some of whom also spoke Turkish) more sharply than any identification through language or common place of residence. If further identification were needed, then they were 'Ottomans'.[2] Such traditional ideas of political identity were shaken by closer contact with the West. The doctrines of national liberation developed in the American and French Revolutions were spread by Napoleon's conquests, as well as by the actual success of the older nation states in Western Europe.

Yet the Napoleonic wars, despite the French excursions into Egypt and Syria, seemed to have left the Ottoman empire relatively unscathed. The empire had managed to remain neutral during most of the war and had prospered accordingly, not least its Greek citizens whose maritime carrying trade had flourished under a neutral flag. The Vienna peace settlement of 1815 which ended the Napoleonic wars included no concessions to the doctrine of nationality. On the contrary, it seemed to reinforce all the conservative tendencies, now paramount again not only throughout Europe but also in Turkey, where attempts at reform had led to a wave of reaction inspired by the usual conservative combination of the Janissaries and the *ulema*, or religious authorities.

Appearances, however, were deceptive. Important changes had taken place both inside the Ottoman empire and in its international position. Some of them were obvious and tangible and others of an imponderable kind. In the first place, the Ottoman empire was in growing isolation as a Moslem power. By 1820 the European powers had already begun to bite deeply into the world of Islam. In Egypt, still nominally part of the Ottoman empire, Mohammed Ali had been left stronger and more independent and, with French help, had begun to modernise his army and administration. The Serbian rising in 1804, although made in support of the sultan against local Turkish rebels, had been a pointer to the future restiveness of the Balkan Christians. And, of more importance to future Greek relations with the empire, the British had kept control of the Ionian Islands which they had taken from the French. Napoleon had seized the islands from Venice and proclaimed them, in one of his grandiose generalisations, to be the key to the Near East. He saw them as the first step on the road to India through Egypt: that road he was fated never to be able to travel.

Most important of all was a change, not yet visible on the map, but destined to alter completely the shape of the Ottoman empire, of Europe and the whole world. The political ideas of national and civic liberty set in train during the French Revolution and the Napoleonic wars had taken deep roots which could not be torn up by the diplomatists at the Congress of Vienna. Nor could they any longer be kept in check within the Ottoman empire by an occasional local massacre. These ideas helped to fuse together already existing elements to form the Greek national movement.

The Greeks' consciousness of their Byzantine heritage had been kept alive by the organisation of their Church. It had been further stimulated by the rise to power of Russia, the biggest Orthodox state, on the frontiers of the empire. Within the empire, the Greeks had enjoyed considerable power and influence both in central and local government. Their dominant position in commerce, especially in foreign trade and shipping, had given them both wealth and contacts with the West. As in other national movements, the revival of literature and language by patriot-writers had played its part. The literary influence was all the stronger since the Greeks could, at that time, claim to be 'the most literate Christian race in Europe'.[3] This was due partly to the popular role of the Church in providing a national framework, partly to the Greeks' own highly developed communal sense, and partly to the fact that, for Christians in a Moslem state, learning was the easiest way to advancement, since the profession of arms was denied them.

Some of these contributory factors to the growth of the Greek national movement also explain why, in the first phase of their revival, the Greeks seemed to be thinking not of a national state of their own—an unfamiliar idea—but rather of greater autonomy under a different imperial sovereignty, such as that of Russia, or—at their most optimistic moments—of taking over from within the empire which they considered had once been theirs.[4] But, eventually, the Greeks were forced to the conclusion that they could build a nation only on territory they themselves controlled—territory torn from the empire they had dreamed they might control again. When they made their bid for independence, they did so in an area equal to only about a third of what is now the Greek state. Most of the war was concentrated in the Peloponnese, Rumelia and the Aegean Islands. As a new dream when the Greek state had been won, there came the idea of pan-Hellenism, the bringing together of all the Greek-speaking territories within one national state.

One of the characteristics of nationalism outside Western Europe has been the attempt, not merely to liberate particular territories from foreign rule, but also to unite all those having a common language, culture and religion within a single national state. Nothing comparable with the idea of an English-speaking Commonwealth has seemed strong enough to satisfy the image of the new nation which has to be recreated. This is especially true of those peoples whose own past has been imperial, for example, the Arabs and the Greeks. The creation of political unity even where it has never before existed seems to be a necessary part of the recreation of the sense of personality and identity submerged by centuries of foreign rule. But it has been a fruitful source of conflict in areas like Eastern and South-east Europe where, unlike the West, the boundaries of language and culture do not follow easy and clear contours but often cut across other political frontiers made desirable by geography, security and economics. Such is the essence of the Cyprus problem, as it was of the conflict in the Balkans which set off the first world war.

The first serious Greek revolt, which took place in the Peloponnese in 1770—only fifty-five years after the Turks had taken this last piece of the Greek mainland from the Venetians—was inspired from Russia. It was supported by the Russian fleet which made an extraordinary voyage from the Baltic to the Mediterranean, passing through the English Channel with the benevolent permission of the British, to operate off the southern Greek and western Turkish coasts. The result was little more than a local rising against the Turks encouraged by the Russians for their own purposes: a practice of which the great powers were to make increasing use during the next one hundred and fifty years, to the advantage of some of the sultan's subjects but to the destruction of others, such as the Armenians. The link with the rising power of Russia was important in several respects. Russia was an Orthodox Christian country, the greatest. Her ambition was to reach Constantinople and control the Straits. Catherine II had in anticipation named her grandson Constantine and had him brought up as a Greek. Greek émigrés had established themselves strongly in Russian commerce, especially in the Black Sea area, and some had risen to high office at the Russian court. It was among the Greek trading community at Odessa that the foundations were laid, in 1814, of the secret nationalist society, the Philiki Hetairea, which spread throughout the Greek-speaking communities and helped to launch the war of independence. The Danubian principalities, the autonomous territories of Wallachia and Moldavia, which formed part of the northern frontier between the Ottoman and Russian empires, were traditionally governed by Greek princes.

It was this latter circumstance which dictated the form in which the Greek national movement first made its eventual bid for freedom. On March 6, 1821, Prince Alexander Hypsilanti, a former Greek *hospodar* of Moldavia and Wallachia and at that time ADC to Tsar Alexander's foreign minister, the Count Capo d'Istria (also a Greek), crossed the River Pruth and raised the standard of revolt in Moldavia. It proved a false move. The rebels were disowned by the tsar and got no support from the Rumanians who disliked their Greek governors. Hypsilanti was defeated at Dragoshan in Wallachia on June 19, 1821, and the remnants of his small force were wiped out four days later after a heroic resistance at Skaleni with their backs to the Pruth.

But on March 25, 1821, almost spontaneously and with little co-ordination with the Moldavian revolt, a more serious national rising had begun in the Peloponnese. The odds against the Greeks were heavy and their assets slight. Europe was then in a period of dark reaction after the defeat of Napoleon. Tsar Alexander had formed, with Austria and Prussia, the Holy Alliance sworn to uphold legitimacy. France was under the Bourbons. Britain did not join with the absolutist powers but her government, bent on subduing radicals in England and nationalists in Ireland, did not dissent fundamentally from the Alliance's attitude to revolution. Moreover, all the powers except Russia were sympathetic to Turkey. The first shocked reaction of the powers to the Greek revolt was to condemn the Greeks out of hand as dangerous rebels who should submit at once to their lawful sovereign, the sultan. But when it became clear that the Greeks were managing to hold their ground against Turkish counter-offensives and had actually gained naval command of the Aegean, the attitudes of the powers began to change. Slowly they moved first towards neutrality and then towards mediation and support for Greece.

There were several reasons for the change. One of the most important was the pressure of public opinion in Europe, particularly in Britain and France. To the voices of liberal-minded supporters of nationalism were added those of people whose classical education had bred in them a reverence for the name of Greece. Philhellenism, embracing the modern in the admiration for the ancient Greeks, brought to the support of the independence movement many who, in other respects, were conservative in outlook. This pressure, together with the Greeks' own spirit and their command of the sea, was the chief asset of the Greek national movement. Commercial expediency was also a factor in Western support for the Greeks, particularly in the case of Britain, who also, with France, was anxious to prevent a war between Russia and Turkey from which the former might benefit. So long as the Greek rebels held command of the Aegean, where Britain had considerable trade, and of the sea approaches to the Ionian Islands, now under British control, it was awkward for the government in London to treat them simply as pirates.

Although, at the outset, the international situation was unpromising for the Greeks, there were some good reasons for their choosing this moment for revolt. It was not because the moment was one of particularly harsh oppression or misgovernment by Turkey. If anything, it was because a growth of Greek prosperity, strength and national feeling had coincided with signs of Turkish weakness. 'Turkish rule was in fact neither effectively harsh enough to ensure subjection nor effectively constructive enough to enable the Greeks to prosper as they might and run their own affairs efficiently.'[5] Although the Greeks had a generous share in the commerce and central administration of the Ottoman empire, and their tax burden was not tremendous, the Turkish administration was corrupt and inefficient. The tax-payers got nothing back in the form of government services, not even security and justice. The judges had to be bribed and security depended on a balance between brigands, the *klephts*, and a kind of gendarmerie called the *armatoli* who were little more than other brigands in official pay. In 1821, the Ottoman empire was under pressure, not this time from the European powers or its own Christian subjects, but from its Moslem neighbour, Persia, and from its nominal Moslem vassals, Mohammed Ali in Egypt and Ali Pasha of Yannina in Epirus. Ali Pasha's defiance of the sultan, in particular, may have encouraged the Greek rising, since it both diverted Turkish troops northwards from the Peloponnese and also faced some of the Greeks with the unpleasant choice between the tyranny of Ali Pasha and that of the Turks, one of which was bound to emerge strengthened from the conflict. In the Peloponnese, the Greeks had their best chance of setting up an embryo state which could hold out long enough to have a chance of winning international recognition. There they had been the shortest time under Turkish rule and had retained a surprisingly complete system of local government of their own. There they already had guerrilla warfare experience through the *klephts* and *armatoli*, and there they had a long coastline in contact with the four wealthy maritime islands which could provide them with precious sea-power.

The war began with sporadic local acts of violence; throughout its seven years it was marked by ferocity, heroism, treachery and incompetence on both sides. It was a religious as much as a national war. Two of the Turkish commanders were Greek Christian converts to Islam, while two of the most effective Greek leaders were an Albanian Christian and a Vlach.* The Greek leadership ranged from aristocrats like Prince Hypsilanti and his brother, and Alexander Mavrocordatos

* The Vlachs are a nomadic people akin to the Rumanians in language.

of an ancient Phanariote family, to local mountain chieftains or ex-brigands, such as Kolokotronis, and buccaneering seamen from the islands. The initial impulse had come from the Philiki Hetairea but it was the local leaders, the peasantry themselves and often their parish priests, who kept the struggle going most fiercely. Within the first year, the Greeks had managed to gain enough ground to hold a first National Assembly at Epidaurus, bringing together representatives from the areas freed in Rumelia, in the Peloponnese and the four islands, the main theatres of war and resistance. On January 1, 1822, the Assembly issued its historic proclamation: 'The Greek nation, under the fearful domination of the Ottomans, unable to bear the heavy and un-exampled yoke of tyranny and having with great sacrifice thrown it off, declares today, through its lawful representatives gathered in National Assembly, before God and man, its political existence and independence.'

Despite many reverses—from Turkish counter-offensives, from the defeat of Ali Pasha, the annihilation of the philhellene International Brigade in the battle of Peta, and the siege of Mesolonghi, a key point on the northern approaches to the Peloponnese—the Greeks managed to hold on until, in 1825, they began to feel the more serious pressure of the French-trained Egyptian army under Ibrahim Pasha, Mohammed Ali's son, which the sultan had been obliged to call to the Peloponnese to help him. Ibrahim had already crushed the Greek rebellion in Crete, the island which had been offered to his father by the sultan as part of the price of his help. At the beginning of 1825, Ibrahim set about the reconquest of the Peloponnese by the same methods of massacre and extermination as he had used in Crete. At first, the Egyptian entry into the war was a serious setback for the Greeks, but at least it ended, for the time being, the virtual civil war which had developed among their own rival leaders. It also brought out the bravest efforts of a people who always seem to be at their most heroic when the odds are heaviest against them. But, perhaps most important of all, it hastened the internationalisation of the war which, in the long run, provided the Greeks' best hope of victory. Ibrahim's massacres and deportations—and especially the brutal sack of Mesolonghi—further roused the public opinion of Europe which had already been moved by such events as the Greek capture of Athens, the Turkish massacre of most of the 28,000 men, women and children inhabiting the island of Chios, and the death of Lord Byron and other philhellene volunteers.

By now, the existence of Greece as an independent state was firmly established in the eyes of European opinion. It was paradoxically clinched by the fall of Mesolonghi which had become, partly through Byron's death there, a symbol of Greek resistance. 'Mesolonghi ranks with Thermopylae and Dunkirk among the great victories that have settled the course of history against their victors.'[6] The European governments were being forced to take note of the pro-Greek feeling among their publics, especially their educated classes. Canning, who had taken over the Foreign Office in London, made the first moves towards recognition of the Greeks and began to sound out the Russians about a possible mediation to end the war. His main purpose, however, was still to prevent the Greek revolt from giving the Russians an excuse for war with Turkey. After becoming prime minister and just before he died three months later, Canning persuaded all the powers except Austria to agree to the Treaty of London on July 6, 1827, which led to joint international intervention with a view to achieving a peace settlement. The treaty and the subsequent instructions sent to the British, Russian and French admirals in the Mediterranean called for an armistice, to be enforced if necessary by a naval blockade but without taking sides in the war. The Greeks accepted but the Turks refused mediation. Whether by accident or design—probably the latter—the allied fleets, commanded by Admiral Sir Edward Codrington, a British philhellene, not only blockaded Ibrahim Pasha in the Peloponnese but also destroyed his Turco-Egyptian fleet in the battle of Navarino Bay on October 20, 1827. Wellington, who had succeeded Canning as prime minister, disapproved of this result of Canning's policy of intervention, since his one aim was to preserve the independence of the Ottoman empire. Britain half-apologised to the sultan and the ruin of Canning's policy brought on the one result it had been designed to avoid: a Russian war against Turkey.

The allied intervention had come just in time to save the Greeks from possible defeat at the hands of the ruthless Ibrahim Pasha. The Russo-Turkish war and Wellington's policy delayed the completion of a Greek settlement. In July 1828, Britain and France agreed on joint action in the Peloponnese. Fourteen thousand French troops were landed there and the Egyptian and Turkish troops withdrawn. In the Treaty of Adrianople, imposed on Turkey by Russia on September 14, 1829, the sultan virtually acknowledged Greek independence. Finally, in the Protocol of London, on February 3, 1830, Greece was declared to be an independent monarchy under the guarantee of three powers: Britain, France and Russia. Meanwhile, Count Capo d'Istria, the former tsarist foreign minister, who had been called from retirement to become first provisional president of Greece, had been busy trying to establish his authority over the several Greek political factions and ensure that the frontiers of the new Greek state were as extensive as could be secured. He had more success with the second task than with the first, and in 1831 he was assassinated by a political rival.

After much haggling, the powers agreed that the new king of Greece should be Otho, the seventeen-year-old son of Ludwig I, the philhellene king of Bavaria. Otho was established in Greece in February 1833 with the help of a regency of Bavarian officials, a contingent of 3,500 Bavarian troops and an international loan from the guaranteeing powers. His new state embraced the Peloponnese, central Greece and the islands of the Cyclades; its northern frontier ran from the Gulf of Arta to the Gulf of Volo. 'It thus excluded much territory which could not be described as anything but Greek, in particular Thessaly, Crete, Samos and the Ionian Islands. It was a settlement which left the majority of Greeks outside the pale of freedom . . . but at least it was a beginning and the nucleus of an independent Greek state had at last been formed.'[7] For the next hundred years, Greece was to have two chief political preoccupations: the extension of national freedom to include these 'unredeemed' territories and the extension of political freedom within the Greek state itself. The two purposes often reacted one upon the other. But for the first half of the century at least it was the second which played the more important role.

Although at first King Otho's Bavarian efficiency helped to bring some necessary order out of the political anarchy in the new Greek kingdom, his autocratic methods began to irk his liberty-loving subjects. On September 15, 1843, he was forced by a bloodless revolution to grant a constitution and replace his Bavarian advisers by Greek ministers. But it was not until 1864, after Otho had been compelled to abdicate in the aftermath of another liberal revolution in 1862, that Greece became a popular constitutional monarchy under a new constitution and a new monarch. The Greeks wanted Prince Alfred, duke of Edinburgh, the second son of Queen Victoria, as their new king, but this was ruled out by the treaty between the guaranteeing powers. Eventually, on British advice, the Greeks accepted instead Prince William of Denmark and, as part of the bargain, the British handed the Ionian Islands to Greece. These had been internationally recognised as under British control since 1815, but when Gladstone went to the Islands on a special commission in 1858, he recommended in his report that the desire of the islanders for union with Greece should be fulfilled. On October 30, 1863, Prince William, aged seventeen, ascended the throne of Greece as George I. On November 28, 1864 the new constitution was promulgated. George I's reign was to last for fifty years, to be marked by a careful respect for the constitution, as well as by a revival of expansionist 'Hellenism', and ended by his senseless assassination.

For the Ottoman empire, the Greek war of independence had three important consequences. First, it stimulated the process of internal reform and modernisation that had begun haltingly in the eighteenth century and had been taken up more vigorously by Sultan Mahmud II. To the example of the European powers themselves, there had now been added the further spur of the successful rebellion of a subject race and the achievement of a Moslem vassal in Egypt on whose help the sultan had had to call. Second, the success of the Greeks inevitably changed the traditional relationships which had hitherto existed between the Moslem ruling power and the Christian minorities and nationalities still left within the empire. In particular, it destroyed the former privileged position of the 'unredeemed' Greeks. It created a new tension between the Ottoman government and the minorities.

This tension expressed itself alternately in efforts to appease the Christians through liberal reforms or greater local autonomy, and attempts to control them more closely for fear that they might try to break away from the empire altogether.

The tension was increased by the role of the European powers whose legitimate concern with the fate of the Christian minorities was often subordinate to their use of these same minorities to strengthen their own influence within the area of the empire. The third consequence of the Greek war was that the intervention of the European powers in Ottoman affairs was greatly extended and increasingly given formal recognition.

The crushing of the Janissaries by Mahmud II—an event known in Turkish history as 'The Auspicious Incident'—was followed by the creation of a new Ottoman army recruited and organised on European lines with the help of Prussian advisers. This was the first step towards the strengthening of the state power which the sultan regarded as necessary in order to carry through a programme of westernisation. A powerful state authority backed by a reliable army was needed to deal with the opposition of the traditionalists led by the *ulema*, and of others whose privileges would be threatened. Before his death in 1839,

Mahmud had abolished the military feudal system which had already fallen into decay, and had begun to modernise the civil service. The old institutions of central government and the Moslem religious establishment were reorganised into ministries, departments and committees with European-style titles. Although Islamic law still remained in force in social and personal questions, Mahmud began to introduce European styles of dress and social manners into public life. Not only was the army dressed in European uniforms but officials were also obliged on public occasions to abandon their traditional robes for European frock-coats. The sultan himself set the example by receiving European guests, including ladies, at social functions. His reign also saw the establishment of a postal system and the publication of the first Turkish language newspaper, *The Ottoman Official Gazette.*

Mahmud's efforts, though hampered by Moslem conservatism which limited the amount of European help he could use, were the prelude to a further programme of reform embodied in a series of imperial decrees known collectively as the *Tanzimat* or Reorganisation. The first of these decrees, the 'Noble Rescript of the Rose Chamber', was issued on November 3, 1839, by the new sultan, Abdul Mejid, who was determined to carry on the reforms begun by his father. The *Tanzimat* introduced both new principles and new institutions. It proclaimed the security of life and property, the abolition of tax-farming, the introduction of orderly recruitment for the armed forces, fair and public trials, and equality of people of all religions before the law. It laid the foundations of a new judicial system to replace, at least in part, the authority of the Islamic law. It established a banking and paper currency system. It also proposed the creation of a new system of centralised provincial administration on French lines.[8] The 'Noble Rescript of the Rose Chamber' was followed by a period of conservative reaction. But a new phase of reform began and was embodied in the 'Imperial Rescript' of 1856: it was marked by special attention to education and land reform.

Sceptical European critics have often pointed out how much of the proposed reforms remained only on paper. They have suggested that the reforms were proclaimed chiefly to appease public opinion in Europe and to stave off European pressure and interference. Undoubtedly, the publication of reform schemes often coincided with Ottoman diplomatic requirements, following or accompanying the negotiations of treaties with European powers. The 'Imperial Rescript', for example, was part of the preparation for the Treaty of Paris which settled the Crimean War. But the failure or slowness of many of the reforms was due not so much to insincerity of purpose as to lack of means. Outside pressures, education and closer contact with the West had set genuine new forces in motion in Ottoman society but the transformation of a huge and naturally conservative empire was an enormous task.

Cyprus shared to a limited extent both in the beneficial and adverse results of the Greek war of independence and in the changed attitudes of the Ottoman authorities and the European powers. The Turkish governor, Küchük Mehmed, had found an excuse for the execution of Archbishop Kyprianos and other Greek notables. He had intercepted contacts between the Greek Cypriots and emissaries of the Philiki Hetairea who were urging the Cypriots to join in the Greek revolt. But the archbishop had told the emissaries that the Cypriots could give only moral and financial support. Because Cyprus was so far from Greece and so near the Ottoman Moslem lands of the Levant, a revolt in the island could only bring a massacre of the Cypriots. In fact, as Sir George Hill sardonically summed it up:

> With the exception of some money subscriptions and a few volunteers, Cyprus contributed little to the liberation of the Greeks except by making itself a nuisance to Turkey. In this the Cypriots compared not unfavourably with the majority of the Greek subjects of the Sultan outside the Peloponnese, Attica and some neighbouring islands and parts of Thessaly and Epirus. Thrace, Constantinople, the cities of the Asiatic littoral and the islands of the Ottoman archipelago all failed to answer the summons to join in the revolt.[9]

This cautious attitude did not save the Cypriots from a massacre, though it may have spared them a holocaust on the scale of Chios. Among those who escaped from the island were the two nephews of the murdered archbishop who both rose to be lieutenant-generals in the Greek war of independence.

At the end of the war, when the Egyptian troops which had been sent to Cyprus had been withdrawn and when Greece had already been recognised by the Porte as a sovereign state, a Greek Cypriot agent was sent to Count Capo d'Istria, president of the new Greek state, to ask him to annex the island to Greece. But the liberation of Cyprus was clearly beyond the means of the new Greek state; there is no evidence that Capo d'Istria even raised the question of Cyprus in the negotiations which fixed the first frontiers of Greece. The Cypriot mission was the first manifestation of the modern 'enosis' movement. Its result was also the first demonstration of a basic fact about Cyprus: that Greece alone is not strong enough to take and hold the island against Turkey; this can only be done with the help of some outside stronger power. The reason lies in the relative military strengths of the Greeks and Turks and in the relative distances of Cyprus from the Greek and Turkish mainlands.

The Greek war of independence had destroyed the powerful position enjoyed in Cyprus by the archbishop. Nor could he any longer gain the ear of the Porte through high Greek officials in Constantinople. But, as part of the Ottoman reforms, the Porte made some effort to improve the administration of Cyprus and to give the islanders some degree of economic autonomy. The Turkish governor remained in supreme authority, however, and when he did try to carry out reforms he would often be obstructed by local notables with vested interests, both Greek and Turkish. The Turkish governors varied in their reforming zeal and their ability. A fairly typical example of the time was Said Mehmed whose career is described by Sir George Hill. He was governor three times, the last time in 1841 at the age of eighty. In the course of his duties he made a fortune said to be £400,000. The leading Turks and Greeks liked him because he let them do as they pleased; the peasants were pleased because he relieved them of 600,000 piastres (about £4,800) of tax which he paid out of his own pocket. 'He was mercenary, ignorant, illiterate but easy-going and sometimes generous. Yet it was also said of him that, since owing to the depopulation of the island, he could not raise enough money by taxation, he would be obliged to "cut down and burn the tree in order to get the ashes".'[10] Some idea of the state of the island's government at this period may be gained from the fact that, in 1858, just after the Crimean War, revenue from taxation was 14 million piastres (approximately £117,000) a year, while government expenditure on maintenance, apart from official salaries, was only one million piastres.

There were several small revolts, chiefly against taxation, and the Greek war left increased tension between the Greeks and Turks on the island. It reached a high pitch during the Crimean War when the excited Greeks displayed portraits of Tsar Nicholas of Russia and only the tact of the Turkish governor saved the archbishop from an angry mob. Turkish anger was roused not only by Greek disloyalty but also by the abuse of the system of 'capitulations' by which Greek Cypriots who obtained European citizenships could claim the protection of their consuls and commercial advantages. But the European consuls were often able to intervene with good reason and good result to mitigate the effect of some official injustice.

Among the early benefits which must be counted to Cyprus from the creation of a free Greece was an improvement in the education and cultural life of the Greek Cypriots under the influence of progress on the Greek mainland. These cultural links were also to provide the foundations for the eventual revival of Greek Cypriot political life.

CHAPTER FOUR

Britain's New Empire

THE GREEK WAR of independence involved the European powers, and especially Britain, France and Russia, more deeply than ever in the affairs of the Near East. The Greek settlement not only brought into being a new state and a new balance of power, but also created new fields of diplomacy. It opened the door to the disintegration of the Ottoman empire in Europe and the establishment of other new states in the Balkans, thus creating a new zone of international instability. Inevitably, as a result of the long repressing of national self-expression, the war set in train a movement for national independence among the Christian, and eventually among the Moslem, subject races of the empire: a movement which, though slow to develop, led eventually to the empire's complete collapse. It introduced into the policies of the great powers towards the Porte a fresh source of rivalry and persistent ambiguities of a moral and practical nature which played a large part in leading the European powers, as well as the Ottoman empire, to subsequent catastrophe. It would be absurd, of course, to seek to trace the causes of the first world war directly back to the Greek war of independence. Even so, the Greek struggle can be seen as symptomatic of a series of situations which were to bring the plight of languishing nationalities to the forefront of world affairs and, eventually, to accomplish the disintegration of established imperialism.

The Greek war and settlement magnified the temptation offered the European powers to use the nationalities of the Ottoman empire as agencies either for dismembering or dominating it. Similarly, movements of reform inside the empire were also capable of being used by outside powers either as a necessary means of saving and supporting the sultan's authority, or as a way of influencing and eventually supplanting it. The powers were faced all the time with a calculation of interest whether to prop up the empire, or to nibble away at it, or simply to catch the falling pieces. There was also a genuine moral dilemma, strong in Britain during the Greek war but also visible in France and Russia. On the one hand, European public sentiment was in favour of helping suppressed Christian nationalities struggling against a Moslem power; on the other, the maintenance of the European balance of power and the pressure of British strategic interests appeared to call for the support of the Ottoman sultan and the maintenance of his dominions.

Much of great power policies was henceforward directed to keeping a balance between these factors. For Britain the moral ambiguities have continued until this day. For Russia the moral dilemma was less acute, since she was less concerned about the weakening effect which support of the nationalities might have on the sultan's power. Nevertheless it existed in the conflict between sympathy with Slav and Orthodox nationalities and the tsarist regime's desire to maintain the European status quo against the pressures of revolutionary nationalism. Moreover, just as Britain, while wishing to preserve the Ottoman empire, did not want it to be *too* strong, so Russia, while seeking to dominate the empire, was often in two minds as to whether she really wanted to destroy it altogether or to inherit it more or less intact. As the Ottoman empire became even weaker from within, the rival protectors became, in time, rival heirs-presumptive, each anxious to make sure that the other did not seize the inheritance.

This rivalry and the ambivalence in Russian policy were demonstrated in a spectacular fashion soon after the Greek war. One of the first paradoxical consequences of the settlement was that two of Greece's protecting powers, Russia and Britain, became rivals for the protection of the sultan against a more formidable 'rebel'. Mohammed Ali of Egypt, whose armies had all but crushed the Greeks in the Peloponnese, was forcibly seeking recompense for his help to the sultan by seizing Syria and advancing on Constantinople. His son, Ibrahim Pasha, twice routed the empire's forces inside Anatolia and obliged the sultan to appeal for help. Britain and France did not at first respond but Russia seized the opportunity to intervene with a powerful fleet followed by the landing of an expeditionary force. The Egyptian advance was stopped. The subsequent settlement gave Mohammed Ali Syria and other territories he had demanded, but it also recompensed Russia by way of an agreement with the sultan—the Treaty of Unkiar Skelessi (July 8, 1833), which gave Russia the strongest position she has ever held in Constantinople. This treaty made the Ottoman empire virtually a Russian military protectorate, and a clause, which particularly alarmed Britain and France, gave Russia exclusive rights in the Straits. 'It guaranteed to Russia a free passage for her warships through the Straits, and it closed the door into the Black Sea to every other power. The day after the treaty was signed the Russian troops re-embarked and the Russian navy sailed back to Sebastopol.'[1] As a diplomatic coup, the treaty was obviously too good to last, unless Russia was prepared to fight the other powers to keep all she had won. Britain, where the energetic Lord Palmerston had taken over the Foreign Office, was determined to upset the treaty and establish the principle that any protection for Turkey must be a joint European affair and not exclusively Russian. This objective Palmerston achieved in the Treaties of London of 1840 and 1841. A European Concert of Powers, consisting of Britain, Russia, France, Austria and Prussia, agreed on a new settlement which forced Mohammed Ali to withdraw to Egypt, and stipulated that the Dardanelles and the Bosphorus should be closed to all foreign warships while the Ottoman empire was at peace.

The attitudes of Russia and also of France, which had favoured the claims of Mohammed Ali, left deep suspicions in London. These fears were not set at rest by the efforts of Tsar Nicholas I to come to an understanding with Britain over the future of the Ottoman empire—this 'very sick man' as he called it—and they contributed to the outbreak of the Crimean War (1854–56) in which Britain and France fought against Russia in support of Turkey. The Crimean War has been described as one of the most unnecessary wars in history—a view from which it is difficult to dissent. Yet it could perhaps be argued that, at least, it served to uphold the principle of collective, rather than unilateral, dealings by the great powers with the Ottoman empire. The principles stated in the Treaty of London in regard to joint action by the powers and to the neutralisation of the Straits were reaffirmed in the Treaty of Paris (March 30, 1856) which ended the Crimean War. The Ottoman empire was also invited to join in the Concert of Europe, whose members promised to guarantee collectively the empire's independence and territorial integrity. At the same time, in return for the sultan's promise of internal reforms 'without distinction of race or creed', the powers renounced their own right to interfere, either collectively or separately, in Turkey's internal affairs. There were, however, some accompanying limitations on this self-denying ordinance. While the Rumanian principalities of Moldavia and Wallachia were to remain under Turkish suzerainty, their privileges, together with those of autonomous Serbia, were to be guaranteed collectively by the powers.

Repudiation of the exclusive pretensions of Russia to a protectorate over Turkey, or of France to a protectorate over Egypt, became the 'key-note of English foreign policy throughout three-quarters of the nineteenth century'.[2] But it is difficult to agree with Marriott's further observation that Britain never 'asserted any exclusive claims on her own behalf', and that 'the principle to which she firmly adhered was that the problem of the Near East could be solved only by the Powers in Concert'. For Britain was herself later to break this principle in the case of both Egypt and Turkey. The first serious breach was the Anglo-Turkish Convention of 1878, by which Disraeli established British control over Cyprus and launched his country on the process by which she became a Middle East imperial power in her own right and the successor to, rather than the protector of, the Ottoman empire in Asia.

Until the late eighteenth century, British interests in the Near and Middle East were purely commercial. Since then the pursuit of hard cash has, of course, never been far distant from British preoccupations in that area, whether in the form of the collection of debts in Egypt at the height of the imperial era or of the protection of the sterling assets in Kuwait in the mid-twentieth century. The Younger Pitt was the first to draw attention to the need for a more active British diplomacy in the Near East, in view of the rising power of Russia, but British political, as distinct from purely commercial, interests in the Near and Middle East developed only gradually. This development was shaped by two sets of circumstances. The Napoleonic wars, the campaigns in Egypt and Syria, the acquisition of the Ionian Islands, and then the Greek war of independence, had involved Britain more closely in the Eastern Mediterranean. At the same time, the development of the British empire in India, where British power had been established throughout much of the subcontinent by 1818, led not only to a greater interest in overland communications and trade routes across Western Asia but also, as the Russian empire spread into Central Asia, to the growth of new anxieties about Russian policy. To the nightmare of Russian dominance over the Straits was added the fantasy of Russia hammering at the gates of India.

On the western approaches to the Eastern Mediterranean, towards Egypt and the Levant, Britain's potential rival remained France. On the eastern approaches, towards the Straits, the Persian Gulf and India, her rival was Russia. Yet Britain, France and Russia, who together had saved Greece, were destined because of the rise of German power to be allies in Europe itself. And, in fact, for all the alarms and excursions of antagonistic diplomacy, these three powers—save for the Crimean War

—never came to blows over the Ottoman empire in Europe, or anywhere else, until the futile Anglo-French intervention against the Soviets in the Russian civil war.

However, it was ostensibly to protect the Ottoman empire in Asia against Russia that Britain went into Cyprus in 1878. And it was no coincidence that the man who put Britain there was Disraeli who, a year before, had added 'Empress of India' to Queen Victoria's titles and in 1875 had bought for the British government the khedive of Egypt's shares in the Suez Canal. Disraeli did not suffer from the moral inhibitions that sometimes affected Gladstone and the Liberals in dealing with the Turks. From then to the 1960s, from Disraeli to Harold Wilson, Britain's policy in Cyprus has been a reflection of her general policy in the Near and Middle East and of the role of Turkey in the area. This policy in turn has been influenced by British interest in the trade routes to and from the Persian Gulf and by imperial and then Commonwealth commitments 'East of Suez', with India as the imagined centre-piece of both. After the second world war, when the Indian empire was replaced by the empire of oil, the Persian Gulf became more important and Kuwait outshone Delhi as the brightest jewel in the imperial diadem. It was then that Cyprus again became a serious international issue, after an interval of seventy-five years, during which time the southern maritime route to India through Egypt and Suez had claimed first importance.

A fascinating example of the rhythm of history may be seen in the fact that Britain's first acquisitions in the Near and Middle East under what became the Disraelian policy of empire are also the last to remain at least partially in British hands: Aden, taken in 1839 and for long governed from India; the Persian Gulf sheikhdoms, first controlled by treaty with the government of India from the 1830s onwards; and Cyprus, acquired from Turkey in 1878, but also first occupied by Indian troops. Within this cycle a vast shadow empire in the Middle East has been won and lost by Britain.

The acquisition of Cyprus developed out of the new imperial policy which Disraeli announced when he came to power in 1874. Later he spoke of 'a new world' in which 'the relations of England to Europe are not the same as they were in the days of Lord Chatham or Frederick the Great. The Queen of England has become the Sovereign of the most powerful of Oriental States.' The Indian empire had created 'vast and novel elements in the distribution of power' and the maintenance of the empire had become Britain's first duty. However, the occasion for acquiring Cyprus was provided in the 'old world' of Balkan Europe, not in the 'new world' of Victoria's empire; and the Anglo-Turkish Convention on Cyprus of 1878 was a compromise between the many factors involved in British and European politics during the famous 'Eastern Crisis' of the 'seventies.

When Disraeli, after a life in opposition with but short tenures of office, at last achieved real power at the age of seventy, he pledged himself to pursue an 'energetic' foreign policy. Scope for an expansion of British influence in Europe was limited by the *Dreikaiserbund*—the league of the Austrian, German and Russian emperors—and by the weakness of France after the Franco-Prussian war. On failing to woo Russia away from its alliance with the central empires in Europe, Disraeli acted on the conviction that the most promising field for an 'energetic' foreign policy lay in Asia, especially in the glorification of the Indian empire, and in countering the Russian challenge in Central Asia—for he believed that Russia's expansionist policy there included designs on India. Although the purchase of shares in the Suez Canal Company had intensified Britain's interests in Egypt, Disraeli regarded Constantinople and the Straits as more vital than Egypt for protecting the route to India. Along with many Near East experts of the day, like Sir Henry Layard, the British ambassador to the Porte, he attached exaggerated importance to the Euphrates and Tigris valleys as overland routes to India. Hence he was, at first, a staunch supporter of the Palmerstonian policy of maintaining the independence and integrity of the Ottoman empire.

But this policy had been overtaken by events and had become outdated, due to the declining power of the Turks and to the ferment of nationalism and protest among the Balkan Christians. The latter movement, which aroused the sympathies of European public opinion, threatened the Ottoman empire in Europe with collapse from within. The Turks had been slow to carry out the reforms promised in the Treaty of Paris and in the 'Imperial Rescript' which accompanied the treaty. Continuing unrest in Crete, where direct Turkish rule had been restored in 1840, spread in 1875 to the Christian communities in the Balkans; first in Herzegovina, then through Bosnia, Serbia, Montenegro and Bulgaria. The Bulgarian rising was suppressed by Turkish irregular forces, the *bashi-bazouks*, with a ferocity which horrified Europe. The Western powers, however, took no action against Turkey, and it was left to Russia to take the initiative in defence of the Balkan Slavs. This she was to do with a will, her military intervention in 1877 shattering the Turks and imposing on them the Treaty of San Stefano, signed on March 3, 1878.

As the crisis in the Balkans intensified, leading to Russian intervention, Gladstone thundered against the Bulgarian atrocities and demanded the departure of the Turks 'bag and baggage' from their European provinces. But Disraeli was less concerned with the iniquities of the sultan and the fate of his victims (for long, he, Layard and other British turcophils refused to admit the extent of the atrocities) than with the diplomatic consequences of Russia's rescue operation and, above all, with its effect on Turkey. Indeed, a justifying motive for the Russian intervention may be ascribed in part to the fact that the Turks, believing they had the support of Disraeli and Lord Salisbury (then at the India Office and later to be foreign secretary) in resisting Russian pressure, rejected the various compromise proposals put forward by the powers for pacifying the Balkans by some measure of European supervision. Disraeli certainly had earlier rejected the 'Berlin Memorandum' of May 1876 proposing a joint European mediation in the Balkans, on the grounds that it would have meant Britain's playing second fiddle to Russia in Europe. He would have liked to intervene openly on the side of Turkey against Russia, despite the tsar's assurances that Russia had no intention of seizing Constantinople for herself and that she regarded the status of the Straits as a matter for Europe as a whole. But the British prime minister was restrained by sharp divisions of opinion among the public at home, in Parliament, and even within his own cabinet. Except among the more extreme russophobes and jingoists (which categories later included Victoria), there was no support for a war with Russia or for an offensive alliance with the Porte, whose troops were massacring Christians. Although not all his colleagues in the Liberal leadership shared Gladstone's fervour against the Turks, most Liberals and many Conservatives believed Britain should maintain a policy of non-intervention. Inside Disraeli's cabinet, the foreign secretary, Lord Derby, put a constant brake on the prime minister's moves towards intervention. Salisbury, who succeeded Derby when the latter eventually resigned, favoured an agreement with Russia and the other powers on the partition of the Ottoman empire rather than a fight with Russia in defence of this empire which was too weak to survive. Salisbury thought the Russian threat to India 'a chimæra', and that the best way to secure the route to India was by sea through the control of Egypt and Crete. It was this view which was eventually to prevail, but with the substitution of Cyprus for Crete. Another school of thought was represented by Layard and Colonel Home, a turcophil adviser to the British government on the Near East. They believed that, with Britain's help, Turkey could be reformed and reinvigorated, as India had been, by British rule. To the sultan, the idea that his empire should be treated by the British as a 'second India' was, not unnaturally, more alarming than reassuring.

Disraeli's main preoccupation, apart from the Straits and Constantinople, was to prevent Russian control of Turkish Armenia from which, it was argued by the more melodramatic British strategists of the day, the (overvalued) Euphrates–Persian Gulf route to India would be menaced. But to act against Russia he needed both a change of opinion in Britain and a 'place of arms' in the Eastern Mediterranean which could provide a naval base for military operations in the Dardanelles or in Anatolia. Such an acquisition would also be a concrete symbol of his new imperialism, serving also to commit popular opinion in Britain to the forward policy he desired to pursue in the Near East. For, as Salisbury shrewdly pointed out in a letter to Layard on April 18, 1878:

> . . . this country, which is popularly governed, and cannot, therefore, be counted on to act in any uniform or consistent system of policy, would probably abandon the task of resisting any further Russian advance to the southward in Asia, if nothing but speculative arguments can be advanced in favour of action. But it will cling to any military position occupied by England as tenaciously as it has clung by Gibraltar; and if any movement were made which would threaten it, while assailing the Ottoman dominions its action might be counted on.[3]

Such a place of arms could also serve either as bargaining-counter for a Russian withdrawal or as partial compensation to Britain for any gains Russia might be able to retain. Disraeli initiated a secret survey by Colonel Home and other officers of possible Mediterranean bases. The terms of reference were bases which should combine technical suitability with least likelihood of offending the French if taken over by Britain. This latter stipulation automatically excluded Egypt as an area of study. At the same time, Disraeli worked to change public opinion and to unite his cabinet. He was helped in this by the rapid advance of the Russian armies at the end of 1877 and by the publication of the terms of the Treaty of San Stefano in March 1878.

This treaty powerfully strengthened anti-Russian feeling in Britain.

It would have virtually wiped out the Ottoman empire in Europe, replacing it by a number of new Christian Slav states with varying degrees of independence but all under Russian or Austrian protection. (Russian diplomacy, clumsy in many respects, had been resourceful enough to seek to attach Austria to the proposed settlement of the Eastern Question.) In the Ottoman empire in Asia, Russia was to be given the Black Sea port of Batum, parts of Armenia and the frontier fortresses of Kars and Ardahan. The sultan was to grant reforms to the Armenians living elsewhere in Turkey. Serbia and Montenegro were to become completely independent, while Austria and Russia would jointly supervise the introduction of reforms into Bosnia and Herzegovina. The Russian gains in Armenia provoked the immediate concern of Britain. The feature of the treaty which aroused most concern among the other powers and the Balkan nation states, especially Greece and Serbia, was the proposal to create a Greater Bulgaria as an autonomous principality stretching from the Danube to the Aegean. This revival of the medieval Bulgarian empire would have included most of Macedonia, in which both Greeks and Serbs had claims based on population, and, as a protégé of the tsar, would have given the Russians an outlet to the Mediterranean, putting them in a dominant position in the Balkans and in Constantinople.

Disraeli, though he had rejected the opportunity offered for joint action with Russia, was no more prepared to accept these results of unilateral Russian intervention than Palmerston had been ready to accept the Treaty of Unkiar Skelessi. Claiming that the Treaty of San Stefano had changed previous treaty relationships among the powers, he demanded that it be completely revised at a congress of the European powers. He backed up this demand by moving 7,000 Indian troops to Malta. Eventually, through Bismarck's acting as 'the honest broker', Russia agreed to come to a congress in Berlin to negotiate a settlement of the situation arising from her military defeat of Turkey.

As the diplomatists gathered for the opening of the congress on June 13, 1878, news began to leak out of a striking coup by Disraeli. On June 4, Britain had concluded with Abdul Hamid II a 'Convention of Defensive Alliance' in which she promised to help the sultan to defend his empire in Asia against Russian encroachment. In return, the sultan agreed 'to introduce necessary reforms, to be agreed upon between the two powers, into the government, and for the protection of the Christian and other subjects of the Porte in these territories'. To enable Britain 'to make necessary provision for executing her engagement', the sultan consented to assign the island of Cyprus for occupation and administration by Britain as a 'place d'armes'. Disraeli had found his Mediterranean base. An annexe to the Convention, signed on July 1, 1878, provided that, if Russia handed back to Turkey her Armenian conquests of Kars, Ardahan and Batum, the Convention would come to an end and Britain would withdraw from Cyprus.* Under the same annexe, the surplus revenue of Cyprus, determined by the average of the previous five years, was to continue to be paid to the sultan. (This annual payment became known as the Tribute.) While the sultan retained de jure sovereignty over the island, Britain was accorded, not only de facto control, but also the right to make laws and international agreements for it.

Cyprus had attracted some slight British attention in the preceding decade as a possible staging post on a projected overland route to the Persian Gulf and India via the Euphrates valley. There had also been anxiety in London in 1860 that the French might seize it in a side-operation of their expedition to support the Lebanese Maronites against massacre by the Druze. But, on the whole, Cyprus remained a neglected backwater of the Ottoman empire. The Turks themselves never felt very strongly about the island, to judge from the serious consideration they gave, from the 1840s onwards, to proposals for pawning or selling it to meet their international debts. Indeed, this is precisely what the sultan did in the 1878 Convention; for the Tribute promised him under this agreement with Britain went, not to Constantinople, but to the British Treasury in London, which used it to pay off the debt owed by Turkey to the holders of Ottoman government bonds. This transaction, incidentally, created one of the most persistent and justifiable Cypriot grievances against the British administration. Whether intended or not, one of the practical effects of Disraeli's occupation of Cyprus had a good deal in common with one of the causes of Gladstone's going into Egypt four years later: it ensured the collection of a debt.

Another similarity between the British occupations of Cyprus and Egypt, both still formally under Ottoman suzerainty, was their original provisional character. But both provided excellent illustrations of the precept that 'rien ne dure que le provisoire'. For the evidence of the Cyprus Convention itself and of the circumstances of the day suggests that, initially—at least in Salisbury's mind—the occupation of Cyprus

* By the terms of the settlement at the Congress of Berlin, Russia returned Kars and Ardahan to Turkey, but retained Batum, which is now part of Soviet Georgia.

was intended to be part of the diplomatic game to be played against the Russians at the Congress of Berlin. The movement of Indian troops in the Mediterranean was part of the pressure applied to bring Russia to the conference table. The Convention itself was drafted in such a way as to be dispensable should something more worthwhile be extractable from the Russians.* On the other hand, Disraeli had already described the island to Queen Victoria as the 'key to Asia'; its occupation certainly fitted in with his general imperial schemes.

The occupation of Cyprus appears to have been first suggested to the British government on March 27, 1878—five days after the terms of the Treaty of San Stefano were published in London—when Disraeli told the cabinet that he intended to send troops from India to occupy the island, together with Alexandretta on the mainland of Turkey. On April 17, the British prime minister announced the despatch of 7,000 Indian troops to Malta. The decision to land a force in Cyprus, rather than at Alexandretta or any other port in the Levant suitable as an advance base against a Russian attack on Turkey, was probably made between April 18 and May 10 as a result of recommendations contained in a report by Colonel Home. Meanwhile, negotiations for the convening of the Congress of Berlin and for the secret conclusion of the Cyprus Convention had been proceeding in parallel. The despatch of Indian troops may have helped to ensure the former, while the latter was clinched by a telegraphed ultimatum from Salisbury in London on May 24. He bluntly threatened the sultan, already terrified by the proximity of Russian troops to Constantinople and the discovery of a plot against his life, that unless he signed the Convention at once, Britain would be compelled to abandon him. The Russians would then be free to enter Constantinople and partition the Ottoman empire at their will. Although Salisbury's threat was toned down by the British ambassador, Sir Henry Layard, to spare the nerves of his friend, the sultan, the latter's agreement to the British demand was secured within the time-limit set. The Turkish Grand Council attempted to delay a decision in the hope that something might still be arranged at the Berlin Congress without involving submission to the British terms for protection. But the pressures on Turkey were too great to admit of delay, and the sultan signed.

Once the Convention had been signed, the British installed them-

* In a letter to the French foreign minister, Waddington, explaining the Cyprus Convention, Salisbury referred to the occupation of the island as 'provisional'.

selves in Cyprus with the utmost speed—presumably because London felt it essential that Britain's presence there be effectively established before the Congress of Berlin ended. Even so, quick as the British were, others had got there before them. Rumours of the change of regime had brought over a swarm of speculators from Constantinople to buy up property, among them Zacharios Vasilios Zachariades who was to achieve fame in later years as Sir Basil Zaharoff, the armaments king.[4] The British advance guard was a naval squadron under Vice-Admiral Lord John Hay. Landing at Larnaca on July 8, 1878, he took charge of the island without any Turkish resistance, proceeding to Nicosia the next day to complete the take-over from the last Turkish governor, Bessim Pasha. The British navy showed its usual resourcefulness. 'The absence of any opposition to the Vice-Admiral's progress may possibly have been due, in part at least, to the fact that he let it be known that the British Government would pay all arrears of salaries. As though in earnest of the promise, he was accompanied by two mules laden with sacks of new sixpences.'[5] The British flag was hoisted in Nicosia on July 12, 1878, and on July 17, 400 Indian troops from Malta landed at Larnaca. They were followed five days later by Lieutenant-General Sir Garnet Wolseley, the new high commissioner and commander-in-chief.

Non-official Turks and Greeks welcomed the change of authority, hoping it would mean the ending of all taxes, at least according to *The Times* correspondent, whose inspiration may have derived from the fact that he was also the private secretary to the new high commissioner. There is no reason to doubt that the Greeks welcomed the change for political reasons also. Not only was the burden of Turkish rule lifted, but there were hopes that the British occupation might be a stage towards the island's eventual union with free Greece. The bishop of Kition read an address of welcome to the new high commissioner in which he is reported as saying: 'We accept the change of Government inasmuch as we trust that Great Britain will help Cyprus, as it did the Ionian Islands, to be united with Mother Greece, with which it is naturally connected.' No one, of course, had consulted the Cypriots themselves about the change of their government and status. Unlike Crete, Cyprus at that time was not considered as a factor in the balance between Greece and Turkey. The fact that the Cypriots were mostly Greek-speaking was never, even by Liberals, considered of importance or even publicly mentioned, except for Lord Derby's prediction, after resigning from the Foreign Office, that in a generation Cyprus would be a Greek, not an English, community. Indeed, one reason why Colonel

Home had recommended the occupation of Cyprus rather than of Crete, with its 'enormous advantages', was that the people of Crete had always sought union with Greece, and so its occupation 'would infallibly produce political trouble'.[6] Clearly, no such cause of trouble was seen among the Cypriots. Some of the European powers, however, felt strongly about Disraeli's action when the facts became known. So, too, did the Liberal opposition in Britain. The French, in particular, always sensitive about their traditional position in the Levant, had to be placated by the offer of a free hand in Tunis. They were also assured that it was precisely to avoid upsetting French feelings that the British had chosen Cyprus as a base rather than Alexandretta, or a port in Egypt or Syria. This may have been partly true, but another reason was British official optimism about the possibilities of the development of Famagusta as a naval base. These possibilities, about which other expert naval opinion was doubtful, were never put to the test, because within a few years the British obtained far superior naval facilities at Alexandria. France withdrew from the joint control of Egypt and, after the British intervened there militarily in 1882, they took charge not merely of an Egyptian port but of the whole country.

In Britain, there was little popular criticism of the Cyprus occupation. Queen Victoria wrote to her cherished Disraeli: 'High and Low are delighted, except Mr Gladstone, who is frantic'. In political circles, however, some Conservatives as well as Liberals were sceptical of the value of the Cyprus Convention. The usefulness of Cyprus as a naval base was questioned and it was not difficult to show its irrelevance to the tasks of defence and reform in Turkey's Asian provinces. The more general criticism in political circles was directed at the wisdom of promising to protect Turkey against Russia. The critics also asked whether Turkey's promise to reform was worth anything in the light of past experience and whether Britain had been wise to take responsibility for ensuring that the reforms were carried out.[7] For Gladstone, the Cyprus agreement was an 'insane convention' and the fruit of 'an act of duplicity not surpassed, and rarely equalled in the history of nations'. Gladstone could not deny that the Congress of Berlin had helped to consolidate the freedom of the new Balkan Christian states from Turkish rule, but he was opposed to the separate British agreement to defend Turkey in Asia. He saw it as a dangerous breach of the principle of concerted European action which was the only effective way to deal with the problems of the Ottoman empire. In the absence of this necessary concerted action, he regarded Britain's assumption of responsibility for ensuring reforms in the Asian provinces of the Ottoman empire as a sham used to justify the acquisition of Cyprus, which was itself worthless. In fact, the attempt of Salisbury and Layard to bring about the promised reforms in Turkey came to nothing. Britain's later inability or unwillingness to intervene in Turkey to prevent the massacres of the Armenians—whose protection the Cyprus Convention had clearly in mind—was to confirm the accuracy of Gladstone's analysis. But when Gladstone returned to power in 1880, he did not repudiate the Convention or give up Cyprus. It was too soon to reverse an act which had both popular feeling and the monarch behind it.

Gladstone's disapproval, the occupation of Egypt, the Tribute, the uncertainty of the British lease—all contributed to discourage both public and private investment in Cyprus, whether military or civilian. British rule brought immediate benefits of law and order, of personal security and civil liberties. But socially and economically, Cyprus remained for long an orphan island among British imperial territories. Typical of the atmosphere of parsimonious impermanence was the prefabricated wooden military bungalow, once destined for Ceylon, which served for years as Government House, until it was burnt down by the rebellious Greek Cypriots in 1931 at the cost of their constitutional liberties.

Because of the island's geographical position (as noted on page 57), it is doubtful whether the Greek Cypriots could ever have liberated themselves from Turkish rule unaided. The Cretans, more warlike and less exposed, could not do so, and it is by no means certain that Greece herself could have finally achieved her independence without outside help. If the British had not taken Cyprus, it is unlikely that the island could have won freedom with the help of Greece alone. It is, of course, conceivable that it might have won freedom as the result of a war involving the European powers, or as part of some general settlement and exchange of territories and populations such as took place after the first world war and the subsequent Anatolian war between Greece and Turkey. But otherwise it would probably have stayed under Turkish rule with the Greeks as a minority within a Turkish state, like the Kurds or like the Arabs in the Hatay. So it could be argued that the British occupation was a necessary stage in the liberation of the Greek Cypriots from Turkish rule, even though, after waiting for seventy-seven years, they finally had to fight Britain to achieve it.

CHAPTER FIVE

Greek Revolt and Turkish Revolution

THE CYPRUS CONVENTION inaugurated a new British policy and eventually a new imperial era in the Middle East. During the next forty years a large part of this area, formerly under Ottoman sovereignty, became in one form or another a huge British protectorate. This quasi-empire has varied in its parts from outright colony to treaty associate, from mandated territory to pseudo-independent state. For more than eighty years, the policy it represented was never entirely abandoned, but it steadily became more of a ghost than a reality as the British power to maintain it shrank. British policy was eventually reduced to an intermittent rearguard action designed to prevent the domination, not of an external major power, but of a local minor power: Egypt, which emerged in the mid-twentieth century as a rival heir to Turkey's Asian empire as she had been a century and more earlier under Mohammed Ali.

Yet at the time it was made, the Cyprus Convention seemed merely a 'sideshow' to the Congress of Berlin. And so it might have remained but for the British occupation of Egypt. Ironically, it was not Disraeli the Imperialist but Gladstone the Liberal who, by his reluctant intervention in Egypt in 1882, laid the real foundations of future British power in the Middle East. It was from this almost accidental action, as much as from Turkey's decision to join Germany's side in the first world war, that Britain was led to pursue in the Ottoman empire precisely that policy for which she had attacked Russia after the treaties of Unkiar Skelessi and San Stefano. Britain and France together destroyed the Ottoman power in Asia—that power which it had once been British policy to uphold—and replaced it by their own.

But in 1878 international attention was still concentrated on what was left of the Ottoman empire in South-east Europe. The Berlin Congress was called primarily to revise the map of the Balkans drawn up in the Treaty of San Stefano. The Treaty of Berlin, signed June 13, 1878, had four main results. It prevented Russian dominance at Constantinople; cut down Greater Bulgaria to a minor principality which was to wait another thirty years to expand and gain complete independence; restored most of Macedonia to Turkey; and recognised the independence of Serbia, Montenegro and Rumania. The treaty was criticised for having left some rebellious Christians, such as the Cretans, under Turkish rule and restored others, such as the Macedonians, to the sultan's authority. The Balkan peoples themselves were scarcely consulted, but the treaty set the pattern in the Balkans for thirty years of comparative peace in the peninsula and in Europe as a whole. This peace was eroded at last by the growing nationalism of the Balkan peoples; by a gathering movement of revolt among the Turks themselves against the absolutism and incompetence of Sultan Abdul Hamid; by the sharpening of unsatisfied Greek irredentism; and by the breakdown of the Concert of Powers through the growing ambitions of Germany in the East.

Greece had acquiesced, not without disappointment, in the British occupation of Cyprus. The island had not been among the Greek claims presented to the Congress of Berlin. None of these claims, which included Thessaly, Crete and Epirus, had been accepted. Greece had gained nothing immediately from the Berlin Treaty except a vague promise of changes in her northern frontier and the fact that the Macedonian Greeks remained under Turkish instead of Bulgar rule, thus giving them a chance for future redemption.[1] The Turkish retention of Crete in particular was a sore blow to Greek pride and to the expansionist hopes of Hellenism. After the accession of King George I in 1863, the Greeks had been chiefly preoccupied with building their young state on a constitutional basis. But they had not forgotten their hopes of achieving the liberation of the other Greeks still left 'unredeemed' under Turkish rule. The new Greek monarch was significantly given the title 'King of the Hellenes' instead of 'King of Greece'. During most of his reign, Greek politics was a struggle between a militant expansionist Hellenism, advocated in an often jingoistic form by Theodore Delyannis, and a policy of cautious national consolidation represented by the more conservative Charilaos Trikoupis.

Although rebellion in Crete may have helped to inspire the insurrections which led to the Congress of Berlin, the Balkan struggle of 1875–78 was largely a Slav affair in which the Greeks had little share. For a time the Greek government, with Trikoupis as foreign minister, resisted popular pressure to join in the fight against the Turks. It relied on the British government to secure Greece proper compensation at the peace settlement for having virtuously resisted the temptation of siding with Russia. But as the Russians neared Constantinople, popular pressure forced the replacement of the government by an interventionist cabinet with Delyannis as foreign minister. The new government encouraged Greek risings in Thessaly and Epirus, and the Cretan Christians also rose again in revolt. But before the Greek army could carry out its declared purpose of occupying Thessaly and Epirus, the Russians and Turks had signed the armistice which was to lead to the Treaty of San Stefano. British mediation helped to end the rebellions in Thessaly and Crete. However, most of Thessaly, a rich agricultural province, went to Greece three years later, after the talks to settle Greece's northern frontier which were agreed upon at the Congress of Berlin. Greece owed this important territorial gain largely to the diplomatic support of Britain and France. In the course of these negotiations, she rejected an alternative offer from Turkey of Crete, some small islands and a minor change in the mainland frontier. The Cretans accepted this decision as being in the general Hellenic interest. 'It was felt that Crete, racially a Greek island, must inevitably one day come to Greece, whereas an increase of territory in the direction of Macedonia and Albania was urgent, for in those regions there were rival races with claims of their own.'[2] This settlement lasted almost unchanged until 1912, except for a slight strategic modification of the frontier in Turkey's favour after the Greco-Turkish war of 1897. The cession of Thessaly, where the Moslems had been large landowners, led to the migration to Turkey of much of the local Moslem population: a phenomenon afterwards often repeated in areas won by the Greeks from the Turks.

Crete, the self-sacrificial victim of the settlement, was left under Turkish rule and in a state of unrest. The difficulties in the way of realising the Cretan hopes for union with Greece were much greater than in the case of the Ionian Islands. They were more comparable with those which later faced the Greek Cypriots. Like Cyprus and the Ionian Islands, Crete had been ruled by Venice. But whereas the Ionian Islands, far from the centre of Turkish power, were never wholly occupied, or for long, by the Turks and had no Moslem population, both Crete and Cyprus, within striking distance of Asia Minor, were conquered by the Turks and had a substantial proportion of Moslem inhabitants. Yet between Crete and Cyprus there were also important differences. Crete was not conquered by the Turks until nearly a century after Cyprus. In Crete the Moslems, who at one time were a majority, were mostly converted Greeks and townsmen, whereas in Cyprus they were Turkish settlers from the mainland and predominantly farmers.

The relative docility of the Cypriots was accentuated by their nearness to the Turkish mainland and their five hundred miles distance from Greece. The aggressiveness of the Cretans, renowned fighters and rebellious by character and tradition, was encouraged by their mountain terrain and their greater proximity to the Greek mainland than to the Turkish coast. Yet local valour or even help from Greece were not enough for liberation in the face of superior Turkish power. Either allies or international support were essential. This, true for Crete, was to be as true for Cyprus in modern times.

Crete had joined in the Greek war of independence in 1821, but after the Christian rising had been crushed by Ibrahim Pasha, the island was united with Egypt as the Turkish payment to Mohammed Ali for his help in the Greek war. Ten years later, when Mohammed Ali was forced by the great powers to withdraw from Syria to Egypt, Crete returned to Turkish rule. Like other groups of the Ottoman empire, the Cretans were promised reforms. In 1858, both Christians and Moslems in the island threatened rebellion if the reforms were not carried out. The Christians were hoping for either union with Greece or the creation of an autonomous Christian principality. The Moslems wanted less taxation. Eight years of further delay by the Ottoman government provoked a Christian rebellion in 1866 which lasted for three years. Volunteers from Greece went to support the rebels, but the Greek government at first was neutral. However, Turkish atrocities, which alternated with conciliation, and the heroic act of Abbot Mareses of Arkadion in blowing up his monastery rather than surrender to the Turks, excited international and Greek opinion. France proposed a plebiscite in Crete and, together with Russia, supported Cretan union with Greece in 1867. Britain opposed this union. Greece drifted nearer to war with Turkey, but in 1869 at a conference called in Paris by Bismarck she promised not to allow action against Turkey by Greek irregulars or warships.

With no prospect of Greek support, the Cretan rebellion died down. Its only success had been to rouse the attention of Europe, which was to prove useful thirty years later, and to extract from the Turks the promise, in 1868, of a new 'Organic Statute'. Under the new statute, the island was to be governed by a *vali* with two assessors, one of them a Christian, and a mixed Christian–Moslem Council of Administration. Greek and Turkish were both to be official languages. There was to be an annual General Assembly and no new taxes. Turkey's refusal to modify this statute led to the Cretan rising of 1878 during which the

Cretan Assembly asked for the island to be given autonomy with the payment of a tribute, a position similar to that enjoyed by Samos. The Ottoman government promised 'in concert with England' to arrange for 'a new form of government for Crete'. Although the promise was not kept, the Congress of Berlin decided that Crete should remain under Turkish rule on condition that the sultan applied the 1868 Organic Statute. The Cretans were, however, given some concessions in the Pact of Halepa which improved the Organic Statute. The pact set up a governor-general (who for some years afterwards proved in practice to be a Greek Christian subject of Turkey), assisted by an assessor of the opposite religion. In the General Assembly the Christians had a majority, and Greek was made the official language of the legislature and the courts. Half of the surplus revenue was pledged for badly needed local government. But, after the Cretans rose again in revolt in 1889, the pact was repudiated by the Ottoman government. A struggle between Christians and Moslems developed out of a party dispute in the Assembly and the Christians called for union with Greece, but the Greek government under Trikoupis held aloof. Turkey then adopted a more conciliatory attitude, appointed a Christian governor and called together the Assembly for the first time in six years.

Cretan discontent was only temporarily appeased and broke out again in a fresh rising on May 24, 1896. This rising led not only to the end of Turkish rule but also to the Greco-Turkish 'Thirty Days War' of 1897 which briefly punctuated the thirty years' peace in the Balkans. The continued struggle of the Cretans to achieve union was also closely linked with the Balkan Wars of 1912–13, which gave Greece her biggest expansion since she became a state. The architect of the Balkan victories was the Cretan leader, Eleutherios Venizelos, and the Cretan question played a part not only in the rise to power of Greece's greatest statesman of modern times, but also in bringing about the revolution in the Ottoman empire which led eventually to the creation of modern Turkey under Kemal Ataturk. Venizelos, then a thirty-two year old lawyer scarcely known outside his native island, was one of the leaders of a handful of Christian rebels who, in February 1897, occupied Akrotiri* and once more made the traditional proclamation of union with Greece. This time the proclamation was at last to bear fruit because, for once, the Cretans' own efforts were supported from outside, not only by Greece but indirectly by the European powers. But this help led in the first place to disaster for Greece herself, and the union was not com-

* The peninsula in Crete which separates the town of Canea from Suda Bay.

pleted until Greece was strong enough, with the help of her Balkan allies, to enforce it without the assistance of the great powers.

When the Cretan chiefs proclaimed enosis, Delyannis was in power in Athens, unchallenged by his old rival Trikoupis who had died in exile in Cannes. Delyannis decided to intervene. A squadron of Greek destroyers was despatched to Crete under the command of Prince George and Greek troops under Colonel Vassos were landed on the island. The Turkish governor, destined to be the last, fled. But the great powers intervened to prevent a Greek annexation of the island, for this, they considered, would have upset the agreed status quo and brought about war between Greece and Turkey. The fleets of the Concert of Europe—warships from Britain, France, Russia, Italy, Germany and Austro-Hungary—were lying off Crete. Their admirals jointly occupied Canea and bombarded the positions of Christian rebels who had raised the Greek flag on Akrotiri. But while the powers were still determined to prevent annexation by Greece, they were no longer willing to restore the island to Turkish rule. Instead, they proclaimed Cretan autonomy and set up a blockade to enforce it.

In Greece, public pressure grew strong for war with Turkey. The king gave way to this pressure, possibly in the hope that the powers might intervene and so enable him to withdraw gracefully before war actually started.

Greek irregulars were sent across the Turkish frontier in Thessaly and regular reserves were mobilised. On April 17, 1897, Turkey replied by declaring war on Greece. The powers, however, did not move. Alone and ill-prepared, Greece was routed on land by the German-trained Turkish army, while she was unable to use her superior sea-power effectively partly because of the presence of the European fleets, and partly also because of the danger to the Greek population along the coast of Asia Minor.[3] After a campaign of only one month, mainland Greece lay at the mercy of the Turkish forces advancing through Thessaly, and was saved from being over-run only by the intervention of the powers. The Treaty of Constantinople (December 4, 1897), which followed this intervention, restored to Greece Turkey's gains in Thessaly, except for certain strategic points along the frontier.

This humiliation had two beneficial consequences for Greece. It led eventually to the Greeks' making efforts to put their house in order and reorganise their governmental system and armed forces. It also led to the end of Turkish rule over Crete. The island, however, had to wait another fifteen years for complete union with Greece. During most of the intervening time, it was under a hybrid, semi-independent regime and an international military force—in this curiously anticipating the situation in Cyprus sixty years later. Partly because of the international military presence in the island, Greece's defeat by Turkey did not end the rebellion in Crete.

Before the end of the Greco-Turkish war, Greece had withdrawn her forces and volunteers from the island, but the Cretans themselves continued their insurrection despite attempts at repression by the great powers. Two-thirds of the Moslem population were concentrated in a cordonned-off enclave round Candia, from which 8,000 Christians had left. In this area there was still a Turkish governor, and elsewhere in the island there were units of Turkish troops which were involved from time to time in minor clashes with the insurgents. The blockade by the fleets of the great powers prevented any reinforcement or rotation of these troops from Turkey. Moreover, the powers were considering the idea of a non-Ottoman and a non-Greek, Christian governor to head an autonomous Cretan state. In the end, however, the final withdrawal of the Ottoman authorities and of Turkish forces from the island was brought about, not so much by European sympathy for the Christian rebels, as by a sudden rising of Cretan Moslems in Candia on September 6, 1898, which resulted in the death of the British vice-consul and of a number of British soldiers. This bloody incident and the accompanying massacre of Christians in the town finally convinced the powers that the island could not be pacified until Turkish rule there had been totally ended. The admirals of the four powers (Germany and Austro-Hungary had withdrawn from the joint operation of the Concert of Europe in Crete) demanded the departure of the Turks, and invited Prince George of Greece to act as high commissioner of Crete for three years on behalf of the powers, while still remaining nominally a vassal of the Ottoman sultan. The last Turkish troops withdrew from the whole of Crete, except for a small island in Suda Bay, and on December 21, 1898, Prince George landed on Cretan soil, to stay not for three years but for eight.

'Thus,' as an English historian observed, 'the loss of a handful of British fighting men had done more to goad Europe into definite action than the massacre during several generations of many thousand Cretans.'[4] Prince George arrived with the best conciliatory intentions and his first five years as high commissioner were relatively quiet. Cretan autonomy was given substance by a new Constitution, together with the outward symbols of a new Cretan flag, stamps and coins and a

Cretan police force trained by Italian carabinieri. The powers withdrew from the districts their troops had occupied but maintained their headquarters at Canea. The British withdrawal from Candia led to a big emigration to Asia Minor of the local Moslems whom the 1900 census showed to have been reduced to only one ninth of the population. But Crete's troubles were not yet over. The Constitution had given Prince George considerable personal influence and his inexperience and temperament led him into an increasingly autocratic use of this power in his dealings with the Cretan politicians. He quarrelled with the Assembly and dismissed Venizelos, the most able of his five councillors. Venizelos and other members of the opposition took to the hills and, in 1905, set up a provisional National Assembly at Therisso, a famous stronghold. They passed the traditional vote for union with Greece but were persuaded by the consuls of the powers to end their resistance and disperse. A year later Prince George resigned from his post of high commissioner and Crete took another step towards the international recognition of union when the four protecting powers allowed King George of Greece to choose the prince's successor. He chose Alexander Zaimis, a competent and moderate politician from an old political family, who had twice before served as prime minister of Greece. Zaimis quietly and tactfully took the administration of the island in hand, and retired Greek officers took over the training of the police from the Italians and organised a Cretan militia.

In Greece itself politics in the decade following the Greco-Turkish war of 1897 were an affair of personalities and rapid changes of government, often on trivial pretexts. Delyannis was the victim of assassination, the first murder of a Greek leader since Capo d'Istria's in 1831. He was killed not because of his adventurous foreign policy but because he tried to suppress the gambling houses of Athens. Macedonia began to take the place of Crete as the chief Hellenic question. It became the battleground of Greek and Bulgarian armed bands supporting the rival claims of the Greek and Bulgar states and churches. The growing chaos there brought the introduction of an international gendarmerie provided by five European powers. As in Crete, Germany held aloof—another sign of her growing effort to woo the Turks, and strengthen her influence at Constantinople.

Macedonia was also the birthplace of the Young Turk revolution of 1908 and the homeland of Kemal Ataturk who was born in Salonika in 1881. It was from Salonika that a group of young Turkish army officers and intellectuals, united in the secret Committee of Union and Progress, sent an ultimatum by telegram on July 21, 1908, to Sultan Adbul Hamid. They demanded the immediate restoration of the Ottoman Constitution of 1876, failing which a hundred thousand troops would march on Istanbul and replace the sultan by the heir-apparent.

The 1876 Constitution had been short-lived. It had been the fruit of an agitation by liberals and reformers of the 'Young Ottoman' movement against the incompetence, over-centralisation and waste of Sultan Abdul Aziz (1861–76). During his reign, increasing reliance on foreign loans brought the Ottoman treasury to bankruptcy and caused it to default on its debt payments. Abdul Aziz was deposed in 1876, and, after a three months' reign by his nephew Murad V, he was succeeded by his younger brother, Abdul Hamid II. As a condition of his accession, Abdul Hamid had promised to set up a constitutional regime. He proclaimed the Constitution on December 10, 1876, and appointed as grand vizir the leading liberal statesman, Midhat Pasha, who had drafted the Constitution together with the Turkish writers and reformist leaders, Namík Kemal and Ziya Pasha. But the new sultan soon showed that he had accepted the Constitution only as a matter of political and diplomatic expediency. He intended it only to facilitate his own assumption of power and to appease European opinion in the international crisis that was threatening with Russia over the ruthless Turkish suppression of the Christian revolt in Bulgaria. As soon as these purposes had been served, the sultan first got rid of Midhat Pasha, whom he sent into exile and later had murdered in prison in Arabia, and then of the parliament which had been elected under the Constitution. This first parliament in Ottoman history, consisting of a Senate and a Chamber of Deputies, lasted only ten months. It was dissolved by the sultan on February 13, 1878, on the excuse that it had been responsible for the disastrous defeats inflicted on the empire by Russia in the war of 1877–78.

For the next thirty years the Ottoman empire was subject to the personal despotism of Abdul Hamid: a ruler of pathologically suspicious nature whose cruelly oppressive regime was supported by a vast network of spies and secret police. The Young Ottoman movement was broken. Some of its leaders accepted office from the sultan, while those who kept their ideals were driven underground or into exile. Nevertheless, a new liberal movement began to take shape inside the empire and abroad. It was spurred on not only by the evils of the sultan's rule but also, paradoxically, by some of its benefits. Abdul Hamid was not opposed on principle to practical reforms, provided they left his political power untouched. During his reign there was a considerable expansion in public education, in the provision of railways, posts and telegraphs, and even in the publication of newspapers, books and magazines, though their political content had to conform to the sultan's rigid censorship. At the same time, the army was being reorganised and trained with German help. By these means the sultan unwittingly prepared the way for his own eventual overthrow, for these improved means of public knowledge and communications, both within the empire and with the outside world, helped the spread of new ideas, despite the censorship. The new higher schools, especially those connected with the army, began to swell the stream of a new governmental and military elite. This new elite was anxious to put into practice the modern ideas it had learned from Europe through teachers who were imbued with the Young Ottoman doctrines of freedom and progress.[5]

'These young men, the future soldiers and administrators of the Empire, were given the most advanced and most modern education that the state could offer; it was inevitable that they and their teachers should, sooner or later, reach some radical conclusions on the conduct of the state which they were to serve.'[6] The first of the new liberal movements was the secret 'Ottoman Society for Union and Progress' founded among the students of the Army School of Medicine in 1889. The society spread to other schools but, discovered by the police, was suppressed. Some of its members fled into exile. They continued their propaganda from London, Paris and other foreign capitals and maintained contact with Turkish students, officials, intellectuals and army officers. The mainstream of the movement in exile flowed through the Committee of Union and Progress in Paris of which the leading figure was Ahmed Riza Bey (1859–1930) who had been director of education at the Turkish city of Brusa. They became known as the 'Young Turks', possibly after the journal *La Jeune Turquie* which had been founded by one of their forerunners in Paris. In 1896 there was an unsuccessful attempt to depose the sultan, after which the organisation became more cautious until, ten years later, the Young Turk movement entered a significant new stage on the road to power with the formation of secret revolutionary cells among army officers in the field. Among the first of these groups was the 'Fatherland Society' which Mustafa Kemal, later Ataturk, helped to found in Syria where he was serving with the army as a cavalry captain. Kemal's group later merged with a committee set up by the officers of the Turkish Third Army Corps in Salonika.[7] The Salonika group in turn merged in September 1907 with the Committee of Union and Progress in Paris.

A number of factors brought the movement out into open revolt. The introduction of constitutional regimes in Russia and Persia in 1908 was an encouragement to action. The Turkish army itself was in a bad state, with the soldiers short of rations and pay. 'Smart young officers, with up-to-date training for an out-of-date army, could not but be painfully aware of the inadequacy of the defences of the empire in the face of the dangers that were looming. Their political ideas were simple and rudimentary—freedom and fatherland, the constitution and the nation.'[8] The revolt was finally precipitated by the sultan himself who, alarmed at reports of unrest among the Third Army Corps, sent two commissions of enquiry to Macedonia. One of the suspected officers, Enver Bey, was asked to come to Istanbul but instead he escaped to the hills. He was followed shortly afterwards by a more senior officer, Major Ahmed Niyazi, who took soldiers and weapons with him and declared his open defiance of the authorities. As the mutiny spread, the Committee of Union and Progress gave it open support and linked with it their demand for the restoration of the Constitution. The sultan tried to temporise and break the movement by intrigue, but on July 24, 1908, three days after the Salonika Committee's ultimatum, he announced that the Constitution had been restored.

CHAPTER SIX

Ottoman Imperialism and Hellenism: Death Throes and Disaster

THE YOUNG TURK revolution began the destruction of the old Ottoman political order, but it was only one, albeit important, stage in the long effort of the Turks to come to terms with Western culture and power: an effort which began two centuries ago and on which, psychologically at least, the Cyprus dispute still has some effect today.

One of the tragedies of this Turkish struggle to adapt and reform is that, as has occurred in other countries, the advent of the reformers often coincided with dangerous pressures from precisely those quarters at home and abroad to which the reformers looked for co-operation and help. The results generally either discredited the reformers at home or provoked them to bitterness and disillusion. For example, the revolt of the Balkan Slavs and Turkey's disastrous defeat by Russia in 1876–78 helped to wreck the first Ottoman constitutional experiment.

When the Young Turk revolution revived the constitutional regime thirty years later, it again immediately faced a crisis in its relations with the Balkan Christians and with Europe. The revolutionary movement was strong enough to survive but only at the cost of becoming more nationalistic and authoritarian. Even before it came to power, the Young Turk movement had been split. One section believed in a decentralisation which would give local autonomy to the subject peoples of the empire. It advocated inviting help from the European powers in carrying out reforms. The other section, which had most support among the army officers, wanted a unified centralised Ottoman state in which everyone would have equal rights and duties, irrespective of race, language or religion. It rejected any foreign intervention.[1]

Before the revolution, a compromise had been reached between the two sections. When Abdul Hamid's despotism was ended and the Constitution restored, there was a genuine feeling of freedom and reconciliation between the different races and religions of the empire. But it did not last long for, while Greeks and Bulgars were waiting to take their seats next to Turks in the new Ottoman Parliament, Prince Ferdinand of Bulgaria was proclaiming his country independent and free of the last trace of Ottoman suzerainty, the Greeks of Crete were announcing their union with Greece, and the Austro-Hungarian empire was annexing the former Ottoman provinces of Bosnia and Herzegovina. Within the next four years, Italy attacked Turkish-controlled Tripolitania and seized the Dodecanese Islands, while Greece, Bulgaria and Serbia united in the Balkan League to attack Turkey and wrest from her almost all her remaining territory in Europe.

The difficulty was that neither the decentralisation plans of the Ottoman liberals nor the ideas of the more nationalist Young Turks could achieve the aim of saving the empire from further disintegration. Nationalism among the Ottoman Christians, backed by the existence of the new Christian states in the Balkans, had already gone too far for them to be satisfied for long with local autonomy. They would inevitably have regarded autonomy as the first step towards separation from the empire and reunion with those of similar race and religion beyond the Ottoman frontiers. Even less were the Christians disposed to accept a new minority status which robbed them of old privileges and protections while offering new freedoms whose application, in practice, was open to doubt. For the nationalists who dominated the Committee of Union and Progress increasingly came to interpret 'ottomanisation' as meaning centralised rule by the Turkish majority and the 'turkification' of the rest of the population. They no doubt considered themselves as genuinely progressive in offering to all Ottoman subjects the privileges of full citizenship, with its duties as well as its rights, which had hitherto been reserved for Turkish Moslems. But at the same time their main purpose was to defend and preserve the Ottoman empire more effectively than the Hamidian despotism had done.[2] In trying to achieve an aim which was no longer possible, they were driven back to a military despotism of their own. Their failure, and the feeling that they had been betrayed by those to whom they had looked for understanding and friendship, gave a new bitterness to their relations with the Christian minorities and those countries outside the empire which supported them. The Armenians were to bear the brunt of this bitterness at the cost of a million dead, but it also affected the Greeks who were still the biggest and most influential Christian minority within the empire. In the eighty years after the Greek war of independence, there had been no great increase in animosity between Greeks and Turks in Asia Minor, despite recurrent crises between Greece and the Ottoman empire over

Crete or Thessaly. Apart from the Thirty Days' War in 1897, there had, indeed, been no war between Greece and the Ottoman empire. But a new bitterness and savagery was to show on both sides in the great Greco-Turkish conflict which, opening in 1908 with the proclamation of Cretan union, closed in 1922–23 with the Greek withdrawal from Anatolia.

The first round of the conflict, however, ended not in tragedy but in farce, largely because of the intervention of the European powers. In Crete, the powers had begun, in the summer of 1908, to withdraw their troops, since Zaimis, the Greek high commissioner, appeared to have the island well under control. But when the Young Turk revolution broke out, the Cretans took advantage of the absence of Zaimis from the island to form a provisional government under Venizelos and five associates. In October 1908, this government proclaimed union with Greece. The Greek constitution was declared to replace that of Crete. The European powers now favoured the union of Crete with Greece, provided the Moslem minority were protected, but the Athens government hesitated to take the final step of accepting the union for fear of Turkish and international reaction to such a fait accompli.

In the meantime, the Young Turks had reacted strongly to external pressures and to an attempted coup by reactionaries in Istanbul. On April 12, 1909 they had deposed Sultan Abdul Hamid, putting the harmless Mehmed V in his place. In response to European pressures to recognise the union of Greece, they had demanded the end of Cretan autonomy and a return to the situation in the island before 1898 when it was still under Turkish sovereignty. Despite the continued deadlock over the international status of the island, the powers completed the withdrawal of their forces from Crete in June 1909 and the Cretans hoisted the Greek flag. When the Turks demanded a repudiation of the Cretan action by Greece, backing up their demand with a boycott of Greek goods and a threat of war, the powers intervened and, as a conciliatory gesture, sent marines to cut down the flagstaff bearing the Greek flag. At the same time they warned both Greece and Turkey not to intervene. They declared both Crete and Macedonia to be matters of European and not merely Greco-Turkish concern.

This humiliation, which the Greek government was forced to swallow, brought to a head the revolt of the Military League in Greece. The League, bearing some resemblance to the Young Turks, was composed of young army officers who disapproved of the conduct of national affairs by the professional politicians and, especially, of their neglect of the armed forces. In August 1909, a group of 500 officers, members of the League, and 1,500 troops, led by Colonel Zorbas, marched out of Athens and encamped on Goudi Hill. They demanded the reorganisation of the armed forces under service ministries headed by professional soldiers and sailors, and the exclusion of the royal family from army commands. The latter demand largely resulted from the fact that Crown Prince Constantine had been held responsible for the main defeats of the Greek army in the 1897 war with Turkey. As a result of the intervention of King George, the reforms were accepted by Parliament. The League then demanded political changes and called on Venizelos to come to Athens from Crete to deal with the political situation.

The energy and intelligence with which Venizelos disentangled the crisis in Athens was the foundation of his political fame. He persuaded the king to accept the calling of a National Assembly to revise the Constitution and obtained the agreement of the Military League, in return, to dissolve itself voluntarily once the Assembly had been called. After the National Assembly, including Venizelos himself, had been elected, Venizelos resigned from the post he still held as head of the Cretan provisional government and was appointed prime minister of Greece on October 18, 1910. When the Assembly refused to accept his view that its task was only to revise the Constitution and not to make a new one, he resigned, advised the king to dissolve the Assembly, and, in new elections was swept back to power with huge public support. The revised Constitution was adopted in June 1911. Among the reforms was the introduction of compulsory primary education and the establishment of a permanent, non-political civil service. In 1912, the National Assembly gave way to an ordinary Chamber of Deputies of whom the great majority were supporters of Venizelos.

At the opening of the Chamber, Venizelos created a sensation by refusing to allow the deputies elected from Crete to take their seats. He did so because he was not yet ready to face the crisis with Turkey which recognition of the Cretan delegates might precipitate. The retraining of the Greek army and navy by French and British missions was still in progress, but, more important, Venizelos was waiting for the completion of the Balkan alliance which he had set in motion in a secret approach to Bulgaria a year earlier. The basic idea of the alliance was to end the divisions among the Balkan states which had been exploited by Turkey against each of them in turn. Greece, Bulgaria and Serbia, who all had claims on Macedonia, were to unite with Montenegro in stripping Turkey of her European provinces in which Greek and Slav

Christians were a majority. They were then to divide the spoils of victory among themselves.

Thus, on March 13, 1912, Bulgaria signed a treaty with Serbia and, seventeen days later, an alliance with Greece. The Greco-Bulgarian agreement contained a clause which released Bulgaria from her obligation to Greece if war with Turkey were caused by the admission of Cretans to the Greek Parliament. The treaties were the prelude to the first Balkan war which international opinion nowadays would probably classify as a carefully prepared war of aggression, despite its aspect of national liberation. Hostilities began in 1912 with a declaration of war on Turkey by Montenegro, as a result of a dispute over the international status of Albania. Ultimatums were promptly presented by Greece, Bulgaria and Serbia and, equally promptly, rejected by Turkey. On October 14, 1912, the same day that he sent the ultimatum to Turkey, Venizelos officially recognised the union of Crete with Greece and allowed the Cretan deputies to take their seats in the Greek Parliament.

The Balkan allies quickly routed the Turkish armies and over-ran almost the whole of Turkey's remaining territory in Europe. The Greeks captured southern Macedonia, including the major prize of Salonika which they occupied before the Bulgarians, their potential rivals in the area. They took part of Epirus, nine Aegean Islands and Mount Athos. Despite the Bulgarian–Serbian armistice with Turkey and the opening of the London Conference on the Balkans in December 1912, Greece maintained hostilities in order to keep control of the Aegean and prevent any Turkish troop movements by sea. After the London Conference broke down, full scale hostilities were resumed in February 1913, and Greek forces took the offensive and captured Yannina, northern Epirus and the island of Samos which, throughout most of the nineteenth century, had been an autonomous principality paying a fixed tribute to Turkey. Albania was proclaimed independent under Italian protection. The Greek victories were marred by the assassination in Salonika on March 18, 1913, of King George. He was shot in the street by a Greek with a personal grievance. His son, Constantine, succeeded him in an aura of popularity won by his command of the troops which captured Salonika and Yannina.

The first Balkan war was brought to an end by the Treaty of London on May 30, 1913. Turkey formally surrendered to the Balkan alliance the island of Crete and all her European territories except Thrace. The future of Albania and its frontiers, and of the Aegean Islands was left to be settled by the great powers. However, the Balkan allies quarrelled over the division of the spoils. Bulgaria, in particular, was dissatisfied with the share of Macedonia which was offered to her, and on June 30, 1913, began the second Balkan war with a sudden attack on the Greeks and Serbs. But she was defeated by her three former allies with the help of intervention by Rumania, while the Turks took advantage of the conflict to recover the city of Adrianople from the Bulgarians. The Treaty of Bucharest, signed on August 10, 1913, confirmed Greek possession of southern Macedonia and part of the coast of Thrace, including the tobacco port of Kavalla. Greece also kept Crete. She remained in occupation of most of Epirus and all the Aegean Islands, except Tenedos and Imbros which guard the approaches to the Dardanelles and the Dodecanese. The latter had been taken by the Italians in their war with Turkey in 1912 and remained under their control. The Greek occupation of the other islands and Epirus was, however, subject to approval by the European powers.

Greece had almost doubled her territory and population within one year. But her success brought new problems in its train, and Venizelos hoped for a generation of peace in which to absorb these gains. Greece's new frontiers in the north were greatly extended, and her two million increase of population included 600,000 Moslems with some Slavs and other minorities. Moreover, the Treaty of Bucharest had created a legacy of bitterness and revenge in Turkey where there were still over two million Christians, the majority of whom were Greek. The treaty also established a new pattern of power in the Balkans which led to the outbreak of the first world war. Despite their warning that they would uphold the integrity of the Ottoman empire, the great powers had been unable to deter the Balkan alliance. It was the continued determination of Austria to curb the influence of Serbia, strengthened by the Balkan wars, that eventually brought the great powers themselves into conflict.

Turkish resentment was strongest at Greece's formal annexation of Crete and occupation of the Aegean Islands, especially Chios and Mitylene. These two large islands lie only a few miles off the coast of western Anatolia and cover the approaches to the port of Smyrna. The Turks feared they might be used as a base to attack Asia Minor—as indeed happened six years later. Turkey's refusal to accept the loss of her Aegean Islands was, in fact, the main cause of the breakdown of the London Conference and the resumption of the first Balkan war. After the Treaty of Bucharest, when the future of the islands was being considered by the powers, Turkey began a campaign to force Greece to withdraw from Chios and Mitylene by a combination of economic and naval pressure and by the persecution of the Greek minority in Asia Minor. (These tactics were to be repeated fifty years later when Turkey began to take reprisals against the Greeks in Istanbul and the islands in order to put pressure on Greece over the Cyprus question.) A boycott of the Greeks in Turkey began in November 1913, and, at the same time, some 30,000 Greeks were deported or driven from their homes on the coasts of Thrace and Anatolia.* The Turkish authorities claimed that their jobs and homes were needed for the Moslem refugees who were pouring in from Macedonia. Turkey began to expand her navy and bought two dreadnoughts which were being built in British yards. In July 1914, Greece countered this show of force by acquiring two secondhand American battleships.

Relations between Greece and Turkey became increasingly strained and on June 12, 1914, Venizelos gave a warning in a parliamentary speech that Greece might be forced to fight to protect the Greeks in Turkey from further persecution. A month later he left Athens in order to meet the Turkish grand vizir in Brussels to discuss a possible settlement of the dispute. But, before they could meet, the Greco-Turkish quarrel was swallowed up in the outbreak of the first world war.

Turkey's decision to side with Germany in the first world war destroyed the traditional British policy of maintaining the integrity of the Ottoman empire. Instead, Britain found herself for the first time at war with Turkey and, moreover, in alliance with Russia, her former chief rival at Constantinople. Her aim now became the dismemberment rather than the preservation of the Ottoman dominions. But the old British policy had always been to a certain extent conditioned by her other role as one of the protecting powers of Greece and by her own ambitions as a Middle Eastern power in her own right. The outcome of the Balkan wars had already dealt a heavy blow at Britain's attempts to keep a balance between her Greek and Turkish interests. Now Turkey's action gave Britain the opportunity of expanding her own Middle East empire, the foundations of which had already been laid—though still in a hesitant provisional fashion—for some time past. For at the outbreak of the first world war, Britain had already been established in Cyprus for thirty-six years, in Egypt for thirty-two, and in the Sudan for sixteen,

* Venizelos claimed at the Lausanne Peace Conference in 1923 that a total of 430,000 Greeks had been expelled from these areas and had taken refuge in Greece in the months just before and after Turkey's entry into the first world war.

following the reconquest of 1898. She controlled the Suez Canal and her fleet dominated the Eastern Mediterranean, the Red Sea and the Persian Gulf. On the day, November 5, 1914, that Britain declared war on Turkey, she also announced the annexation of Cyprus and the establishment of a protectorate over Egypt. Both territories had, until then, remained formally under Ottoman sovereignty though occupied and controlled by Britain.

In August 1914, both Turkey and Greece at first maintained a position of neutrality in the world conflict. But it was clear from the start that the military oligarchy led by Enver Pasha which had come to rule in Turkey favoured Germany, while the policy of the Greek prime minister, Venizelos, was to side with the Entente powers—Britain, France and Russia.

Turkey entered the war on October 28 when her fleet bombarded Russian ports on the Black Sea. Resentment at Britain's refusal to deliver two battleships ordered for the Turkish fleet has been cited as an excuse for the Turkish government's decision to abandon its neutrality. But Turkey had already become heavily dependent on Germany for financial help and military supplies, and she now saw Germany as her chief ally against her traditional enemy, Russia. Her military leaders, themselves German-trained, believed Germany would win. But, even so, a more cautious man than the impulsive, ambitious Enver, who had emerged as the decisive figure among the Young Turks, would probably have hesitated longer before committing himself.

Greece's entry into the war on the Entente side was to be brought about only after a bitter and confused struggle inside Greece lasting for nearly three years in which Venizelos and the Allied powers were pitted against King Constantine. At first, Constantine and Venizelos agreed that Greece should remain neutral and that she must, above all, avoid a clash with the Allies, who controlled the seas round the long Greek coastline. But Constantine did not share Venizelos's belief that the Allies would win and that Greek neutrality should therefore be benevolent towards them. Both Venizelos and the Allies saw Greek neutrality as useful so long as it was a factor in keeping Bulgaria out of the war, but they believed that if Bulgaria attacked Serbia, Greece should go to the help of the Serbs in fulfilment of her treaty with them. Constantine, however, considered that Greece should remain neutral even if Serbia were attacked—though he was also accused of waiting to bring Greece in on the German side at a favourable opportunity. The king's attitude was blamed on his personal germanophil preferences and the influence of his German wife; but a convincing case can also be made that, if he erred, it was not as a result of such personal reasons but from a mistaken view of the Greek national interest.

As long as there seemed to be any chance of keeping Bulgaria out of the German camp, by either threats or promises, Allied pressure on Greece to abandon her neutrality was not heavy and differences between King Constantine and Venizelos were not acute. But, as hope of influencing Bulgaria diminished, the Allies began a more serious effort to bring Greece into the war on their side, so as to provide support for Serbia. In January 1915, the British foreign secretary, Sir Edward Grey, offered Greece 'important concessions on the coasts of Asia Minor' if she would join in a concerted Allied action in the Balkans. This was the first indication for the Greeks that the possibility of their acquiring territory in Asia Minor could be taken seriously. Venizelos pressed the king to accept this unexpected offer 'in order to save the Greeks in Turkey and create a Great Greece which would include nearly all the provinces where Hellenism flourished through the long periods of its history'. He suggested ceding the port of Kavalla to Bulgaria in order to get the latter's co-operation. The king agreed to this, but the Bulgarians were not to be tempted.[3]

The Allied offer, though not immediately accepted, was the beginning of the great Greek adventure which was to end, seven years later, in disaster in Anatolia. Even at this time, the Greek general staff under Colonel Metaxas warned that the conquest and control of western Asia Minor, which Venizelos envisaged claiming, would be an enterprise far beyond Greece's own resources. To accomplish his aims, Venizelos was counting on help from the Allies, and in a memorandum to the king on January 17, 1915, he wrote:

> The proposal that very wide territorial concessions would be made to us in Asia Minor proves to me without the slightest doubt that the activities displayed by the New Hellas have attracted the confidence of certain Powers who consider her an important factor in the settlement of the Near East at the moment of collapse of the Turkish state. The support of these Powers provides us with the financial and diplomatic means to cope with the inherent difficulties of such a sudden increase of territory. Confident in this support, Greece can follow boldly the new and wonderful paths opening out for her.[4]

On March 1, 1915, Venizelos proposed that a Greek army corps be sent to support a renewed Allied naval attack on the Dardanelles. (The first ttack, begun by warships on February 18, 1915, had been inconclusive.) 'ut the very next day, Russia vetoed the proposal, making it clear that ı no circumstances would she allow Greece to take part in an Allied ttack on Constantinople. The Russians now saw the Greeks as potenial rivals in their own newly formulated claims to Constantinople nd the Straits. The Greeks assured the British that their interest in Constantinople was merely sentimental: they only wanted to march ıto the city and be the first of the victorious troops to take Holy Comıunion in Saint Sophia. But they did not wish to stay there, and indeed vould not accept the city if it were offered them.[5] Such was the arguıent of the Venizelists, but the Russian veto was reinforced by the bjections of the Greek general staff.

On March 6, King Constantine rejected the Venizelos proposal, vhereupon the premier resigned. In new elections he was returned to ower. When Bulgaria mobilised on September 12—a month after the Greek elections—Venizelos asked for an Allied expeditionary force of 50,000 men to be sent to Greece. But the king objected that the landng of these forces would be a breach of Greek neutrality unless Bulgaria ttacked Serbia to which Greece had treaty obligations. However, the Allied force was already at sea and, despite a formal protest from Venizelos, British and French troops landed at Salonika on October 5, 915. The same day Venizelos resigned once more after the king, gnoring a parliamentary vote of confidence in the prime minister, had old him he opposed his policy of fulfilling the Serbian treaty.

In a further attempt to gain Greek support for Serbia, Sir Edward Grey offered, on October 16, to transfer Cyprus to Greece. But eight lays later the new Greek government of Alexander Zaimis, backed by he king, formally refused the offer.[6] The British foreign secretary's nitiative, agreed upon at an informal meeting of the 'War Committee', vas criticised both in the cabinet and in the House of Commons for ıaving been taken without proper cabinet consultation. But, in fact, ıs Roy Jenkins points out in his biography of Asquith, the Cyprus offer ıad been thoroughly discussed by the cabinet in January 1915. George V's secretary, Lord Stamfordham, had then written to Asquith:

> The King desires me to express the earnest hope that the Government will, on further consideration, decide to support Sir E. Grey's proposal and offer Cyprus to Greece on condition of her joining the Allies. . . . Financially Cyprus is I suppose a loss to this country. Strategically, HM understands that it has proved a failure; the har-

bours impracticable and ships obliged to lie off six miles from the coast.[7]

The defeat and occupation of Serbia by the Austro-German armies forced the thirteen Allied divisions (eight French and five British) in Greece to withdraw into a fortified camp at Salonika and to treat the Greek government and army as potentially hostile. The Allies instituted a partial economic blockade of Greece, and sent an ultimatum to Athens demanding demobilisation of the Greek army, new elections and a truly neutral government.

Following an Allied offensive in Macedonia and a counter-offensive by the Bulgarians, in which 8,000 Greek troops were taken prisoner and interned in Germany, part of the Greek garrison in Salonika went over to the Allies. Venizelos then raised the standard of rebellion in Crete and from there sailed to Salonika to set up a pro-Allies provisional government. For eight months Greece was split between the Athens government and the Venizelist nationalist movement. The country hovered on the brink of civil war until, on June 10, 1917, the Allies forced the abdication of King Constantine. He was succeeded by his second son, Prince Alexander, and ten days later Venizelos once more became prime minister. By then, 60,000 Greek troops of the Venizelist National Army were fighting beside the Allies in Macedonia. By September 1918, 250,000 Greek troops were engaged in the Allied offensive launched by General Franchet d'Esperey on the Macedonian front, which knocked Bulgaria out of the war. The Bulgarian armistice on September 30 was followed, a month later, by the armistice signed at Mudros between Turkey and the Allies. Greek warships were part of the Allied fleet which sailed up to the Golden Horn. Greek troops shared in the triumphal entry into Constantinople led by General Franchet d'Esperey 'riding without reins on a white horse and thus aspiring to lay the spectre of Fatih, the Moslem conqueror of Byzantium, who had done the same'.[8]

Although the victories in Macedonia helped to bring about the collapse of Turkish resistance, the main blows against the Ottoman empire were struck elsewhere. In the first months of the war, the Turks, under Enver Pasha, boldly took the offensive against both the Russians in the Caucasus and the British in Egypt, but were repulsed on both fronts with heavy losses. For the next two years Turkey held the Allies at bay, with notable victories at Gallipoli where Mustafa Kemal, the future

Ataturk, first made his reputation in forcing a British and ANZAC withdrawal, and in Mesopotamia, where the British and Indian garrison at Kut was obliged to surrender. The Russian revolution in March 1917 relieved the pressure on Turkey's eastern front from Russian armies in the Caucasus, but the respite was short-lived; the Turks could not redeploy enough forces to meet the growing threat from the British in the south. The Turkish armies were exhausted, food was short and transport ill-organised; reinforcements which should have been available to resist the British were wasted by Enver Pasha's reckless decision to pursue the disintegrating Russian armies into the Caucasus, in the hope of fulfilling his dreams of a new pan-Turkish empire.[9]

In 1917, the British under Maude and Allenby began their offensives northwards through Mesopotamia and Palestine, capturing Baghdad and Jerusalem. The army of the Arab revolt, led by Emir Feisal and Colonel T. E. Lawrence, took Mecca and moved up through the Syrian desert towards Damascus, operating as raiding forces on General Allenby's right wing. After a pause, Allenby resumed his offensive in September 1918 and drove the Turkish army out of Damascus and up to the hills north of Aleppo. The remnants of the Turkish forces under Mustafa Kemal had taken up positions covering what is now Turkey's southern frontier when news came of the fall of the Turkish government, of the flight of Enver and his two closest associates, Talat and Jemal, and of the signature, on a warship off Mudros in the island of Lemnos, of an armistice with the British. The armistice was purely military; it provided for the demobilisation of the Turkish army and for Allied control of all important strategic points, including the Dardanelles. But Constantinople was not to be occupied and the Allies promised not to interfere in Turkish internal affairs, unless the Turks themselves failed to maintain law and order.

The Mudros armistice roused bitter feelings among Turkish nationalists, and Mustafa Kemal at once began secret preparations to resist what he feared to be the impending complete subjugation of Turkey. Bitterness and fear were greatly increased when the Allies came to discuss peace terms for Turkey and, above all, when they authorised the landing of Greek troops at Smyrna in western Anatolia on May 15, 1919. In Constantinople, the sultan dismissed the last representative Ottoman government and dissolved parliament, relying on the Allies to save his throne. But elsewhere in the country, especially in the unoccupied interior of Anatolia where two Turkish armies were still in being, the nationalist resistance movement began to spread and the armistice terms were systematically evaded.

Apparently unaware of the extent of this resistance, or considering European affairs of far greater urgency, the Allies wasted a precious year before getting round to serious discussion of a Turkish peace. They then produced, in the Treaty of Sèvres signed on August 10, 1920, a drastic settlement which would have reduced the former Ottoman empire to a small state in central Anatolia under foreign economic and military control. At the San Remo Conference of April 1920, the Allies had already disposed of the former Arab provinces of the Ottoman empire. France had been given a mandate over Syria, and Britain mandates over Palestine and Mesopotamia (now Iraq). The Treaty of Sèvres confirmed these provisions and recognised the Arab kingdom of the Hejaz as an independent state.

The Turks had already resigned themselves to the loss of these Arab territories, but the other provisions of the Treaty of Sèvres exceeded their worst expectations. An independent Armenian republic and an autonomous Kurdistan, both intended to be under American mandate, were to be carved out of eastern and southern Anatolia. Almost all Turkey's remaining territory in Europe, apart from Constantinople and a small enclave round it, was to go to Greece, which was also to receive the islands of Imbros and Tenedos, commanding the entrance to the Dardanelles. Worst blow of all to the Turks, the Greeks were to occupy and administer Smyrna and a substantial hinterland in western Anatolia. While Turkey might retain a nominal sovereignty over it, the Smyrna area would be autonomous: it would have its own parliament and the right to decide, by plebiscite after five years, whether or not to unite with Greece. Cyprus was to remain British and the Dodecanese Italian. The latter islands were to be subject to a separate agreement between Greece and Italy about their future. The Straits were to be open to ships of all countries and controlled by an international commission. Turkey's army, reduced to a token force, was to be placed under Allied supervision. The economic carve-up of Turkey was equally drastic. France and Italy were to have large zones of influence; the hated Capitulations—special concessions to foreign traders—were to be extended; and the national finances of Turkey supervised by the Allies.

The Treaty of Sèvres was the sum of three factors: 1. The various claims of Britain, France and Italy arising from secret wartime agreements among themselves and with Russia for the partition of the Ottoman empire. 2. The claims of Greece for the fulfilment of promises made to her in return for her participation in the war. 3. President Wilson's concern for the principle of ethnic self-determination in accordance with his Fourteen Points.

For Greece the treaty appeared to be a spectacular victory, vindicating the Venizelos policy of supporting the Allies in the war. With Smyrna and its hinterland, Greece would acquire a large and valuable territory and another 1,720,000 inhabitants, making a total population of 6,540,000, compared with 4,820,000 in 1913 after the Balkan wars and 2,760,000 in 1911. But the great gain was to remain a paper triumph and a prelude to disaster. The treaty left out one other vital factor: how it was to be enforced. This omission was all important, since, in the period following the secret partition agreements, and especially in the twenty-one months following the Mudros armistice, significant changes had taken place in the military and political situation, not only in Turkey, but also among the Allies themselves.

The first unforeseen development was the Russian revolution which had led to Russia's withdrawal from the war and from the making and the enforcement of the peace. This not only removed a serious threat to Turkish national resistance but eventually provided it with positive help in the form of Russian arms and money. An independent Armenia or Kurdistan, without support from Russia—which was not forthcoming—had no chance of survival, unless one of the other great powers was prepared to make a heavy long-term military and financial commitment in eastern Anatolia. President Wilson asked Congress to consider an American mandate for the Armenians and the Kurds, despite advice that it would need at least five American divisions to enforce the mandate and to garrison Constantinople. But the president fell ill and his proposal was rejected by the Senate. Marshal Foch estimated that it would require a total of twenty-seven divisions to bring Turkey under complete control and enforce peace terms.[10] Nor were the other Allied powers in any hurry to commit more troops to Turkey when they were all facing mounting pressure from their war-weary populations to bring their troops back home. Indeed, Italy and France, after having tried to establish their claims to zones of influence in southern and southwestern Turkey by force of arms, had come to realise the strength of Turkish nationalist resistance and had already begun to make separate peace arrangements with Mustafa Kemal. Italy was also incensed at the Greek occupation of Smyrna, which she considered should have gone to her under one of the wartime agreements.

The Greek landing at Smyrna, with the ensuing slaughter of civilians

7—CAPOA

and humiliation of Turkish officers by the Greeks, had greatly accelerated the Turkish nationalist movement. Four days after the landings, Mustafa Kemal escaped from Constantinople to eastern Anatolia and assumed the political and military leadership of the nationalists. The British had been forced by growing unrest and the guerrilla activities of the nationalists to withdraw their control officers from their exposed positions in Anatolia. In defiance of both the Allied occupying powers and the sultan's government in Constantinople, the nationalists elected their own parliament in Ankara on April 23, 1920, under the presidency of Kemal. An earlier nationalist congress at Erzerum had already drafted the 'National Pact' which was to be the basis of Kemal's diplomacy and his political aims. The National Pact called for the restoration of Turkey's frontiers to include all non-Arab Moslem subjects of the former Ottoman empire, and rejected any privileges for non-Turkish minorities.

When the terms of the draft Treaty of Sèvres leaked out in May 1920, the Kemalists gained much popular support in Turkey. Their troops broke through the forces still loyal to the sultan and advanced on Constantinople where the British two months earlier had seized key points and deported a number of leading nationalist parliamentary deputies. To relieve the threat to Constantinople and the Allied positions on the Straits, Venizelos offered to send two of the five Greek divisions in Smyrna to attack the Kemalists, and another division to eastern Thrace. Despite opposition from the British and French military staffs, Venizelos, with the active support of the British prime minister, Lloyd George, persuaded the Allied Supreme Council to authorise a Greek offensive. Lloyd George had consistently backed Greek claims in Asia Minor. He did so partly out of pro-Greek and anti-Turkish sentiment, partly as a means of limiting French and Italian influence in Turkey, and partly because he saw the Greek army as a useful and inexpensive means of enforcing British policy. There was also the consideration that a refusal of Smyrna to Greece might have brought down the Venizelos government in Athens, since Smyrna had been the prize offered to win Greek support for the war. But both Venizelos and Lloyd George greatly underestimated Turkey's power of resistance. They ignored warnings from their military advisers about the difficulty which would be experienced by the Greeks in holding their gains on the Asia Minor coast, let alone subduing, virtually single-handed, the vast Anatolian interior. Admittedly, the civilian optimism at first seemed to be justified. In the summer of 1920, the Greeks occupied Thrace and advanced all along the line in Anatolia, and the Turkish nationalists withdrew on to the Anatolian plateau. On August 10, the sultan's government signed the Treaty of Sèvres, and Venizelos returned to Athens in triumph. But within a few months he was out of office. Within two years his dream of a greater Greece on both sides of the Aegean was utterly shattered.

The death of King Alexander of Greece, from a pet monkey's bite, brought up the question of royal succession. It revived old accusations that Venizelos had been imposed on Greece by foreign bayonets when the former king, Constantine, had been forced by the Allies to abdicate. The Greek prime minister had also lost touch with the home political scene in his preoccupation with international diplomacy. In an election fought on November 14, 1920, on the issue, 'Constantine versus Venizelos', he was heavily defeated. Venizelos resigned and left Greece. Within three weeks of the election, the Greeks voted in plebiscite by a large majority to recall Constantine to the throne.

The Greek army in Asia Minor had meanwhile resumed the offensive and continued its advance towards the railway line running from north to south between Eskishehir and Afyon Karahissar. But, as a result of pressure from the French and Italians, the Allied Supreme Council stopped the Greek advance, leaving the Greeks holding a dangerously extended and vulnerable line. The fall of Venizelos and the return of Constantine gave France and Italy an opportunity to wash their hands of what now began to look like a rash Greek adventure in Anatolia. But Lloyd George still believed that the Treaty of Sèvres was enforceable and encouraged the Greeks to carry out the enforcement. Greece faced a difficult choice. To hold her position in Asia Minor against the Kemalist challenge she needed a large army of her own and substantial Allied support. A withdrawal of Greek forces would mean exposing the now heavily compromised Greek population of Asia Minor to possible massacre by the Turks. In the winter of 1920, during their campaign in eastern Anatolia to crush the attempt to create a separate Armenian state, the Kemalists had massacred Armenians wholesale, thus proving —though the details were not known in Europe until more than a year later—that they were quite as ruthless as previous Turkish governments. Possibly overestimating the amount of military support they could expect from Britain in a crisis, the Greeks decided to try to improve their position by a new spring offensive.

But before the offensive began, the Allies made a new attempt at a peace settlement at the London Conference in February 1921. The conference was attended by Turkish delegations from both the Ottoman and the Kemalist governments. The Allies proposed a revision of the Treaty of Sèvres which would have made concessions to Turkey on the questions of the Straits, Constantinople, Armenia and Kurdistan. They also proposed an international enquiry into the ethnic statistics of eastern Thrace and the Smyrna region: a proposal accepted conditionally by the Turks but rejected by the Greeks. (Greece claimed that there were Greek or non-Turkish majorities in these areas. Arnold Toynbee, then in the Smyrna region, formed the impression that there was a clear Turkish majority there.[11]) The Allies then suggested 'an equitable compromise' for the Smyrna region, based on Greek autonomy. This was rejected by the Turks. The conference ended without agreement.

On March 23, 1921, the Greeks began their offensive. They aimed at capturing Eskishehir, Afyon Karahissar and other key points on the railway, their ultimate objective being an advance on Ankara. But they were repulsed with heavy losses before Eskishehir, at Inönü, where the Turkish commander, Ismet Pasha, earned his present name. The Allies, including Britain, declared their neutrality in this conflict outside their zones of occupation in the Straits. This confirmed the character of the struggle as an isolated war between Greeks and Turks: a war of extermination, fought with the bitterness of those who feel their national existence is at stake. The Greek general staff and army command, diluted by political appointments of loyal royalists, were inexperienced and absurdly over-confident. Although the Greek forces were about equal in strength to Kemal's regular forces, they were badly equipped and short of munitions. Greece had 300,000 men under arms but no money in her treasury. In June 1921, the British foreign secretary, Lord Curzon, offered to try again to negotiate a peace settlement but the Greeks rejected the offer.

On June 11, King Constantine and his prime minister, Gounaris, left Athens for Smyrna, and four days later there began 'the greatest campaign undertaken by Greece since classic times'.[12] The new Greek offensive was at first successful. Afyon and Eskishehir were captured and the Kemalists forced to carry out a strategic withdrawal to the line of the Sakarya river, a hundred miles to the east and only fifty miles west of Ankara. The Greek commander-in-chief, General Papoulas, wanted to halt the advance at Eskishehir, but Theotokis, prime minister and minister of war, with the acquiescence of the king, insisted on pursuing the Turks in the hope of driving Kemal out of his political base in Ankara. The Greek army resumed its advance on August 13,

1921. After ten days' march across the hot, dusty Anatolian plateau, with little food or water, the exhausted Greeks launched an attack on the strong defensive positions held by the Kemalists in the loop of the Sakarya river. The battle was fought with immense courage and heavy casualties on both sides. It lasted for twenty-two days and nights—the longest pitched battle in history, according to Mustafa Kemal.[13] Having gained only ten miles in ten days of fighting, the Greeks were finally forced to retreat back across the plateau to the line of Afyon and Eskishehir.

The Greek government now sought Allied help to save it from the dangerous situation into which its political ambitions and military recklessness had drawn Greece. But by this time there was no common policy discernible among the Allies. One of the first fruits of the Kemalist victory was the signature of what was to all intents and purposes a separate peace treaty between France and the Ankara government. Under the Franklin Bouillon Agreement of October 20, 1921, France withdrew its forces from Cilicia in southern Turkey, though keeping the port of Alexandretta and the surrounding province of the Hatay within her Syrian mandate, and gave the Kemalists large quantities of arms and ammunition. Kemal was also able to buy arms from Italy with money from Russia and from the contributions of Moslems in India. France at first refused to take part in a meeting of the Allied foreign ministers to discuss new terms for a peace treaty with Turkey; but eventually, on the insistence of Lord Curzon, a conference met in Paris on March 22, 1922. Curzon, Conservative foreign secretary in Lloyd George's coalition government, proposed an armistice to be followed by peace talks which would provide for the Greek evacuation of Anatolia. The conference broke down when the Turks declared that the Greek evacuation must come before the armistice. In the meantime, the Greeks continued to hold on to a front three hundred miles long, and a new government in Athens, instead of preparing for a withdrawal, appointed a new commander-in-chief, General Hadjanestis and, in July, proclaimed the independence of the Smyrna vilayet.

The catastrophe in this Greek tragedy was approaching. In a surprise attack at sunrise on August 26, 1922, the Kemalists broke through the southern flank of the Greek front, surrounded and destroyed half the Greek army and drove the rest headlong back to Smyrna and the coast. In Smyrna harbour lay the yacht from which the Greek commander-in-chief, General Hadjanestis, incompetent and almost insane, had directed the fatal battle.[14] In their retreat the Greeks left a trail of burned towns and villages and massacred Turkish civilians; 40,000 Greek troops escaped from Smyrna in Greek warships, leaving another 50,000 as Turkish prisoners. When the Turks entered Smyrna on September 9, 1922, the city was packed with refugees. The Turks began to deport all able-bodied Christian men to the interior, killing Greeks and Armenians and looting and setting fire to their houses. The flames from the burning houses spread into a great fire, destroying most of the city and driving thousands of people into the sea.

After Smyrna, the next Turkish objective was to recover control of Constantinople and of the area of eastern Thrace, including Adrianople, which was still in Greek hands. But when the Kemalists advanced towards the Allied neutral zone round Constantinople, they were stopped by the British at Chanak on the Asian shore of the Dardanelles. A minor international crisis ensued with a threat of renewed war between Britain and Turkey. France and Italy advocated a peace conference with Kemal and withdrew their support from Britain when the British government sent a division of troops to reinforce the Chanak garrison. A compromise was reached by which, pending the organisation of a peace conference, the Turks would occupy eastern Thrace together with an Allied detachment. The Greek population of eastern Thrace began to move out to Greece and preparations were put in hand for a peace conference at Lausanne.

In Constantinople, the Kemalists gradually took over power, leaving the sultan isolated. Kemal then proposed, and the Ankara Assembly accepted, the abolition of the sultanate but leaving the caliphate still in being. On November 4, 1922, the Kemalists formally took over from the Ottoman government in Constantinople. The last Ottoman sultan, Mehmed VI Vahdettin, was smuggled out of the city on a British warship into a comfortable exile on the Italian Riviera.

The sultan's government was not the only victim of the Anatolian débâcle. In Greece, a military revolution under General Plastiras had overthrown the government, tried and shot General Hadjanestis, Gounaris and four other ministers and sent King Constantine once more into exile. The revolutionists asked Venizelos to return to Athens, but he replied that he had finally retired from public life. He agreed, however, to represent Greece at the Lausanne Conference. Lloyd George's Near Eastern policy was in ruins and the Chanak crisis finally brought him down. He was replaced as prime minister by the Conservative leader, Bonar Law, who had declared in a letter to *The Times*: 'we cannot act alone as the policeman of the world'.[15]

In the Treaty of Lausanne, signed on July 24, 1923, Greece renounced all claims to Asia Minor and to eastern Thrace beyond the Maritza river. Her only territorial gain was a small area of western Thrace. Turkey thus secured frontiers consistent with the principles of the National Pact: that is, frontiers embracing all—or almost all—non-Arab Moslem subjects of the former Ottoman empire. She kept possession of the Straits, but formally agreed to their being demilitarised and to the establishment of an international commission to ensure freedom of passage for ships of all nations. Greece's sovereignty over the Aegean Islands, save for Tenedos and Imbros, was confirmed, but she had to agree not to put naval bases or fortifications on the islands of Mitylene, Chios, Samos and Nikaria. Turkey recognised British sovereignty over Cyprus, and the Dodecanese remained under Italy.

Greece and Turkey also agreed at Lausanne to a 'gigantic and unprecedented barter of populations'.[16] Before the Anatolian war there had been over 2,000,000 Greeks and about 600,000 Armenians left in Asia Minor. Several hundred thousand had subsequently lost their lives and another million or more Greeks had fled as refugees to Greece. Most of the refugees were old men, women and children, since many of the younger men had either fought in the war or had been deported into the interior of Anatolia by the Turks. Greece asked that these refugees be returned to their former homes but the Turks refused to have them back; so Greece demanded the compulsory emigration of 400,000 Moslems from Greece, chiefly from Macedonia, to make room for the Greek refugees returning to Greece. The Turks, who needed people, accepted the deal although they claimed that 1,500,000 Moslems had disappeared from the Greek-occupied areas of Asia Minor as a result of massacre or deportations. The only Greek and Turkish minorities on either side who were not compelled to move were approximately 100,000 Greeks who had stayed in Constantinople and in the islands of Imbros and Tenedos, and some 124,000 Moslem Turks of Western Thrace. These minorities were guaranteed equality as citizens and the right to use their own language and their own educational and religious institutions. But otherwise all special communal arrangements such as had existed under the Ottoman empire were abolished together with the Capitulations. Under pressure from European and American opinion, Turkey dropped a proposal to remove the Orthodox patriarchate from Istanbul, but it was agreed that the patriarchate should be a purely spiritual and ecclesiastical institution, with no political or administrative role.

The departure of the Greeks from Asia Minor ended a long historic association for both the Greeks and Turks. Anatolia was the main reservoir of power for both the Byzantine and Ottoman empires. 'It was the birthplace of the Modern Greek people and the backbone of the medieval Greek state.'[17] After the Ottoman conquest most of the unconverted Christians in Anatolia adopted Turkish as their language, which they wrote in Greek script. Similarly, many of the Moslems in Greece spoke only Greek and wrote it in the Turco-Arabic script. So 'what took place was not an exchange of Greeks and Turks, but rather an exchange of Greek Orthodox Christians and Ottoman Muslims. A Western observer, accustomed to a different system of social and national classifications, might conclude that this was no repatriation at all but two deportations into exile—of Christian Turks to Greece, and of Muslim Greeks to Turkey.'[18]

Six weeks after the signature of the Lausanne Treaty, the Allies withdrew from Constantinople. Mustafa Kemal, recognising that Anatolia had now become the backbone of the modern Turkish republic, decided to make his capital at Ankara. So ended what a Greek writer has described as the second part of the struggle for the Ottoman succession. The first part was the Balkan war of liberation to free the homeland of the Greeks, the Serbs and the Bulgars. The second part was the struggle for territories with mixed populations, such as Macedonia, Thrace and finally Asia Minor. This struggle began in 1912 with the Balkan League against Turkey, and ended with the Greek disaster in Anatolia in 1922.[19]

Or so it seemed. But in the Near East, history has a habit of lingering on. Scarcely noticed in the turmoil of war and the making of the peace was another territory with mixed population where the struggle between Greek and Turk had not been settled: Cyprus.

CHAPTER SEVEN

Colonial Interlude

IN THE UPHEAVALS of the first world war and the Greco-Turkish conflict, a new Turkish state was born and an old Greek dream of empire died. In Turkey, a republic founded on the principles of secular nationalism took the place of a multiracial Islamic empire. The withdrawal of the Greeks from Asia Minor meant the end of the *Megali Idea*, the Great Idea of Greece's re-establishing the lost Byzantine empire with Constantinople once more as its capital. Greece still held the territories she had won in the Balkan wars and had a greatly increased population. But with more than a million refugees, she faced vast problems of social and economic reconstruction.

Britain, despite the failure of Lloyd George's policy on Asia Minor, emerged as the dominant power in the Middle East during the next generation. In addition to gaining full sovereignty over Cyprus and a formal protectorate over Egypt, she had acquired mandates over Iraq, Palestine and Transjordan, and was the paramount power in the Persian Gulf and the Arabian Peninsula. Cyprus was a small and neglected colony in a corner of this valuable, but turbulent, new empire.

If Cyprus under the British flag had escaped the terrors as well as the glories of the great Greco-Turkish struggle, it was not by choice of the Greek Cypriots. Though welcoming the arrival of the British in 1878 as a release from Turkish rule, they had never ceased to make plain their desire for enosis—union with Greece. Their hope was that British occupation would be a stepping-stone to enosis, as it had proved in the case of the Ionian Islands. Although the intensity of the agitation for enosis varied during the period of British rule, scarcely a year passed without at least a memorandum, resolution or manifesto demanding union with Greece and, additionally or alternatively, self-government by majority rule. Sometimes there were demonstrations, occasionally riots; in 1931 there was a minor rising; and finally, from 1955 to 1959, there was a major rebellion. Almost invariably, a Greek Cypriot declaration in favour of enosis would be matched by a protest from the

Turkish Cypriots, asking to remain under British rule or for the island to return to Turkish sovereignty. Similarly, from 1882, when the island was given its first Constitution on crown colony lines, the Turkish Cypriots opposed rule by an elected majority or proportional representation in the legislature on the grounds that this would put them at the mercy of the Greek majority, whose aim was independence and eventually enosis.

The struggles between Greeks and Turks outside Cyprus intensified the racial–religious division among Cypriots. But it must be admitted that the British government on the whole showed itself more ready to make use of this division rather than to take any determined steps to overcome it. As regularly as the Greek memoranda with the Turkish counter-memoranda would come the replies from the colonial secretary in Whitehall or his officials on the island to the effect that no change in the status of Cyprus was or could be contemplated; that Cyprus could not have representative self-government, either because it was not 'ready' for it or because of the need to safeguard the rights of the Turkish minority. The British arguments varied somewhat at different periods of the occupation according to diplomatic and political circumstances. From the beginning of the occupation in 1878 to annexation in 1914, the Anglo-Turkish Convention was still legally in force, and Cyprus was still, juridically, a part of the Ottoman empire on lease to Britain. During this period, enosis was rejected on the grounds that it would be a breach of the Convention. If Britain gave up the lease, the island must inevitably return to Ottoman control.

In practice, the Cyprus Convention lost a good deal of its relevance soon after it was made. Because of Britain's acquisition of Egypt, with the fine harbour of Alexandria, the island was never developed as a base for the defence of the Ottoman Asian provinces against Russia. Nor did the sultan, Abdul Hamid, carry out in these provinces the promised reforms, implementation of which was supposed to be ensured by the British presence in Cyprus. On the contrary, his reign marked the beginning of the extermination of the Armenians in Turkey which his successors were to complete. Although Gladstone had condemned Disraeli's acquisition of Cyprus as worthless and the Convention as a sham, and had later publicly advocated the union of the island with Greece, he did nothing to alter the Convention when he returned to power in 1880. Popular feeling in Britain, backed by Queen Victoria, was by now too deeply imbued with the new imperialistic spirit for the British flag to be withdrawn whence it had so recently been hoisted. In everything except the letter of the international law, Cyprus was effectively under British sovereignty. Although the island was not formally declared a crown colony until 1925, it was administered as such from 1880 onwards in all save two important respects: it was denied the prospects of eventual self-government; and its economic development was hampered by the uncertainty of British tenure under the terms of the Convention, and by the unprecedented additional financial burden of the Tribute. (See chapter 4, page 68.)

In the Legislative Council set up under the first Constitution of 1882, there were six official members and twelve elected members. Nine of the latter were Greeks, the other three were Turks. This division of elected members corresponded to the proportions of the population at that time when, out of a total population of 186,084, the Greeks numbered 136,629 and the Turks 46,389.[1] In the powers given to the Council, the Gladstonian Constitution was more liberal than any other constitutions offered by Britain seventy years later. But the Council's powers were more apparent than real, for its composition meant that, in practice, the British official members and the Turkish elected members could together, backed by the casting vote of the high commissioner, exert a permanent veto over the Greek elected members. In cases of persistent deadlock in the Council, executive authority could be exercised by Orders in Council issued by the high commissioner, later known as the governor.

This power-pattern became a permanent feature of the administration of Cyprus, even when the proportions of the population changed more heavily in favour of the Greeks. It became a source of intense frustration to the Greek Cypriots and served to widen the gulf, politically, between them and the Turkish Cypriots. It robbed of some of their value the real benefits which the Greek Cypriots obtained from British rule: impartial justice; physical security; an incorruptible administration and tax system; and—at least until 1931—freedom of speech and of the press, and the liberty to develop their education and culture on Greek lines.*

In effect, under the British the Greek Cypriots had freedom to speak, but not to act politically, since Britain believed that the sole aim of her Greek subjects in Cyprus was the replacement of British by Greek rule in the form of union with Greece. It was not surprising, therefore,

* The Greek Cypriots followed the curricula of the Ministry of Education in Athens, and pupils at the *gymnasia* (high schools) took the matriculation examinations set by Athens University.

that a longstanding alliance developed between British officials and Turkish Cypriots to prevent enosis. It does not require any suggestion of especially machiavellian conduct on the part of British governments to explain why Turkey herself came into the game against the enosists in the final struggles of the 1950s. To justify their policy, the British would argue—sometimes not without reason—that Greek Cypriot political leaders were not really interested in effective self-government but only in agitation for enosis. Sometimes this argument would be supported by others of a less worthy kind, to the effect that the Greek Cypriots, because of their racial origin, and the fact that they had never been ruled from mainland Greece, were not really Greeks at all; that enosis was simply the parrot-cry of a few town politicians which left the peasant masses unmoved (this is one of the classic theories held by colonial administrations about nationalist movements); or that the Cypriots were not politically mature enough for self-government. This latter proposition was never stated with more glacial sanctimoniousness than by the Labour colonial secretary, Lord Passfield (the former Sydney Webb of Fabian renown) who, in reply to a Greek Cypriot appeal in 1929, declared: 'There is much to be said for the view that what Cyprus needs at present are fewer occasions for political discussion and more occasions for constructive work.'

The first argument was answered with some dignity in 1911 by the Greek members of the Legislative Council who said in an address to the high commissioner:

> Forming, as we do, Your Excellency, an inseparable part of the Greek race, it is natural that we should feel, in a strong and irresistible manner, the desire that our fatherland should be annexed to the Hellenic Kingdom. The fulfilment of these, our aspirations, we base on the strength of our rights and the magnanimity of the English nation. But we will be sorry if it be supposed that these aspirations prevent us from co-operating with the Government for the promotion of the manifold moral and material interests of the country.[2]

Yet great men of the English nation, like Gladstone and Winston Churchill (who visited Cyprus as colonial secretary in 1907) did not stoop to the insult of denying a man's identity or distorting his motives in order to refuse his demands. Answering a Greek Cypriot petition, Churchill said it was only natural 'that the Cypriot people of Greek descent should regard their incorporation in what they call their mother country as an ideal to be earnestly, devoutly and fervently cherished.

Such a feeling is an example of the patriotic devotion which so nobly characterises the Greek nation.' But union with Greece, he added, would mean the abrogation of the Convention with Turkey and create a permanent and dangerous antagonism between the two sections of the community.[3] The most sensible comment on the racial argument came from Sir Ronald Storrs, governor of Cyprus from 1926 to 1932: 'The Greekness of the Cypriots is, in my opinion, indisputable. . . . A man is of the race which he passionately feels himself to be.'[4]

The struggle in Crete for autonomy and then union deeply stirred the Greek Cypriots, intensifying their own agitation for enosis. Several hundred volunteers from Cyprus went to fight with the Greek army against the Turks. In 1899, the bishop of Kition, one of the leading men in the Cyprus Church, tried to form a new political organisation among his Greek compatriots, but his activities led to a schism in the Church over the election of a new archbishop: a dispute which dominated the island's politics for the next decade. The hope of the enosists that union with Greece might develop out of the Balkan settlements between Greece and Turkey in 1912 and 1913 was disappointed. During the London Conference at the end of 1912, Lloyd George was reported by Venizelos to have suggested that Cyprus might be ceded to Greece in return for the right of Britain to use Argostili in the Ionian island of Cephalonia as a wartime base. But the proposal seems to have had the approval neither of the British nor the Greek foreign minister.[5]

Cyprus itself played no great part as a base in the operations of the first world war, but 11,000 Cypriots served in the war as auxiliary troops. The annexation of Cyprus on November 5, 1914, was welcomed by the Greek Cypriots as destroying what had hitherto been the main official argument against enosis: that it would be a breach of the Anglo-Turkish Convention and lead to the island's return to Turkey. They found an even greater encouragement for their hopes in the British government's offer of the island to Greece in October 1915 in return for a Greek pledge to go to the help of Serbia. (See above, page 93.) Although Athens rejected the offer because of the price demanded, the Greek Cypriots took the offer as confirmation of their argument that the British Government was now free to grant enosis if it wished. The Turkish Cypriots were correspondingly apprehensive, for their position had been weakened by Turkey's entry into the war against Britain. The Peace Conference in 1919 gave the Greek Cypriots a new opportunity to lobby London and Athens for enosis. A delegation, headed by the archbishop, saw Venizelos in Paris and the new British colonial secretary, Lord

Milner, in London. But, although Lloyd George had privately echoed Gladstone's sympathies for enosis, the War Office opposed on strategic grounds any change in the island's status. The Cyprus question was soon overshadowed for both Lloyd George and Venizelos by their preoccupations with the Greek position in Asia Minor. On July 1, 1920, the British government stated officially that no change in the status of Cyprus was contemplated.

In the island the campaign for enosis was intensified, culminating in the demand for a plebiscite, the formation of a 'National Council' headed by the archbishop, and a boycott of the elections to the Legislative Council and local bodies. This boycott lasted until 1923. But when the Greek defeat in Asia Minor and the Treaty of Lausanne made the prospects of enosis seem remote, the Greek Cypriots turned their main attention to demands for greater self-government, while the Turkish Cypriots asked for the return of the island to Turkey. The Conservative government in London rejected the plea for a more liberal constitution and declared that the question of enosis was closed. This position was also taken by the first Labour government under Ramsay MacDonald in 1923, although the Labour Party had supported self-determination for Cyprus in 1919. The same position was maintained even more strongly by the second Labour government in 1929. Two years later, under the philhellene governor, Sir Ronald Storrs, Greek Cypriot frustration flared up into an open revolt in which a mob set fire to Government House in Nicosia. The outbreak appears to have been largely unpremeditated. In retrospect its scale and nature would hardly seem to have justified the long suppression of constitutional liberties in Cyprus which the British government later imposed. In this respect, the British government's treatment of Cyprus during this period compared unfavourably with its attitude in Egypt and Iraq, both of which were recognised as independent, sovereign states, though bound to Britain by military treaties. A closer parallel was Palestine, where the British also held back the development of self-government for the majority in order to maintain the international status of the country and to protect the interests of a minority.

Although the enosis agitation was the revolutionary spark, there were other causes of discontent in the island which prepared the ground for the 1931 riots. The passage, against the opposition of the Greek members of the Legislative Council, of a bill taking primary education out of the hands of local committees and putting it under direct government control had aroused some fears of an attempt at 'dehellenisation'.

Then the effects of the world economic depression on the island sharpened public reaction to the budget of 1931. The budget introduced new customs dues and taxation and was imposed against the vote of the legislature by an Order in Council of the governor. An added irritation was connected with the ending of the hated Tribute. As already stated (see page 68 above) the Tribute, intended to be paid from Cyprus to the Turkish government under the Cyprus Convention, went in fact to the British Treasury to pay off bondholders of the Ottoman debt. The Cypriots had long protested against this payment and had been supported in their protests by successive high commissioners. Eventually the British government agreed to make a compensatory annual grant to Cyprus which covered most of the Tribute. Payment of the Tribute had stopped during the first world war after the annexation of Cyprus, but was resumed in 1923 on the grounds that, as one of the successor states to the Ottoman empire, Cyprus had to assume a share in repayment of the Ottoman debt—an obligation that no other of the successor states, such as Iraq, ever fulfilled. Sir Ronald Storrs succeeded where his predecessors had failed. He secured agreement from Whitehall to the final abolition of the Tribute in return for a contribution from Cyprus towards the cost of imperial defence, amounting to £10,000 a year: a sum about equal to the gap already existing between the British grant-in-aid and the Tribute. But the Treasury had yet to reveal a final piece of meanness. When the Cypriots asked for the surplus which had been accumulated from the small annual difference between the Tribute and the debt payments, the Chancellor of the Exchequer disclosed, in 1931, that the surplus no longer existed—it had already been used for the sinking fund of the Turkish loan.

Before the disturbances of October 1931, the bishop of Kition and the other Greek members had resigned from the Legislative Council. On October 17, the bishop issued an inflammatory manifesto calling for national liberation through union with Greece and declaring that the foreign ruler 'to whom and to whose illegal laws we owe no obedience' must be forced to leave the island. A speech by the bishop on similar lines three days later at a meeting in Limassol appears to have aroused only moderate excitement except in the breast of a reporter for the Greek press in Nicosia. A dramatic story in the morning newspapers of the capital was followed by the outbreak of rioting in Nicosia on the evening of October 21. The riot was led by a prominent Orthodox priest of Nicosia who brought out the Greek flag and declared that the revolution had begun. The rioters burned down Government House in

Nicosia and the trouble spread to other parts of the island. British troops were brought in from Egypt to strengthen the tiny garrison of one company. Law and order were quickly restored. There were no government casualties but six Cypriots were killed, and over thirty wounded. The bishops of Kition and Kyrenia and eight other Greek Cypriot religious and political leaders were banished for life from the island. Two thousand others were sent to prison and fines amounting to £66,000 were imposed on the Greek Cypriots to pay for the damage. Constitutional government was suspended, the Legislative Council and local councils abolished, political parties banned and the press put under censorship. The governor was empowered to rule by decree. The Colonial Office promised to review the constitutional future of the island but no new constitution was put forward until 1948. Until then the only modification of the governor's rule was the appointment in 1937 of an Advisory Council and the revival of municipal elections in 1943.

The 1931 rising and its suppression aroused strong emotions in Greece. There were public demonstrations and a press campaign in support of the Cypriots. A secret committee was formed to send a thousand volunteers to Cyprus, but it came to nothing. Venizelos was then in power again in Athens. He took a bold stand in favour of the national interest rather than national sentiment. He declared that Greece as a state could do nothing to help the Cypriots, however sympathetic she might feel about their aspirations. British friendship was vital for Greece; so long as Britain believed her interest demanded the continued occupation of Cyprus, she would not be influenced by Greek agitation. Venizelos added, however, that he hoped that the idea of ceding Cyprus to Greece need not be given up for ever, and hinted at a solution that the British government was in fact eventually to adopt in part—but not until twenty-eight years later after much blood had been shed in the island. He suggested that if Britain found she could satisfy her military requirements by having the use of a part instead of the whole of the island as a base, then it was possible that Cypriot aspirations might be fulfilled, provided violence were avoided.

In Greece, the end of the Anatolian war and the overthrow of King Constantine had been followed by a difficult period of political instability. Political life was dominated by the breach between royalists and Venizelists which was not healed until 1935 when the restoration of the monarchy was recognised by Venizelos. 'During the fourteen years which followed the *débâcle* in Asia Minor, there took place nineteen changes of Government, three changes of regime (the institution of the Republic in 1924, the Dictatorship of General Pangalos in January 1926 and the restoration of the Monarchy in November 1935), seven military revolutions or *coups d'Etat*, and innumerable minor acts of sedition due to the constant intervention of military juntas in the government of the country.'[6] To these Greek governments and regimes of the interwar years must be added the dictatorship of General Metaxas which lasted from August 1936 to his death in 1940 during the war with Italy. The abolition of the Greek monarchy and the proclamation of a republic on March 25, 1924, had been preceded by the brief return to Athenian politics—for one month only—of Venizelos. He did not return again until 1928 when he became prime minister again for four years.* In the meantime Greece had been rescued from the follies of the five months' dictatorship of General Pangalos by the intervention of another and more able army officer, General Kondylis. The country had also been saved from bankruptcy by a capable finance minister, Kaphandaris, who secured a settlement of her war debts and obtained international loans for the stabilisation of her currency and the resettlement of her refugees.

The exchange of populations between Greece and Turkey, agreed upon at Lausanne, proceeded rapidly with the help of a League of Nations Commission under Fridtjof Nansen. But there were a number of difficulties with Turkey before a final settlement was reached in 1930. One of them concerned the patriarchate in Istanbul. When a new patriarch, Gregorios VII, was appointed in December 1923, his appointment was attacked by Papa Eftim, the head of the self-styled 'Turkish Orthodox Church' in Anatolia. Papa Eftim considered the Greeks of Asia Minor to be Turks who had been converted to Christianity. He seized the headquarters of the patriarchate in the Phanar but was driven out by the Turkish government which had agreed, at the Lausanne Conference, to allow the patriarchate to stay in Istanbul as a purely religious institution. But when Gregorios died and was succeeded in December 1924 by Constantine VI, the Turks refused to accept the new incumbent. They argued that he was not an 'established' resident of Istanbul in the terms of the Lausanne Treaty, and so not one of the Greeks entitled to remain in Turkey. On January 30, 1925, the patriarch was expelled to Greece amid loud protests from churches

* He was associated with an unsuccessful republican revolt in 1935, was sentenced to death in absentia, later pardoned, and died on March 18, 1936 aged seventy-two.

throughout the world. He was obliged to abdicate in favour of the metropolitan of Nicaea, Basil Georgiadis, whom the Turks considered to be 'established' and not 'exchangeable'.

A well-timed gesture by Venizelos paved the way to a final settlement and the beginning of reconciliation with Turkey. He refused to spend money on adding another battleship to the Greek fleet to match Turkey's reconditioning of the wartime dreadnought *Goeben*. Venizelos told the Greek parliament he was confident that Turkey's intentions were not aggressive and that it would be wiser for Greece to resume the negotiations with Ankara which had broken down over the return to Istanbul of Greeks with Turkish passports. A Greco-Turkish convention, signed on June 10, 1930, settled the remaining problems connected with the exchange of populations, such as the value of properties left behind on both sides, and the position of the Greeks in Istanbul and the Turks in Thrace who had not been exchanged. The convention was followed four months later by the visit of Venizelos to Ankara where he signed a treaty of neutrality, conciliation and arbitration, and an agreement to limit naval armaments. At a banquet given in his honour by Mustafa Kemal, the Turkish president, Venizelos is reported to have declared that his presence in Ankara 'signified the end of a conflict between Greece and Turkey which had lasted for ten centuries'.[7] To symbolise the reconciliation, Mustafa Kemal ordered Santa Sophia in Istanbul, the great Byzantine cathedral converted into a mosque after the Turkish capture of the city in 1453, to be turned into a museum.[8]

The exchange of populations, involving the resettlement in Greece of nearly a million refugees, transformed the ethnic character of both Greece and Turkey. At the cost of vast human suffering, they became compact and homogeneous national states. Anatolia, except for its Kurdish fringe, became completely Turkish for the first time in history. Greek Macedonia became almost wholly Greek for the first time since the Slav invasions of the sixth and seventh centuries.[9]

This state of affairs was in accord with the new concept of Turkish nationalism which inspired Mustafa Kemal, the founder of the Turkish republic. Before the Young Turks' revolution, the dominant nationalistic ideas of the Turks were either pan-Islamic or based on 'Ottomanism': the idea of an Ottoman society in which members of all races would be equal citizens. However, the revolution brought to the fore a more specifically Turkish concept, expressed at first in political pan-Turkism and in a Turkish cultural revival stimulated by the research of European and Russian scholars on the language and history of the Turkish peoples.

The collapse of the Ottoman empire and the Bolshevik revolution in the Russian empire, where most of the other Turkish peoples lived, put an end to pan-Islamic, pan-Turkish and 'Ottomanist' ideas. Encouraged by the Anatolian war and by Mustafa Kemal's own vision of a 'westernised', secular Turkey, there emerged the idea of a purely Turkish patriotism, of a territorial nation-state based on the Turkish people in Turkey. This idea of Turkey—the land of the Turks—was so novel that there was no name for it in the Turkish language, though there had been earlier suggestions of 'Turkestan' or 'Turkland'.[10]

It was not easy for educated Turks brought up in the Ottoman tradition to get used to the new limits of their state and the old association between the Turks and Islam died hard. In law, the new Turkish republic provided complete equality for all its citizens, irrespective of race or creed. In the Lausanne Treaty, Turkey had accepted international obligations under the League of Nations for the rights of her minorities in the matter of language, education and religious and personal status. But, in practice, though the minorities were not actively persecuted (except to some extent the Kurds, who were Moslems), they remained second-class citizens. 'The old idea that only Muslims can really be Turks still permeated even official policies and actions', despite the efforts made by Mustafa Kemal to destroy the Islamic basis of Turkish society and state.[11] The leader of the new Turkey had followed his ending of the sultanate by the abolition of the caliphate and the Moslem religious establishment, the *sharia* courts, the religious foundations and the dervish brotherhoods. He developed his drive for westernisation by promoting the emancipation of women, forbidding the wearing of the fez and traditional costume. He ordered the 'purification' of the Turkish language from Persian and Arabic words, and introduced a new Latin alphabet instead of the Arabic script in which Turkish had been written for centuries past. He decreed that all Turks must have western-style surnames, and took for himself the name 'Ataturk'—meaning 'Father of the Turks'.

But one aspect of Western society eluded him: the creation of political democracy. Two attempts at a 'managed' opposition broke down. But since his failure coincided with the abandonment of democracy by large parts of Europe in favour of authoritarian or totalitarian regimes, Ataturk found that his one-party dictatorship was not so unwestern after all. His People's Republican Party had as its symbol the Six Arrows, signifying Republicanism, Nationalism, Populism, Etatism, Laicism and Reformism.[12] Dictator though he was, Mussolini and Hitler aroused his contempt; but Stalin he admired and he tried to keep on friendly terms with Soviet Russia.

'It was a cardinal point of Ataturk's foreign policy to remain on good terms with [Turkey's] nearest great sea power, Britain, and her nearest great land power, Soviet Russia.'[13] In 1926, he settled the dispute with Britain over Mosul and the Iraqi frontier which had been left over from the Lausanne conference. In the tripartite Anglo-Iraqi-Turkish Treaty, signed on June 5, 1926, Ataturk accepted the decision of the League of Nations that the disputed area should go to Iraq. Ten years later he secured a revision of the Dardanelles Convention. A new agreement, signed at Montreux on July 20, 1936, and still in force, re-established full Turkish sovereignty and military control over the Straits. In peacetime, merchant ships of all countries and warships of the Black Sea powers are allowed to pass freely. In time of war or threat of war, Turkey may impose certain specified restrictions on foreign shipping.

Only in one respect did Ataturk deviate from his policy of relinquishing irredentist claims for territory, formerly under Ottoman rule, where non-Arab Moslems were not a majority. This was in the case of the Hatay, the province in the south-west corner of Turkey, on the Syrian border. This question merits special attention here, not only because the port of Alexandretta lies so close to Cyprus, but also because the methods used to obtain the return of the Hatay to Turkey throw some light on official attitudes in Ankara to the Cyprus problem.

Under the Franco-Turkish agreement of 1921, the Hatay remained part of French-mandated Syria, but under a special administration which safeguarded the rights of the local Turkish population. The Ankara government considered the Turks in the Hatay to be in a majority (they were in fact about 40 per cent of the population, the majority being Arab and Armenian). When in 1936 France planned to give independence to Syria, the Turkish government asked for the cession of the Hatay to Turkey on the grounds of national self-determination by majority. The Syrians were strongly opposed to the cession, not only because of the Hatay's actual non-Turkish majority but also because Alexandretta was the main port for northern Syria and for Aleppo, the largest Syrian city. The French, however, were anxious to appease Turkey in order to secure her signature to a military alliance in view of the looming threat of war in Europe. The dispute was brought before the League of Nations and negotiations led, in 1937, to a form of autonomy for the Hatay. The territory was to have full internal self-government, with both Turkish and Arabic as official languages, but it was to be linked by a customs and monetary union with Syria which would also be responsible for its foreign affairs. This arrangement, which bears a striking resemblance to later Turkish proposals for a confederal state in Cyprus, was clearly intended by Ataturk as merely the first step towards annexation. He knew the French were in a weak bargaining position. When the international commission sent by the League to supervise the elections in the Hatay produced electoral registers showing the Turks to be in a minority, there were demonstrations by the Turks in Antioch against the electoral register. Ataturk ostentatiously moved Turkish troops towards the Hatay and the Syrian frontier. Under pressure the French yielded the next step. In July 1938, they agreed to the entry of Turkish troops to police the Hatay jointly with French troops and to a joint guarantee of its autonomy. When new electoral registers were produced, they showed a Turkish majority. In the elections held in August the Turks won twenty-two out of the forty seats in the local assembly. They promptly exercised their right of self-determination and proclaimed the Hatay an independent republic. This was followed, on June 29, 1939, by the union of the republic with Turkey—what the Greeks in the case of Cyprus would call enosis. No one then made much fuss about the rights or future protection of the Arabs and Armenians who claimed to be a majority. Most of the Armenians trekked across the border into Syria when it became clear that the Hatay would become Turkish.

Ataturk died on November 10, 1938, before his diplomatic coup had been completed. France reaped her reward on October 19, 1939, when the treaty of alliance between France, Britain and Turkey was signed in Ankara. But in the world war which had just begun, Turkey's neutrality was to prove the alliance to be a recompense of limited value.

CHAPTER EIGHT

World War, Civil War and Aftermath

FROM the second world war, as from the first, Cyprus emerged unscathed and, on the surface, little affected by the vast convulsions which had taken place throughout Europe and the Mediterranean. Except for a short period after the German occupation of Greece and Crete in 1941, the island was never in serious danger. It was used as a base for Allied commando raids on German and Italian forces in the Aegean Islands and the Dodecanese. Cypriots enlisted and fought bravely in the Allied ranks. But otherwise the war in the Mediterranean passed Cyprus by, which was further demonstration of its minor importance as a military base in comparison with the mainland of Egypt and the Levant.

The war nevertheless left its mark in several ways. Economically, the island prospered from a wartime boom; local industries and services were developed to replace those no longer available from abroad. The British administration, though lacking a representative basis among the Cypriots, encouraged social and economic development within its limited available resources. In the years immediately before and during the war, there was a big expansion of trade unions and co-operative societies; road-building, afforestation and agricultural improvement schemes were extended. One of the most striking signs of progress was the liquidation of peasant debts; this had the effect of encouraging farmers to carry out long-term improvements on their land.

Although there was no return to constitutional government or any yielding by the British over enosis, the wartime alliance between Britain and Greece produced a political relaxation on both the British and the Greek Cypriot sides. When the glories of the Greek victories over the Italians and later of the Greek resistance movement against the Germans were part of the canon of Allied propaganda, and with Turkey obstinately neutral, it was difficult for the British to enforce the laws which forbad the flying of the Greek flag and treated talk of enosis as sedition. On the contrary, official recruiting posters called on the Greek Cypriots to volunteer to save the Greek motherland.

In 1941, political parties were allowed again. The first to make a legal appearance was a new communist-controlled party: the Progressive Party of the Working People, known, from the initial letters of its Greek title, as AKEL. It had close links with the main trade union group, the Pan-Cyprian Labour Federation. AKEL was soon followed by the pro-enosis rightwing organisation, the Cyprus National Party (KEK). Both parties were opposed by the Turkish Cypriots, whose leading political group was the Turkish National Party. By the end of the war, there were thirty-four Greek and three Turkish Cypriot parties, though the three just mentioned remained the most important. In 1943 AKEL made important gains in the first municipal elections held since 1931, winning control of two of the five main towns, Famagusta and Limassol. Enosis figured in the election campaign, but the demand for it was not seriously pressed during the war. There was a general expectation on the part of the Greek Cypriots that, since Greece had fought by Britain's side, and in view of Allied declarations about national freedom and liberation, like the Atlantic Charter, the British would, without question, permit the union of Cyprus with Greece once the war was over. This feeling was strengthened when it appeared probable that the Dodecanese Islands would be given to Greece. It is, indeed, conceivable that these expectations would have had a good chance of being realised if Greece at the end of the war had not been torn by bitter civil strife. Her need of British help and the danger of her falling under communist control weakened Greece's position in regard to the question of enosis in the immediate post-war years.

Cypriot political life reflected not only the main currents in the wartime world but also, in particular, the attitudes of Greece and Turkey. The Turkish Cypriots were affected by Turkey's neutrality and her intermittent sympathy with Germany. They also feared that the Anglo-Greek alliance might lead to enosis at the end of the war. Among the Greek Cypriots, the division between right and left was deepened by the politics of the Greek resistance movement, the conflict over the liberation and the later civil war.

The bitterness of the political conflict in Greece was partly a legacy of the inter-war years, reflecting both the pre-war antagonisms and post-war hopes of Greek politics. The Franco-type dictatorship of General Metaxas had destroyed the more moderate political parties, leaving the extreme rightwing royalists and the communists as the only effective political forces in the country. The wartime resistance in which the communists took the lead, the entry of Russia into the war and the British government's controversial support for the exiled Greek king, George II, who had been associated with the repressive Metaxas regime, combined to superimpose a new conflict between communists and anti-communists on to the old rift between royalists and republicans.

Fear of the return of the king and his extremist supporters had the effect, in the first round of the conflict during the wartime resistance, of pushing many non-communist republicans into alliance with the communists. In the second round, after the liberation of Greece, the communists lost some of their republican allies. But the fact that right-wing extremists took the lead among the anti-communists and began a reign of terror against former resistance members, contributed to keeping many non-communists in the communist camp. It was not until the third round—a full-scale civil war by communist guerrillas supported from Yugoslavia, Albania and Bulgaria—that the communists were finally isolated. By then Britain had become deeply and bitterly involved in Greek politics.

On April 13, 1939, six days after Italy seized Albania, the British government, together with France, had given a guarantee to Greece and Rumania against any threat to their independence. Greece did not ask for the guarantee and the Metaxas regime, up to that time, had close economic links with Germany. Britain's association with Greece became further involved as a result of the treaty of alliance, signed in Ankara six months later, whereby Turkey promised aid to Britain and France in the event of war in the Mediterranean or of war arising from their guarantees to Greece and Rumania. The alliance also included a protocol releasing Turkey from any action that might involve her in war with Russia. When the second world war broke out, both Greece and Turkey remained neutral. Italy's entry into the war against Britain on June 20, 1940, bringing hostilities to the Mediterranean, should have activated the Turkish alliance, but Turkey still stayed neutral, invoking the protocol about Russia as her excuse for inaction. Turkish neutrality was maintained when Italy attacked Greece on October 28, 1940, and was continued for almost the entire duration of the war. Turkey did not declare war on Germany and Japan until February 22, 1945, after the Yalta Conference had ruled that only those countries which declared war on the Axis powers by March 1 of that year would be invited to become founding members of the United Nations at the San Francisco Conference. The British view was stated by Churchill and

Eden, both of whom made it clear that they hoped Turkey would enter the war in 1944.

Ismet Inönü, who had succeeded Ataturk in 1938 and remained president of Turkey throughout the war years, has claimed (in an interview with the author in June 1965) that the Allies showed a full understanding of Turkey's position, which was 'theoretically belligerent but in practice waiting for the right moment to act'. Other Turks have argued that their country's neutrality helped to shelter the Allied position in the Middle East when the Germans were threatening it from several directions: from the Balkans, the Caucasus and North Africa. The Turkish attitude, at least in the early years of the war, is most easily explained by the changed situation created by the defeat of France and other German successes in Europe, which brought the Germans to Greece and left Syria under the Vichy regime, and, above all, by the German attack on Russia. In June 1941, Turkey signed a non-aggression pact with Germany, and the swift advance of Hitler's troops into southern Russia must have strengthened the belief that Germany would win the war. Even so, the Turkish attitude did not change after the Germans had been driven back in Russia and North Africa, and Italy had been knocked out of the war. It should be noted here that one consequence of German influence in Turkey was a departure from the principles of equal treatment for minorities laid down in the Treaty of Lausanne and in the Turkish Constitution. This was the imposition by the government in Ankara of a capital levy which discriminated against non-Moslem Turkish subjects and foreigners. Greeks, Armenians and Jews were the principal victims. Those who could not, or would not, pay the exorbitant sums demanded of them were sent to work on the roads in Anatolia.

Greece had at first refused British help—except for four squadrons of bombers—in dealing with the Italian invasion, hoping that she might thus avoid German intervention. But the magnificent Greek performance against the Italians, and Hitler's determination to control the Balkans before invading Russia, provided the catalyst which precipitated the German invasion of Greece on April 6, 1941. By then, the German occupation of Bulgaria had resulted in an agreement whereby Britain was to send three divisions and an armoured brigade to Greece. British troops began to land in Greece in March 1941. Churchill took this decision largely for political reasons: to encourage the confidence of Turkey and other Middle Eastern countries in the credibility of a British guarantee. The British did not then know the full purpose of the

German entry into Bulgaria, taking it to be the prelude not only to an attack on Yugoslavia and Greece, but also to the domination of the Bosphorus and the Dardanelles by intimidation or force. 'The last thing we wanted', wrote the British commander in Greece, General Wilson (later Field-Marshal Lord Wilson), 'was a German walkover in either country; the only way it could be prevented was by our presence in Greece, as on that moral factor alone depended the hope of building up a southern front against Germany. If the German forces in Bulgaria were to be used against three countries, the odds against our being able to hold them were not so hopeless.'[1]

In the event, the Germans left Turkey alone, singling out Yugoslavia and Greece for attack. Britain's military support for Greece proved, militarily, a bad investment. The war cabinet in London had overestimated the value of Yugoslav and Greek troops in action against the Germans; it had not been accurately informed of the heavy toll taken of the Greek army in its victories over the Italians and in the bitter winter conditions of the Albanian mountains.[2] The decision to weaken Britain's meagre forces in Libya in order to support Greece paved the way for her defeats in the Western Desert by Rommel's Afrika Korps which eventually forced her troops back into Egypt. Greece itself was over-run by Hitler's army within three weeks, and 57,000 British troops had to be withdrawn under fire. On May 20, 1941, Crete had to be evacuated in the face of a German airborne attack. But the heavy losses suffered in Crete by German paratroops—estimated as being between 12,000 and 15,000 men—coupled with Hitler's diversion of aircraft for the invasion of Russia, probably saved Cyprus from a similar assault. The British used the breathing space to capture Syria from its Vichy administration with the help of the Free French, and to seize control of Iraq from the pro-German regime of Rashid Ali.

Anglo-Greek friendship was strengthened by the fact that for eight months in 1940–41 Britain and Greece were alone in the fight against the Axis powers. But the friendship was to be sorely tried by the political disputes which developed out of the relations between the Greek resistance movement—itself divided between right and left groups, royalists and republicans—and the Greek king and government in exile. As the chief military support of the rival resistance groups in the field and the main political prop of the king and the government in exile, the British found themselves painfully involved, first in attempted conciliation, and finally in arbitration by armed force. A detailed account of these disputes, of which a brief survey has been given earlier in this chapter, is beyond the scope of this book. It is still a matter of controversy whether the rising of the leftwing EAM and ELAS resistance forces against the returned Greek government and the British army which liberated Greece in 1944 was provoked by fear of a British-backed royalist repression, or was simply an attempt by the communists at a revolutionary seizure of power. The ferocity with which the communists and their guerrilla supporters fought the subsequent civil war between 1946 and 1949 owed something, no doubt, to the severity of their repression by rightwing governments after the liberation rising.*

Here we are more concerned with the effects of these troubles on the post-war situation in Cyprus and on the British position in the Near and Middle East. There were three main effects. First, the attention of the Greek and British governments was diverted from the revived demands of the Greek Cypriots that their union with Greece should form part of the post-war settlement. In the Italian peace treaty signed in Paris on February 15, 1947, Italy ceded the Dodecanese Islands to Greece. Turkey, from whose coast most of the islands are only a few miles distant, raised no objections, for her wartime record, compared with that of Greece, left her in a weak position to protest. Despite this, Britain showed no signs of willingness to hand over Cyprus to Greece. A delegation to London and to the conference of the deputy foreign ministers of the Allies at Paris in 1946, led by the acting archbishop of Cyprus, asked for enosis. It was rebuffed. The new Labour government in Britain repeated the time-worn formula that no change in the status of the island was contemplated; but it allowed the former exiled Cypriot leaders to return, and offered a new Constitution. The Greek government, heavily dependent on the support of British troops and on economic aid from Britain, was in no position to exert pressure on behalf of the enosists.

The second effect of the Greek troubles was on the attitude of the communists and their sympathisers in Cyprus. While the civil war was raging in Greece, AKEL campaigned for Cypriot self-government through constitutional advance rather than for immediate enosis. So long as the political future of Greece was still in doubt, they could afford to wait for enosis, and in the meantime consolidate their local position in the island.

* The period between the second and third rounds of the civil war were notable for the emergence of Colonel Grivas, later to become leader of the EOKA rebellion in Cyprus, as the head of the extreme rightwing royalist organisation, 'X'.

But after the communists were defeated in the civil war, AKEL switched back to supporting enosis. There was no point in waiting for a communist government in Greece, and, moreover, by that time the attempt to introduce a new Constitution had failed. Their chief political rivals in the island were intensifying the enosis campaign; support for 'constitutional advance' would have put the communists on the right of their opponents.

The third effect was perhaps the most far reaching. It was nothing less than the virtual end of Britain's role, for more than a century past, as the main protecting power of Greece and the chief support of Turkey. It was also the beginning of the end of the position Britain had come to occupy as the dominant power in the Middle East.

At first sight, Britain's position in the Near and Middle East at the end of the second world war was stronger than ever. British troops, diplomatists and other officials were in control of the whole area, except Turkey, from southern Iran to North Africa, and from northern Greece to the southern Sudan. Britain's old rival, France, had been forced out of Syria and the Lebanon, more through French political blunders in dealing with the Syrians and the Lebanese than through British design. But it was an illusion of power, for a number of reasons.

1. The economic weakness of Britain herself, drained of resources by the war, meant that she could not for long sustain alone the burden of keeping large numbers of troops in Greece and the Middle East and of providing economic and military aid for Greece and Turkey.

2. The climate of political opinion had changed in Britain, in the Middle East and in the world at large. Empires and colonies had become less respectable. Stimulated by the collapse of Europe and by wartime propaganda for liberation, such as the Atlantic Charter, the nationalist movements were pressing forward against the old imperial and colonial powers. There was a widespread feeling that in the post-war world there should be a fresh start and an end to old relationships and treaties based on the domination of one people by another. Moreover, it was clear to all that a new power situation existed in the world. Europe had been devastated; France had been conquered; Germany now lay broken and Italy's pretensions had been shown to be hollow. Britain was financially, if not physically, exhausted; her power had revealed its limitations and her ultimate need for reliance on the United States had been demonstrated. America and Russia had emerged as the dominant powers in the post-war world.

3. In the light of these changes and considering the state of her own

public opinion. Britain had decided to withdraw from her Indian empire and to give independence to India, Pakistan, Ceylon and Burma. In doing so, she gave up a great part of the power, notably the Indian army, which had enabled her to hold the Middle East. She also gave up one of the main motives for having a dominant position in the Middle East: the need to hold the route to India—although communications with Commonwealth countries and the remaining imperial possessions east of Suez were still an argument for a British military presence in the Middle East. There were, moreover, new factors exerting powerful influence: the development of the cold war between the West and Stalinist Russia; and the importance to the post-war economy of Europe as a whole of Britain's huge oil investments in Iraq and the Persian Gulf. Assured supplies of Middle Eastern oil were considered vital for the reconstruction of a Europe already heavily dependent on American aid. For Britain herself, both the oil itself and the profits from it were one of the few bright features in the country's economic situation.

In retrospect it can be seen that Britain at first attached too high a priority to the defence of the Middle East against a possible direct military attack from Russia and neglected the more important task of keeping in step with the political evolution of Middle East countries. Her efforts to hold on to military bases consequently brought her into conflict with local nationalism and, as local hostility grew, so the British military presence came to be regarded, by both sides, more as a means of controlling the governments and policies of countries in the area than as a defence against external attack. Yet in the immediate post-war years Britain did make an attempt to adapt her Middle East policy both to local opinion and to her reduced resources. This she tried to do in two ways: first, by building a new system of military alliances with the states in the region which she had hitherto virtually controlled directly; and secondly, by bringing in the United States to take over or share responsibility.

Britain's first step towards shedding some of her burdens in the Middle East was the attempt to secure American co-operation in a joint mission to Palestine. This move also represented an attempt to allay pro-Zionist criticism in the United States of British policy in Palestine in that it sought to involve Washington in dealing with the Zionist-Arab conflict. The failure of this mission led to Britain's decision in 1948 to relinquish the Palestine mandate in the face of Zionist rebellion and Arab counter-attacks. The British government had by then signed a new treaty setting up Transjordan as an independent allied kingdom, and had begun negotiations with Egypt for a revision of the Anglo-Egyptian treaty of 1936. Egypt was pressing for an end of the agreement by which Britain was allowed to station a limited number of troops in the Suez Canal Zone for the protection of imperial communications. The Egyptians wanted the withdrawal of all British forces from their country and the ending of an occupation which had begun as a 'temporary' intervention in 1882. Egyptian feelings were aggravated by the fact that Britain, after the war, was maintaining in the Zone many more troops than had been permitted under the 1936 agreement, and by the increase in the size of the Suez base itself following the withdrawal thither of troops and stores from Palestine.

While grappling with Palestine and Egypt, the British government told the United States that it could not continue its aid to Greece beyond March 1947. The United States had by then become involved in resisting Russian pressures on the outer rim of the Middle East. For example, it had supported Iran when, by a stratagem, the Iranian prime minister, Qavam es Sultaneh, secured the withdrawal of Russian troops from Azerbaijan in May 1946. But Soviet pressures continued not only against Iran but also against Turkey—from whom the Russians demanded the cession of the frontier districts of Kars and Ardahan, and also a revision of the Straits Convention—and against Greece, where the communist rebellion was being supported from the neighbouring communist countries. The American response was the 'Truman Doctrine'. On March 12, 1947, President Truman asked Congress to grant $400 million in aid to Greece and Turkey. The president made it plain that the Eastern Mediterranean must now be considered a vital American interest. He formulated the doctrine that 'totalitarian regimes imposed on free peoples undermine the foundations of international peace and hence the security of the United States'. He thereby inaugurated a new phase in American foreign policy, not only for the Middle East, but for the whole world. The Truman Doctrine led eventually to the creation of an American-backed chain of anti-communist alliances around the globe. The first of these alliances was NATO, to which Greece was admitted in the autumn of 1951 and Turkey in February of the following year. Greek and Turkish forces were included in a new South-East Europe command of NATO which was set up at Izmir (formerly Smyrna) in Turkey in July 1952. Henceforward, in any question affecting Greece and Turkey, such as Cyprus, the views of the United States could not be ignored.

The British withdrawal from Palestine in May 1948, left Cyprus as the only territory in the Eastern Mediterranean under British sovereignty. For military purposes, Britain relied on her bases in the Suez Canal Zone and Iraq, but increasing Egyptian pressure for the withdrawal of British troops from Egypt enhanced the possible future strategic value of Cyprus and caused the British government to make further efforts to resolve endemic problems on the island. A new British governor, Lord Winster—a Labour peer—arrived in Cyprus on March 27, 1947 to implement the reforms promised by the British government. These entailed the calling of a representative Consultative Assembly to draw up proposals for a new Constitution, including the re-establishment of the legislature, suspended since 1931, and the repeal of laws blocking the elections of a new archbishop. The acting archbishop was elected to the post but died a month later and was succeeded by Bishop Makarios of Kyrenia. But Archbishop Makarios II (not to be confused with his more famous successor, Makarios III, later president of Cyprus), and the Greek Cypriot nationalist parties rejected the constitutional reform plans. They feared their acceptance would mean admitting that enosis, their real political aim, was ruled out.

Only the leftwing, together with four Greek independents and Turkish Cypriot representatives, accepted invitations to take part in the Consultative Assembly. The leftwing argued that self-government would be a step towards enosis, and when the Assembly met on November 7, 1947, eight Greek representatives, forming a majority, insisted on discussing full self-government. The chairman of the Assembly, Sir Edward Jackson, chief justice of Cyprus, declared that self-government went beyond its terms of reference. There followed six months of deadlock until, on May 7, 1948, the British government put forward its own proposals for a constitution. It offered an important step forward. For the first time, the Greek-elected members of the legislature would be able to form an effective majority which could no longer be blocked by the traditional combination of British officials and Turkish-elected members. The legislature was to consist of twenty-two elected members, eighteen elected on the general electoral roll and four from the Turkish communal roll—and only four officials. Moreover, the casting vote would no longer belong to the governor but to an independent chairman chosen by him. At the same time, though an important step forward, the Winster Constitution barred any discussion of the status of Cyprus —nor did it provide for full self-government. The British governor was to have reserved powers over defence, external affairs and finance, as well as over laws affecting minorities and the Constitution itself.

These two limitations ensured the rejection of the British plan and the boycott of the Consultative Assembly by both right and left elements among the Greek Cypriots. It was accepted by the Turkish Cypriots whose six representatives, together with one Maronite and four Greek independents, voted the proposals through the Assembly by an unrepresentative majority. The Assembly was dissolved on August 12, 1948 and thereafter the campaign for enosis began to gather strength, now backed by the left as well as by the right.

In retrospect, the Winster constitution can be seen as one of the biggest lost opportunities in the Cyprus dispute. A chance for a peaceful evolutionary settlement was missed because neither the British nor the Greek Cypriots had yet fully understood the changes which the post-war world had brought to each other's political ideas. The Greek Cypriot nationalists were obsessed with the idea of achieving enosis by a simple transfer of sovereignty such as had returned the Dodecanese or the Ionian Islands to Greece. They did not realise that, in the new traditions of colonial government developing in the post-war Commonwealth, an elected majority might open the way to eventual self-government by a whittling down of the governor's reserved powers. Nor did they appear to realise that even the ban on discussing the status of Cyprus within the Commonwealth did not constitute an irrevocable barrier to enosis, for it did not rule out the achievement of independence for Cyprus within the Commonwealth. As the example of Burma had shown, an independent country could not be prevented from leaving the Commonwealth and then joining up with another country if it chose to do so.

Only the Cypriot leftwing seemed to understand the opportunity which was offered by the prospect of eventual self-government. But they were alienated by the failure of the British government to understand that, in the post-war political climate, the constitution it was offering was too restricted. It compared unfavourably with the independence or full self-government being offered to other former colonies or imperial territories which were far less politically and materially advanced than Cyprus. Moreover, the British government went out of its way unnecessarily to affront Greek Cypriot opinion by its repeated public assertion that the enosis question was closed.

Later on, both the Greek Cypriots and the British had cause to modify their attitudes. The former recognised the essential importance of a constitution with an elected Greek majority, and the latter admitted that the door to enosis was not closed. It was on this basis that, in February 1956, Archbishop Makarios III and the British governor, Field Marshal Sir John Harding, were to come the closest that Britain and the Greek Cypriots ever came to a direct bilateral agreement on the future of Cyprus. But by then the relations between Britain and Cyprus and between the two communities in the island had been gravely impaired by developments arising from the missed opportunity of 1948.

The failure of the Winster Constitution led to the organisation by the nationalists and the Church of a plebiscite on enosis on January 15 and 22, 1950. Out of 224,747 Greek Cypriots eligible to vote, 215,108, or 96 per cent, were said by the organisers to have signed the petition for enosis. The Church was accused of putting pressure on its congregations during the voting, although the archbishop had challenged the British authorities to conduct the plebiscite themselves. Makarios II died on June 28, 1950, and it was the bishop of Kyrenia who, in July, took to Athens the books containing the signatures in favour of enosis, presenting them to the president of the Greek Chamber of Deputies. The Greek prime minister appealed for restraint in Greece over Cyprus.

The plebiscite is said to have been suggested by the young bishop of Kition who, after his return from university theological studies in Boston in 1948, had begun to make political contacts in Greece on the Cyprus question. On October 18, 1950, then aged thirty-seven, he was elected archbishop as Makarios III. Ten years later he was to become the first president of the Cyprus Republic. The Greek Cypriots had found a leader.

9—CAPOA

CHAPTER NINE

Enter—and Exit—the Archbishop

THE IDEA of an archbishop as a political leader, particularly as the leader of a militant nationalist movement employing terrorist methods, is strange and, indeed, repellent to most modern Anglo-Saxon minds. The idea of the political cleric may perhaps be less strange to those who recall the role of the great prelate in England's past—Becket, Wolsey and Laud, for example—and reflect that bishops still sit in the House of Lords where many of them have voted in favour of their country's arming itself with nuclear weapons.

To the mind of the modern Kemalist Turk the idea is doubly abhorrent. The exclusion of the Islamic religion from Turkish politics is part of the essence of Kemalism. To have to deal politically with a priest is hard enough for the Kemalist Turk to endure, but when the priest is also a Greek Orthodox Christian the burden of prejudice is added to the weight of principle.

Under Ottoman rule, however, the priest-politician was an accepted feature of public life. In Cyprus the archbishop was recognised by the Turks as the 'ethnarch' or leader of his people. He was in the fullest sense the representative national leader of the Greek Cypriots. This position he retained in their eyes when Britain took over the island from Turkey. His compatriots would have found it shocking if Makarios III had not assumed the leadership of the national movement, though his ecclesiastical dignity made his task in diplomacy more difficult than that, say, of Venizelos in the liberation of Crete.

The election of Archbishop Makarios marked the beginning of a decade of political struggle which ended—though only temporarily—in the creation of an independent republic of Cyprus. It was a decade of consolidation and reconstruction in Greece after the turmoil of the civil war, and a decade of great changes in Turkey and in British imperial affairs.

Turkey was engaged in her fifth attempt since the 1876 constitution to create an effective parliamentary democracy. At the same time her economy, especially her agriculture, was being revitalised by large-scale

American aid. At the end of the second world war Turkey had been transformed by a remarkable bloodless revolution from a one-party dictatorship into a multiparty democracy. Even more remarkable was that in the elections of 1950 the old ruling party, the Republican People's Party headed by Ismet Inönü, had been heavily defeated and replaced in power by the new Democratic Party, led by Adnan Menderes, with a programme of greater freedom in business, religion and politics.

Britain was increasingly in conflict throughout the Middle East with the rising forces of Arab nationalism and neutralism, which eventually focused on the Egyptian revolutionary leader, Gamal Abdul Nasser. This conflict reached its first climax in the Anglo-French intervention at Suez in November 1956. Its second and most decisive climax—and that which probably had the most direct influence on Cyprus—was the Middle East crisis created in 1958 by the civil war in the Lebanon and the revolution in Iraq. It was then that the Western powers and Russia confirmed their tacit recognition of the neutrality of the central Arab area of the Middle East and the undesirability of unilateral military intervention there. When Egypt and Syria merged in the United Arab Republic in February 1958, the Western powers and Russia alike had been obliged to accept the fact that Nasser had successfully driven 'a neutralist wedge into the heart of the Arab world'.[1] The confirmation of this came when, at the time of the Iraqi revolution in July 1958, the Americans and British limited their intervention to the Lebanon and Jordan, and did not press further east to Damascus and Baghdad. The consequence of the new situation was a gradual British disengagement from Arab affairs, except in the oil sheikhdoms of the Persian Gulf and round the fringes of the Arabian peninsula, and, to a limited extent, in Libya. By the end of the 'fifties, British military commitments in the Middle East had shrunk to cover only these remaining areas of direct or indirect economic and political interests.

The Greek Cypriot struggle took place against the background of this broader conflict. It was profoundly influenced by it, and at times—as during the Suez crisis—was overwhelmed by it. The long British retreat in the Middle East and its effect on British politics, especially within the Conservative Party, made a solution of the Cyprus problem more difficult. It concentrated attention for too long on the inessential question of maintaining British sovereignty over the island at the expense of the more important need to secure agreement between Greece and Turkey and between Greek and Turkish Cypriots. Such agreement was essential for Britain's own interest both in maintaining stability in the Near East and in securing the co-operation necessary to operate a military base in the island. By the time Britain had recognised that her military needs did not require maintenance of sovereignty over the whole of the island, great damage had already been done to Greco-Turkish relations. The settlement, when it came, rested on shaky foundations.

Indeed, one of the most tragic aspects of the Cyprus dispute is that it developed during a period when the prospects of improving relations between Greeks and Turks ought otherwise to have been brighter than ever before. Greece and Turkey had become partners in the Western alliance, and both had strongly pro-Western governments with similar outlooks in economic affairs. But for Cyprus, they would have been able to expand further the friendly relations which had been re-established after the interruption of the second world war. While their membership of NATO may have helped them to avoid more serious conflict with each other over Cyprus, the Cyprus question inevitably became entangled at critical moments with the domestic politics of Greece and Turkey, as it did with those of Britain.

Although the Greek Cypriot campaign for enosis was launched in 1950, it did not really gather momentum until the autumn of 1954. It was at its peak from then until the beginning of 1959 when the Zürich and London agreements on an independent Cyprus were signed. During this period of about four and a half years, riot and rebellion, guerrilla warfare against the British and finally communal strife between Greek and Turkish Cypriots, alternated with intervals of truce, negotiation and an annual political agitation at the United Nations. There were five main bouts of negotiation or sets of proposals offered. They reflected to a large extent the British government's gradual advance from the position that its sovereignty over Cyprus would never be changed. The first step forward was when Britain hinted, in the Harding-Makarios talks in January 1956, that she might be prepared to give up her sovereignty at some indefinite future date. But this was followed by a step backwards when, in December of the same year, she offered the Radcliffe Constitution, which stipulated continued British sovereignty, and at the same time declared that self-determination would inevitably mean partition of the island between Greeks and Turks. Later on, in plans put forward in 1958, Harold Macmillan, then British prime minister, proposed virtually a sharing of sovereignty between Britain, Greece and Turkey in a political formula almost as subtly obscure as one of the more recondite heresies of the Trinity. Finally, the recognition by Britain that a small sovereign area would meet her strategic requirements just as well, if not better than sovereignty—whole or shared—over the entire island, paved the way for the Zürich and London agreements in February 1959.

Between 1950 and 1954 the Cyprus question only rarely broke through the surface of international politics. The world itself was preoccupied with much bigger things. During the last years of Stalin the cold war was at its height. The Korean and Indochinese wars were raging, and Greek and Turkish troops were fighting in the United Nations army in Korea, the Turks with particular distinction. Greece and Turkey were busy with their own political and economic affairs. Elsewhere in the Middle East, attention was focused on the crises faced in Egypt and Iran by an expiring British Labour government and a new Conservative administration. Apart from two minor public occasions and one private, the Cyprus issue seemed to be dormant. On February 11, 1951, the Greek prime minister, Venizelos, son of the great Eleutherios Venizelos, asked in Parliament for the union of Cyprus and Greece. But his speech was an unavoidable reply to a statement made in the House of Commons by the British minister of state, Kenneth Younger, who had said that no official demand for enosis had been received from the Greek government. In November 1951, Greece raised the Cyprus question in the Trusteeship Committee of the United Nations during the meeting of the General Assembly in Paris. The Greek delegate pointed out that, while Libya had become an independent state, Cyprus—though more advanced in every way—was still a British colony.

In between these two public interventions, there was a hitherto unrecorded private encounter during a NATO meeting in Rome in November 1951 between Eden, then British foreign secretary (later raised to the peerage as the earl of Avon) and Averoff, later to be Greek foreign minister but at that time an under-secretary in the Foreign Ministry.* The meeting was arranged by the British ambassador in Athens, Sir Charles Peake, who had been disturbed by the effect on Greek opinion of the Cyprus plebiscite in the previous year and the subsequent vote in favour of enosis in the Chamber of Deputies. According to Averoff in an interview with the author in June 1965, he proposed to Eden that, in return for the union of Cyprus with Greece, Britain should keep what bases she needed in the island. In addition, she should be granted bases on a ninety-nine years' lease in four places

* This encounter is not mentioned in *Full Circle*, the volume of Lord Avon's memoirs dealing with this period.

in Greece, including Cephalonia in the Ionian Islands and Suda Bay in Crete. Averoff reports Eden's reaction as being rough and angry: 'The British empire is not for sale. The Cyprus question does not exist.'

During this period of changing coalition governments in Greece, Archbishop Markarios began to make contacts among Greek political leaders. He also met, in July 1951 in Cyprus, the Colonel Grivas earlier mentioned as leader of the extreme rightwing royalist organisation 'X' in Greece after the second world war. Grivas, a former career officer in the Greek army, born and bred in Cyprus, had already begun secret planning with a group of Greek nationalists and Cypriot exiles in Athens for an armed struggle to drive the British out of the island. His meeting with Makarios occurred in the course of a visit to Cyprus to spy out the land. Himself a man of fanatical and ruthless temperament, he found the archbishop full of 'grave doubts' about armed action. But a year later the archbishop became chairman of a revolutionary committee set up by Grivas and his associates in Athens.[2]

In the meantime both Grivas and Makarios had contacted Field Marshal Papagos, the former commander-in-chief—hero of the nation in the Albanian war against Italy and of the anti-communists in the Greek civil war. Papagos had become the leader of a new Gaullist-type political party: the Greek Rally. The new party was openly backed by the Americans, who wanted a 'strong' government in order to achieve political and economic stability. Grivas claims in his memoirs that, in January 1951, he was given a promise of full support by the Greek chief of staff, General Kosmas, who was close to Papagos. But as Papagos came nearer to the responsibilities of political power, he kept aloof from Grivas' plans, though remaining sympathetic. Makarios secured a promise from Papagos that, when he came to power, he would take up the Cyprus question.

In October 1952, Grivas went to Cyprus to begin a five-months' study of a possible armed campaign and to plan the smuggling of arms into the island. Young men of the two Greek Cypriot youth movements, OXEN and PEON* were chosen to receive and store smuggled arms. The preparations continued throughout 1953 for action in Cyprus on two levels: the public level of diplomacy and the secret level of armed conspiracy. Grivas returned to Greece in February 1953 with a completed plan for military action, a copy of which he sent to Makarios. According to Grivas, the archbishop at first accepted the need for the

* OXEN: Orthodox Christian Youth Union; PEON: Pan-Cyprian National Youth Organisation.

use of force but wanted to confine it to sabotage, excluding guerrilla operations. He began to draw back from this position, however, when the new Papagos government sought to discourage the whole enterprise, making it plain that it did not wish to be involved.[3]

While Grivas was in Cyprus, the Greek elections of November 16, 1952 had resulted in a landslide victory for Papagos and the Greek Rally. Aided by a new electoral law, the party had gained half the total vote and 239 out of the 300 parliamentary seats. Makarios asked Papagos to redeem his pledge and bring the Cyprus question before the United Nations. In an interview with the author in June 1965, Stefanopoulos, foreign minister in the new government, stated that Papagos insisted that Greece should first make a direct approach to Britain, whom he considered to be friendly to Greece and to himself. The opportunity to do so arose in the autumn of 1953 when Eden visited Athens during a convalescent cruise in the Mediterranean following a serious illness. A meeting between Eden and Papagos was arranged by Peake, the British ambassador. It proved a disaster. Eden refused to discuss Cyprus, which—he said—Britain would never give up. In the words of Stefanopoulos: 'Eden was ill and Papagos, a blunt soldier, was not very diplomatic. Eden pronounced the fatal word "never". Papagos came back and said to me in an outraged voice: "He told me *never*—not even *we shall see*".'

Papagos was a vain man, and at that time he was still a symbol and hero of the anti-communist struggle. His pride was wounded. The rebuff certainly stimulated Greek official support for the enosists. Greece raised the Cyprus question at the United Nations General Assembly in the autumn of 1954. It is still a matter of conjecture how far Eden's refusal to discuss matters with the Greek leader also led to secret official encouragement for Colonel Grivas to organise an armed revolt in Cyprus and go to the island to lead it in person.

Grivas had gone ahead with his plans. With the reluctant agreement of Makarios, the first shipload of arms and explosives was landed secretly from a Greek caique in March 1954. The colonel was urging that action should start as soon as possible, but in April he was told by Stefanopoulos that violence would cause 'incalculable damage to diplomatic progress on the Cyprus question'. Papagos insisted that Grivas do nothing to upset Britain. There was a pause in the conspiracy as the Greek appeal to the United Nations was prepared. But in October 1954 a second shipload of arms was smuggled into the island. Makarios now told Grivas that both he and Stefanopoulos were eager for him to go to

Cyprus at once, for they thought that some action before the UN debate would impress the Americans.[4] Grivas landed secretly from a caique on November 10, 1954, and at once began to recruit his first guerrilla units from among the young men of the two Christian youth organisations. The extent of the subsequent link between Grivas and the Papagos government is difficult to assess conclusively. Such as it was, it existed through secret service organisations from which the Greek government could dissociate itself when necessary.

There were other factors contributing to the gradual intensification of the struggle in Cyprus throughout 1954. In June, as part of the preparations for a new agreement with Egypt providing for the replacement of British troops in the Suez Canal Zone by civilian technicians, it was announced in London that British Middle East Land and Air Headquarters would be transferred to Cyprus. The misgivings aroused among the Greek Cypriot leadership by this news were strengthened a month later. On July 28, 1954, the minister of state for the Colonies, Henry Hopkinson, announced the offer of a new Constitution for Cyprus. It provided for a minority of elected members in the legislature, and so was a step backwards from the Winster Constitution rejected by the Greek Cypriots in 1948. This was bad enough, but worse was the accompanying statement in the House of Commons in which the minister said of Cyprus: 'There are certain territories in the Commonwealth which, owing to their particular circumstances, can never expect to be fully independent'. The word 'never' now uttered again but this time in public, was glossed over later in the debate by Sir Winston Churchill, then still prime minister. But it powerfully stirred feelings in Cyprus and in Greece.

At the UN Assembly in the autumn of 1954, Cyprus was put on the agenda, but a Greek resolution calling for self-determination was shelved by the Political Committee. The tactics of treating Cyprus as a straight 'colonial' question and of seeking self-determination through the United Nations were suggested by Archbishop Makarios. Throughout the Cyprus dispute Makarios showed a shrewd appreciation of the kind of approach most likely to win broad international support, especially among the growing number of new Afro-Asian countries. He realised that for Greece simply to ask for enosis could be regarded as annexation and so have no international appeal. The desire for annexation was indeed the charge levelled against Greece by the British delegation during the UN debate.

Selwyn Lloyd, minister of state at the Foreign Office, also set out in this debate the British strategic arguments for retaining sovereignty in Cyprus which were later to be repeated many times. Cyprus, he said, was needed so that Britain could fulfil her treaty obligations to the Arab states, NATO, Greece, Turkey and the United Nations. 'Cyprus', he declared, 'is vital to the discharge of those responsibilities . . . there is no acceptable alternative in the circumstances to sovereignty. Full administrative control is necessary because leases expire, treaties have a habit of being whittled away and . . . Greek governments, like other governments, change.'[5] This was the British answer to the Greek argument that Britain did not need sovereignty over Cyprus for strategic purposes. The Greek foreign minister, Stefanopoulos, had said that his country never expected the British to withdraw their forces from Cyprus, but a military base could work only with the support of a co-operative population, and for this self-determination was necessary. The experience of the Anglo-Egyptian Treaty, however, had strengthened the belief of the British government that nothing less than sovereignty would do for their military purposes. But they neglected the other lesson of their forced withdrawal from the Suez Canal Zone: that a military base surrounded by a hostile population is not worth having.

The Conservative government may have underestimated the amount of trouble it could expect in Cyprus from a small and hitherto relatively docile population. But there were other factors involved. At this time, the government saw in the political scene at Westminster and in the Middle East reasons which were political rather than military for trying to hold on in Cyprus. The new agreement with Egypt had aroused bitter opposition from the 'Suez rebels' on the Conservative back-benches. A further concession in Cyprus would, it was thought at Westminster, be interpreted as a sign of weakness, not only by Conservative members of parliament, but also by Britain's remaining allies in the Middle East—especially Iraq, which was being groomed to replace Egypt as the main prop of British influence in the Arab world.

Turkey, too, was becoming of increasing importance in British as well as American plans for the Middle East. The US secretary of state, John Foster Dulles, wanted to switch the emphasis in the strategy for this area away from the British obsession with the Arab states and toward the new concept of the 'Northern Tier'. He wanted an American-backed alliance between Turkey, Iran and Pakistan to close the gap in the ring of containment around Russia. Eden seized the opportunity to combine the American and the British concepts by encouraging the creation of the Baghdad Pact, signed in March 1955. This was an alliance of Britain, Turkey, Iraq, Iran and Pakistan, of which America was a member in all but name. The pact enabled the Iraqi premier, Nuri Said, to terminate the unpopular Anglo-Iraqi defence treaty while yet maintaining the essentials of the alliance under a slightly less old-fashioned title. The British hoped that the new grouping of forces would help to ensure political stability in Iraq by strengthening the country's resistance both to communism and to the appeals of pan-Arab nationalism. Until the Iraqi revolution of 1958 destroyed both Nuri Said and the Baghdad Pact, one of the main considerations governing Britain's refusal to give up the sovereignty of Cyprus was the possible weakening effect this would have on Nuri Said's position.

Turkey played a leading part in the formation of the Baghdad Pact. Whereas in NATO, although an important contributor of troops, Turkey was a junior partner, the Baghdad Pact made her a senior member of what the British regarded as very much their own special alliance. Turkey assumed a greatly increased—indeed, a vastly exaggerated—political and military significance in the eyes of the British government. It saw the pact not so much as a defence against Russia as a means of maintaining friendly governments in the oil countries of the Middle East. With the evacuation of Egypt and the creation of the Baghdad Pact, British policy began to show signs of reverting, after more than seventy years, to the original idea which had inspired the Cyprus Convention: protection of and support for Turkey as the shield for British interests in the Middle East, seen once more as lying chiefly in the Persian Gulf and what is now Iraq. The mid-'fifties saw the abandonment of this idea's supplanter: the policy of control in Egypt, which had earlier been accompanied by conflict with Turkey in Asia. Eden was to write later in respect to Cyprus: 'I regarded our alliance with Turkey as the first consideration in our policy in that part of the world'.[6] In the opening sentence of the chapter on Cyprus in his memoirs, he notes that his only visit to the island was in 1941 for a meeting with the Turkish foreign minister, Sarajoglu. Eden adds, without intentional irony, that the Greek Cypriot crowds then were shouting for Turkey to come into the war on the side of Britain and Greece against Germany and Italy.

Eden's account of his Cyprus policy constantly reveals more concern than the Turks themselves then showed for advancing the Turkish case on Cyprus. He utters not one word of sympathetic understanding for the feelings of the Greek Cypriots or Greece herself. He regarded even the more extreme attitudes adopted by Turkey as natural, reserving his scorn for Greek 'extremism' and for those who thought that the troubles in the island were due to British imperialism. Yet if imperialism consists of one people's ruling another against the latter's will for the sake of the former's strategic or economic interests, then there never was a more clear-cut case of it than Cyprus. Whether such imperialism may sometimes be justified on the grounds of its preventing worse evils than it entails—that is another question. Eden writes:

> The action which the British Government could take was circumscribed by international considerations. First came the strategic value of the island. Our military advisers regarded it as an essential staging point for the maintenance of our position in the Middle East, including the Persian Gulf. There must be security of tenure. It was not then thought enough to lease certain sites on the island from some future administration on whose policies we could not depend.[7]

The desire not to offend Turkey merged imperceptibly into the more positive recognition that Turkish objections to Greek control of Cyprus could be used to preserve the British position in the island. It is scarcely surprising that, so constantly assured by London that Turkey was indispensable, Ankara should have begun to put up the political and economic price of its support.

Turkey's primary interest in Cyprus—apart from simple national pride—was concern for her own security. The future of the Turkish Cypriot community seems to have been of secondary importance. The concern for security evinced in Ankara was based on old suspicions of Greek expansionism and on new fears arising from Greek weakness. These motives were apparently contradictory but the contradictions resolved themselves in the argument that the combination of a weak Greece and a strong great power, brought about either by alliance or conquest, posed a serious threat to Turkey. The Turks recalled that the alliance between Greece and Britain had led to the campaign in Asia Minor after the first world war. They pointed out that the German conquest of Greece in the second world war had brought German forces to Crete and the Aegean Islands. Next time, they argued, it might be Russia, a more formidable enemy, who would make use of Greek territory. Had not the communists still a powerful influence in Greece and Cyprus, despite their defeat in the Greek civil war? Greece already controlled islands covering all Turkey's major Mediterranean outlets except for her southern ports of Mersin and Alexandretta. These ports, vital for the supply of central Anatolia and the eastern frontier, would be vulnerable to air attacks from Cyprus. Greek control of Cyprus therefore threatened Turkey with complete encirclement from the West. It was true that Greece and Turkey were now allies in NATO against Russia—but NATO might not last for ever.

Senior Turkish officials with whom I have discussed this period of history insist that Turkey's interest in Cyprus was not created by Britain nor was it only a result of British stimulation. Britain, they say, stressed the Turkish interest for her own purposes, but this interest already existed independently of Britain. From 1950 onwards the Turkish Foreign Ministry had seen the way the wind was blowing over Cyprus, but the Turkish government made no move because it trusted Britain to stay in control of the island: a situation which was acceptable to Turkey and to the Turkish Cypriots. But when Cyprus was put on the United Nations agenda in 1954, Turkey was obliged to take a more active role. There then began a close Anglo-Turkish co-operation. At first, Turkey supported the British argument that Cyprus was a domestic issue for Britain and so beyond UN jurisdiction. She also argued that enosis would be a breach of the Lausanne Treaty of 1923, in which Turkey had recognised British sovereignty over Cyprus. In the event of a change of the treaty, Turkey had some grounds for claiming that Cyprus should return to her. (It could also be argued that, in recognising British sovereignty over Cyprus in the Lausanne Treaty, Turkey thereby relinquished any legal standing in the future disposal of the island, for Britain was entitled in the exercise of her sovereignty to hand over the island to Greece.) The legalistic argument was developed when the Turkish government realised that it had to find a new attitude for the United Nations, in order not to appear to be defending a colonial power or to be itself indifferent towards Cyprus. It was some time before Turkey hit on the more plausible idea of partition which she was later to adopt as her Cyprus policy. (How she came to do so is part of an historical controversy of which I shall give some details later on.)

The failure of the Greek appeal to the United Nations at the end of 1954 encouraged the trend towards violent action in Cyprus. A general strike and demonstrations by schoolchildren were followed by the worst riots in the island since 1931.

Archbishop Makarios returned to Cyprus from the United Nations on January 10, 1955. The next day he met Grivas in the bishop's palace at Larnaca and told him that Marshal Papagos, a very sick man, was now in full agreement with Grivas' activities. Grivas suggested the name of *Ethniki Organosis Kypriou Agoniston* (EOKA)* for the underground guerrilla organisation. The two men discussed the starting date for the revolution. Makarios wanted it to begin on March 25, the anniversary of Greek independence. Grivas wanted it sooner.[8] But the start of the rising was delayed by the capture off Cyprus of the caique bringing the third shipload of explosives into the island. However, 'by the middle of March', writes Grivas, 'my preparations were complete and after consultation with Makarios I decided on March 31 for the start of the struggle.'[9]

During the early hours of April 1, 1955, a series of bomb explosions wrecked government offices, police stations and military premises throughout the island. The same day EOKA proclaimed its existence in leaflets signed DIGHENIS—the name of a legendary Cypriot hero—later to be revealed as the pseudonym of Colonel Grivas.

Three months later, Sir Anthony Eden invited Greece and Turkey to a conference in London on political and defence questions affecting the Eastern Mediterranean, including Cyprus. No Cypriot representatives were invited. By then the Baghdad Pact had been safely formed, and Britain faced the prospect of a new United Nations debate on Cyprus in the autumn. Greece objected to the absence of Cypriot delegates and the inclusion of Turkish representatives, for this gave Turkey her first official standing in the Cyprus dispute. Archbishop Makarios condemned the conference as an attempt to impair the Greek appeal to the General Assembly. However, Greece accepted along with Turkey the invitation to the conference, because to have refused negotiation would have looked bad at the United Nations.

The conference opened on August 29, 1955. Eden's tactics were to hold back the British proposals until the Greeks and Turks had shown how wide apart their positions were. In this context, the British would appear moderate and reasonable. Eden was later to write: 'We knew how wide the difference of opinion was between the Greeks and Turks, but the world did not. Too many thought our troubles due to old-fashioned British colonialism. By securing a precise definition of those differences we hoped to show the true nature of the problem. The exact terms of our proposals for the future could then be presented.'[10] He had already shown some alarm at Turkish official passivity, and, in the light of this welcomed warnings in the Turkish press that a form of autonomy for Cyprus which opened the doors to enosis would mean

* National Organisation of Cypriot Fighters

that Britain's alliance with Turkey would have no more than paper value. Eden commented: 'It was as well, I wrote on a telegram at the time, that they should speak out, because it was the truth that theTurks would never let the Greeks have Cyprus'.[11]

At the London Conference, the Turks took the cue promptly. Not only did Zorlu, the Turkish foreign minister, claim that, if the British gave up sovereignty over Cyprus, the island should go back to Turkey: he also threatened to repudiate the whole of the Treaty of Lausanne. The Greeks, on their side, pressed for self-determination for Cyprus: which was a way of presenting the demand for enosis in a form more acceptable to international opinion. The possibilities of an accommodation seemed remote. In a curious foreshadowing of his attitude during the Suez intervention in 1956, Eden tried to make Britain appear the arbiter between two intransigently hostile forces, and unswayed by a primary preoccupation with British interests.

The stage was thus set for the British proposals. On September 6, Harold Macmillan, then foreign secretary, put forward his two-part plan. This envisaged a form of constitutional self-government, limited but in some ways more liberal than the previous constitutional schemes. A standing tripartite committee would study the Constitution and watch over the progress of self-government. But the question of the future status of Cyprus should be shelved. The three powers would simply agree that acceptance of self-government would leave their conflicting attitudes to sovereignty unchanged. Macmillan said that when the new Constitution was working in Cyprus, the British government would be ready to call the conference together again and to invite elected Cypriot representatives to take part. But he added, in reply to questions from Zorlu, that he saw no prospect of any change 'in the foreseeable future' in Britain's view that she must keep her sovereignty over Cyprus. 'We do not accept the principle of self-determination as one of universal application.'

This statement, together with the proposal to give Turkey a share in supervising self-government in Cyprus, would of itself have been enough to ensure the rejection of the plan by Greece and the Greek Cypriots. But on the same day that Macmillan presented his plan there came news of the widespread anti-Greek riots in Istanbul and Izmir. These wrecked millions of pounds' worth of Greek property and also the London Conference. The riots followed a bomb outrage at the Turkish consulate in the Greek city of Salonika. The Greeks claim the bomb was planted by a Turk—and, indeed, the Turkish prime minister, Menderes, was later accused in Turkey of having instigated the Istanbul riots. He probably planned a demonstration of Turkish national feeling to influence the London Conference, but it got out of hand and revealed a depth of hatred which genuinely shocked him. The Turkish government apologised to Greece and offered compensation. But the day after the riots the London Conference was suspended. Makarios rejected the British plan for Cyprus and called for a campaign of passive resistance. There were more bomb explosions and attacks on British soldiers in the island.

The breakdown of the London Conference led to the appointment of Field Marshal Sir John Harding, former chief of the imperial general staff, as governor of Cyprus. Harding brought in more British troops to deal with what was rapidly becoming a full-scale national rebellion. A state of emergency was proclaimed, giving the governor the right to detain and deport anyone without trial and to impose the death penalty for possessing firearms and explosives. The leftwing AKEL was banned and 135 of its members arrested.

At the same time, Harding began talks with Makarios on the basis of granting a 'wide measure of self-government' and of keeping the door to self-determination neither fully closed nor fully open but ajar. Makarios at first insisted on British recognition of the right to self-determination before he would co-operate in a 'measure of self-government'. The British reply was to offer, on October 20, 1955, a draft statement of policy which did not exclude the possibility of self-determination. But this draft, though regarded privately by the Greek government as 'constructive', was rejected by the archbishop. Makarios also wanted to exclude the Turkish as well as the Greek governments from talks on the Cyprus Constitution. This the British rejected.

> I considered it capital [wrote Eden] that we should carry the Turks with us in any new move. . . . We had in fact gone to Turkey's limit to find a basis for co-operation with the Greek-speaking Cypriots on a plan for self-government. We could not afford to take Turkish friendship and understanding for granted. . . . The Cyprus dispute could never be settled until the importance of the Turkish position was understood and accepted. This meant that Enosis must be ruled out as a solution.[12]

To meet Greek criticism, the British amended their draft policy statement on self-determination to include a reference to a 'final solution' in accordance with the wishes of the people of Cyprus. But it was still cautiously vague. 'I was always on the watch', Eden recalls, 'to see that we did not get into the position of approving a form of words which would divide us from the Turks.'[13]

In January 1956, after consultations in London, Harding sent Makarios a letter in which he offered a concession in the form of a double negative. The letter said that it was not British policy that the principle of self-determination could never be applicable to Cyprus. The British position was that self-determination 'is not now a practical proposition on account of the present situation in the Eastern Mediterranean'. Harding's statement also repeated the British position at the London Conference, that 'discussion of the future of the island could take place only after self-government had proved itself capable of safeguarding the interests of all sections of the community'. The declaration on self-determination went some way to meet the needs of Makarios. The archbishop was willing to accept a period of self-government with Britain in charge of the island's defence and foreign affairs, but he had to have some concession by the British government about future self-determination in order to keep the support of EOKA and other extremists who were pressing for enosis or nothing.

The negotiations came very near to an agreement. There were three main points left to be settled when the colonial secretary, Lennox-Boyd, flew out to Cyprus to join the talks on February 26, 1956. They were: the control of internal security, which the British wished to keep in the governor's hands for as long as he thought it necessary; the scope of an amnesty for terrorists; and the composition of the elected majority in a Cyprus legislature, which Makarios wanted defined in advance of the drafting of the full Constitution.

But after a single meeting between Makarios and Lennox-Boyd, the British broke off the talks. Twelve days later they deported Makarios and the bishop of Kyrenia to internment in the Seychelles Islands in the middle of the Indian Ocean.

What was the reason for this sudden change of British policy? According to the official explanation in London, the talks confirmed that Makarios, whom the British authorities believed to be secretly in contact with the EOKA terrorists, was not to be trusted. Lennox-Boyd told Eden on his return to London that he thought Makarios did not want to reach an agreement. The British interpreted the archbishop's bargaining technique to mean that every concession they made would immediately be followed by a new demand. But the decisive point, they claimed, was the objection of Makarios to their proposal that the governor should decide when the time was ripe for control of internal security to be handed over to the elected Cypriot government. 'We could not agree', comments Eden, 'that the security of the island should depend on the Archbishop's timing.'[14] A minute from Eden to Lennox-Boyd before the colonial secretary's departure for Cyprus suggests that the prime minister had already decided on a show-down with Makarios, though he was still prepared for an agreement with the archbishop on British terms. 'My own instinct in this business now', he wrote, 'is that we should let the world know what we have offered and see how the medicine works.'[15]

The Greek Cypriots and the government in Athens saw other reasons for what both have since agreed was a tragically missed opportunity of agreement. Archbishop Makarios told me in June 1965:

> When Lennox-Boyd came to Cyprus I got the impression that he or the British government thought Harding had gone further than they wanted, and, although on some points we had already reached agreement, I discovered there was a change of mind on the British side. It is possible that it was connected with outside events, such as Jordan—some people have said so.* Anyway, at the meeting with Lennox-Boyd we didn't agree and went a step backwards. But when I left the meeting I expected another one. I didn't think the British government would send me into exile. Perhaps they thought others would come forward to negotiate. In that case they were wrongly advised and made a mistake.

The Greek government urged Makarios to accept the Harding proposals. But, in the view of men who were then ministers in Athens, Makarios was obliged to ask for better terms because of pressure from the Cypriot extremists. With stronger backing from Athens, Makarios might have been able to over-ride the extremists. But a new prime minister, Karamanlis, had only just come to power. He did not yet feel strong enough to impose his will on the Greek opposition who were staging demonstrations in Athens and accusing him of preparing a betrayal of Cyprus. As a result, Makarios held on too long and the

* On December 1955 nationalist riots in Jordan had stopped British efforts to bring the country into the Baghdad Pact, and in March 1956 the young King Hussein abruptly dismissed Glubb Pasha, the British commander of the Arab Legion.

10—CAPOA

British government changed its mind. If he had been able to clinch the deal with Harding a fortnight earlier, all might have been well.*

There is no doubt that a settlement at that time, which would have given Cyprus some years of self-government and peace before the question of its status was raised again, would have been far better for the Greek Cypriots than what then followed. Although it would have merely postponed a final solution, it would have enabled the Greek and Turkish Cypriots together with Greece and Turkey to have regained some confidence in each other. In a final settlement it might then have been possible to dispense with some of the elaborate and crippling guarantees of Turkish rights which were to make the future Zürich and London agreements so difficult to work. There is also little doubt that the chance was missed partly because of extremist pressures on Eden as well as Makarios. Rightwing Conservative opinion in Britain was looking for a show of force from the prime minister to reassert British prestige in the Middle East. It was outraged by Nasser's campaign against the Baghdad Pact, and the last straw was King Hussein's expulsion of Glubb Pasha. Eden could not send Nasser or Hussein into exile, but he could make an example of Makarios.

* This estimate is based partly on the author's conversations in June 1965 with Theotokis, who was Greek foreign minister at the time, and with his successor, Averoff.

CHAPTER TEN

Suez, Radcliffe and 'Partition'

THE DEPORTATION of Archbishop Makarios marked the beginning of a tougher British policy in the Middle East. This policy culminated in the fiasco of the Anglo-French intervention at Suez in October 1956, more than three months after Nasser had angrily nationalised the Suez Canal Company.

In Cyprus it meant there was no Greek Cypriot leader with whom the British could now negotiate. It also meant an intensified battle between British troops and EOKA which continued through the rest of the year, except for a ten-day truce called by EOKA in August. During October and November 1956, when British troops and planes were using Cyprus as a base for the Suez operations, terrorist actions reached a new peak. In November, there were 416 acts of violence and 693 people were held in detention. The intensive British security measures led to some successes against EOKA, but the continuous arms searches, mass interrogations, curfews and other collective punishments produced the inevitable effect of such repression. The Greek Cypriot population were driven into closer support of EOKA and alienated still further from the British administration. Even more ominous for the future, the year saw the first serious outbreak of communal fighting between Greek and Turkish Cypriots. EOKA's policy was to leave the Turks alone and concentrate on the British. But increasing numbers of Turks were being recruited for the police force and Turkish policemen were among those killed in EOKA attacks. With secret help from Turkey, the Turkish Cypriots had created their own underground organisation, VOLKAN. They had also set up the 'Cyprus is Turkish' party with branches also among the Turkish Cypriots in Turkey. VOLKAN now began to take reprisals when Turks were killed.

The announcement by Lennox-Boyd on December 19, 1956, of new constitutional proposals for Cyprus, drawn up by Lord Radcliffe, an eminent British judge, did nothing to improve the situation. The proposals were rejected by the Greek government even before the Cypriots had seen them, and even, it is said, before the Greek prime minister, Karamanlis, had read them.[1] They were shown to Makarios in the Seychelles but he refused to discuss them while still in detention. They were accepted by the Turks, with reservations.

Lord Radcliffe's terms of reference had included the conditions that Cyprus must remain under British sovereignty; that Britain must have the use of the island as a military base; and that external affairs, defence and internal security were to remain in British hands. He also had to ensure that the special interests of the various communities on the island were protected. Within these limits he produced a Draft Constitution which gave the Greek Cypriot majority more power than they had ever been offered before. There would have been an effective Greek majority in a fully elected Assembly, except that the consent of two thirds of the Turkish members of the Assembly would be needed for any law affecting Turkish communal affairs. There was to be one Turkish minister in the cabinet ex officio. He was to head an office of Turkish Cypriot affairs, with its own budget allocation, which would deal specially with education. Guaranteed Turkish communal rights were to be watched over by two institutions: a Supreme Court and a 'Tribunal of Guarantees'—both of which would have equal numbers of Greek and Turkish members with a neutral chief justice for the former and a neutral chairman for the latter. Both these institutions, with some variations and a change of title, were later incorporated in the Constitution of the Republic of Cyprus.

The rejection of the Radcliffe Constitution by Greece and the Greek Cypriots was ensured by the political climate of the time, especially the detention of Makarios, and above all by the speech in which Lennox-Boyd introduced the proposals to the House of Commons. The Radcliffe proposals had made no mention of future self-determination. The colonial secretary did, but in terms which aroused violent hostility from the Greeks. He declared that self-determination would lead inescapably to 'partition', if, when the time came for a vote to be taken on the island as a whole, the Turks were to decide that they did not wish to follow the Greek majority but to join Turkey. This was the first official public reference to 'partition' though it had been suggested unofficially in Britain before.

Since it was adopted as official Turkish policy and was to play a vital part in subsequent events, some interest attaches to the official origins of the partition idea. The Turks say it was first suggested by the Greek government, but the Greeks deny this. There is some evidence that the public floating of the partition idea was the result of a policy agreed between the British and Turkish governments.

There is no disagreement about the fact that partition was first discussed in official exchanges on Cyprus in a private conversation in Athens in September 1956 between Averoff, the Greek foreign minister, and Iksel, the Turkish ambassador to Greece. Not surprisingly, the Greek and Turkish versions of this tête-à-tête are different.

According to Averoff (in a talk with the author in June 1965), the discussions were a repetition of familiar arguments from each side,'with the Turkish ambassador continually hinting at new solutions at which we must work with imagination'.

> I told him that if what you say means the idea of partition mentioned in the British Parliament, I must tell you that Greece is ready to accept whatever solution the Cypriots accept. We are ready to accept a plebiscite on the questions: first, enosis with Greece; second, enosis with Turkey; third, independence; and fourth, partition. Whatever the Cypriots accept, we shall accept.
>
> The diplomatic meaning was very clear. Iksel began to speak about partition. He said that partition on the thirty-fifth parallel was being studied—which meant practically equal shares. I told him: 'Look, what I have said is already very plain. But if the partition is on a fifty-fifty basis, everyone will think I am completely mad'.
>
> My conclusion was that the purpose of the Turkish ambassador's visit was to find out our attitude to partition. I gave what I thought the best answer I could. I appeared as not rejecting anything but as proposing a plebiscite which could lead only to enosis.
>
> But I must recognise now that my answer left open some possibility of misunderstanding. When I rejected partition on a fifty-fifty basis, it could have been interpreted to mean that I might consider partition on a basis more favourable than half and half.

According to Turkish diplomatic sources, Averoff himself suggested partition as part of 'a Byzantine manoeuvre'. His aim, they thought, was probably both to sound out the Turkish attitude and also, if the Turks agreed to partition, to show Turkey up at the United Nations as a country seeking territorial annexation and aggrandisement, and not self-determination for Cyprus.

It was the British, these sources claimed, who showed Turkey how to use the partition idea without falling into the Greek trap. The following version was given the author by a senior member of the Turkish Foreign

Ministry who has been closely concerned with Cyprus affairs. He said that when Iksel heard Averoff's suggestion of partition, he had reacted coolly, 'as a talented diplomatist should'. He reported the suggestion to Ankara. There was then a discussion in Ankara and contact was made with the British government. Everyone said partition would be the best solution. During the visit to Ankara of Lennox-Boyd in December 1956 to discuss the draft Radcliffe proposals, the British colonial secretary came to an understanding with the Turkish government on 'a very clever formula': if the right of self-determination were to be applied in Cyprus, the Turkish community should have the same right as the Greeks to decide their own future. So the direct proposal of partition could be avoided. 'This was the idea Lennox-Boyd put forward in the House of Commons in December.'

From then on the Turkish government pressed the case for partition with full vigour. But at the United Nations neither partition nor the Greek demand for self-determination won majority support when the Assembly's Political Committee came to debate the Cyprus question in February 1957. Instead the Committee adopted an Indian resolution which merely expressed the hope that negotiations would be resumed. The Greeks interpreted this to mean negotiations between Britain and the Cypriots, and on March 14, 1957, EOKA offered a truce—to facilitate negotiations—'as soon as the archbishop is released'. There were also good military reasons for offering a truce. In his offensive between December 1956 and January 1957, Harding had dealt some telling blows at EOKA. He had rounded up the majority of the mountain guerrilla bands and arrested leading members of the EOKA group in Nicosia.

The British, like the Turks, claimed that the UN resolution meant negotiations between the three governments. They accepted a proposal for conciliation by the NATO secretary-general, Lord Ismay. At the same time, Lennox-Boyd announced that Makarios would be released from the Seychelles. The archbishop would not be allowed to return to Cyprus for the time being, but he would be free to go anywhere else. Grivas and other EOKA terrorists were also offered a safe-conduct out of Cyprus, but the state of emergency was maintained. The safe-conduct offer was refused by EOKA, but Makarios arrived in Athens on April 17, 1957, to a hero's welcome.

CHAPTER ELEVEN

Turkey Takes a Hand

THE RELEASE of Archbishop Makarios was one of the first major decisions of the new British prime minister, Harold Macmillan, who had replaced Sir Anthony Eden at the head of the Conservative government after the Suez war. It was a move away from the tough policy of the past year which had led Britain to disaster in the Middle East. Its first fruit was more trouble for the Conservative Party. Lord Salisbury, lord president of the Council and leader of the House of Lords, resigned from the government on March 29, 1957, in protest. But it also produced a lull of six months in the violence in Cyprus, though during this time no basis could be found for resuming negotiations. The constant British aim was to have tripartite talks which would keep Turkey in and the Greek Cypriots out when the status of the island was being discussed. The Greeks, on the other hand, were trying to keep the Turks out and get the Greek Cypriots in.

Tension began to rise again in the autumn of 1957 as the UN Assembly meeting came round again and Turkey prepared for new elections. The Menderes government was in economic difficulties and under attack at home for its increasingly dictatorial attitude towards the opposition parties and the press. It had begun to disappoint those who had seen Menderes and the Democrat Party as the pioneers of a new Turkish liberalism. After a stormy election campaign, the Democrats, with the help of a new electoral law, won 70 per cent of the seats in the National Assembly while receiving only 48 per cent of the total vote. The Menderes government retained power but its standing in the country was weakened and more sensitive to foreign troubles. It noted with angry disapproval the replacement in Cyprus of Sir John Harding, the soldier, by Sir Hugh Foot, colonial civil servant with a liberal reputation. Ankara's apprehension that Britain might no longer be counted on to hold Cyprus was increased by the resolution of the Labour Party Conference which called for self-determination for the island after an interim period of self-government.

There is some evidence that a settlement based on independence for Cyprus was even then being discussed privately by the governments concerned. In his memoirs, Grivas refers to a letter written to him on July 25, 1957, by the Greek consul-general in Cyprus, Vlachos, suggesting that he should persuade Makarios to accept independence for Cyprus on the understanding that enosis would not be finally excluded. A month later, Averoff wrote to Grivas: 'Most of the allies now believe that a solution must be found on the basis of an independent Cyprus, without a guarantee of independence for all time. The British seem agreeable on the understanding that they keep their air bases in the island and that Turkey consents.'[1] This reference suggests that the British government may by then have already taken the important decision that it no longer needed complete sovereignty over Cyprus for its strategic purposes.

The Turks felt that it was time for them to put on the pressure. The Ankara government began to campaign more intensively for partition and the Turkish Cypriots adopted a more aggressive attitude. Throughout the following year, until the beginning of the Greco-Turkish talks at the end of 1958 which led to the Zürich and London agreements, it was Turkey who dictated the course of diplomacy over Cyprus while the British and the Greek Cypriots continued to claw at each other in the island. The purpose of the Turks was to block any deal between Britain and the Greek Cypriots which would open the door to enosis. For this purpose they had two weapons. The first was diplomatic pressure on Britain. The other was violent action in Cyprus to show that the Turkish Cypriots could not be ignored and to prove that coexistence in the island between Greeks and Turks was impossible without partition. Fighting between Greek and Turkish Cypriots resulted from demonstrations which accompanied the opening of the United Nations debate on Cyprus in December 1957. The debate led to a resolution which was a partial political victory for the Greeks. It expressed the hope for further negotiations 'with a view to having the right of self-determination applied in the case of the people of Cyprus'. But it was passed without the two thirds majority needed to give it force as a recommendation.

Sir Hugh Foot, the new governor, arrived in Cyprus on December 3, 1957, and began to prepare the ground for renewed negotiation. In an attempt to improve the atmosphere he released a hundred detainees and toured the island on horseback and on foot, talking to people everywhere he went and listening to their views. At the end of the year he went back to London to talk to Harold Macmillan. A new British plan was being hatched. It was based on the idea of self-government for an interim period of five or seven years before any final decision about the island was taken. It included three other points suggested by Foot as essential: an end to the state of emergency and the return of Makarios to the island; negotiations in the island with the leaders of the two communities to work out a system of self-government; and an assurance that at the end of the interim period no final decision would be taken which was not accepted by both Greeks and Turks.[2] But first the new ideas had to be tried out on the Turkish and Greek governments.

On January 26, 1958, Foot accompanied the foreign secretary, Selwyn Lloyd, to Ankara where a Baghdad Pact conference was being held. During the four days of the conference, they had talks with Menderes and Zorlu. They found the Turkish ministers in an uncompromising mood and insistent on nothing less than partition. In his book, *A Start in Freedom*, Sir Hugh describes their treatment by the ruthless Zorlu—'the rudest man I ever met. Once in Ankara when we had sat up most of the night drafting a statement of the British position and when we had gone back to the final conference with our Foreign Minister, Selwyn Lloyd, and our Ambassador in Turkey, Sir James Bowker, Zorlu flicked through the pages of the document and threw it contemptuously on one side without even reading it.' Foot pays tribute to Zorlu's patriotism and his courage in bringing about the Zürich and London settlements. But he adds: 'We in Cyprus had no reason to love Zorlu. He had, I have no doubt, known of and perhaps himself given the order for the Turkish riots and the attempt to burn Nicosia.'[3] While the Ankara talks were in progress, Turkish Cypriots had staged demonstrations and riots in favour of partition.

On February 11, 1958, Foot and Selwyn Lloyd went to Athens for discussions with the Greek government, and Foot had a private talk with Makarios. But the initiative planned by Foot had been wrecked by Turkish opposition. The British government had to think again and it was not until June that a new British plan was announced to the House of Commons by the prime minister.

In the meantime, communal tension was increasing in Cyprus and EOKA had begun an intensive campaign of sabotage. During the first ten days of April, there were more than fifty bomb explosions. The governor sent a secret message to Grivas appealing to him to stop the campaign and offering to meet him personally, unarmed and alone.

Grivas did not take up the offer of a meeting but he called off the sabotage campaign.

The Macmillan plan, announced on June 19, was based on an idea put forward by Foot that, in default of negotiations with Greece and Turkey or the Cypriots, the British should work out a constitution themselves and begin to apply it, with or without the agreement of the other parties.[4] It embodied the main ideas of the first Foot plan and proposed a 'partnership' between the Greek and Turkish communities in the island and between the British, Greek and Turkish governments. For seven years the international status of Cyprus would be unchanged. Each community would run its own communal affairs through its own separate House of Representatives. The administration of the island as a whole would be directed by a Council composed of the governor, representatives of the Greek and Turkish governments, and six Cypriot ministers, four elected from the Greek House of Representatives and two from the Turkish. The governor, in consultation with the representatives of the Greek and Turkish governments, would have reserved power to deal with external affairs, defence and internal security. The representatives of the Greek and Turkish governments would be able to require any legislation they considered discriminatory to be submitted to an impartial tribunal. The British government said it would welcome any arrangement which would give Cypriots Greek or Turkish nationality while enabling them to retain British nationality.

The plan was quickly rejected by the Greek and Turkish governments and by Makarios. The archbishop described the idea of 'partnership' as the imposition of a 'triple condominium'. The Labour opposition in Britain criticised the plan as more likely to divide the Cypriot communities than bring them together. In Cyprus, the reaction was an increase in violence. Twelve days before the Macmillan plan was announced, Turkish Cypriots had started fires in Nicosia and begun two months of bitter Greek–Turkish strife in which fifty-six Greeks and fifty-three Turks were killed. More British troops and police were sent to Cyprus, bringing the total there to twenty thousand men.

In August, Macmillan visited Athens, Ankara and Cyprus and announced some modifications to his plan. The most important was that the representatives of the Greek and Turkish governments would not be members of the governing council of the island but would have direct access to the governor. The revised plan was still unacceptable to Archbishop Makarios and to Greece. But a few weeks later the Turkish government announced that it would co-operate with the British in implementing the plan. On October 1, 1958, the date fixed by Britain, Turkey appointed a representative for this purpose in the island.

The Macmillan–Foot plan had several attractions for the Turks which initially also made it appear the worst of all the British plans from the Greek Cypriot point of view. It offered Turkey a voice as of right not only in international negotiations about Cyprus but also in the actual government of the island. The plan not only postponed a decision on self-determination for seven years but virtually ensured for Turkey a veto on enosis at the end of that time. It provided no central legislature which could be controlled by a Greek majority. On the contrary, its provision of separate communal assemblies and the later addition of separate municipalities provided useful stepping-stones to partition should it need to be pursued in the future. Understandably, the plan increased Greek suspicions that the British and the Turks were working together against them. On August 21, 1958, EOKA called for a total boycott of the British administration and of Commonwealth goods, as part of resistance to 'Anglo-Turkish collusion'. A truce, which had lasted from the beginning of August in response to appeals from the Greek and Turkish prime ministers, came to an end. It was followed by months of violence which created not only a threat of civil war between the Greek and Turkish Cypriots but also a deepening gulf of bitterness between the Greek Cypriots and the British. The boycott and noncoöperation with the British were ruthlessly enforced by EOKA. In reprisal for the alleged ill-treatment of Greek suspects by British troops, EOKA began to attack British civilians as well as soldiers. The murder in Famagusta of Mrs Cutliffe, the wife of a British soldier (for which EOKA denied responsibility), led to reprisals by British troops. Scores of Greek Cypriot men in the town were beaten while being rounded up for questioning. One man was killed and many others injured. Throughout the island at that time at least two thousand Cypriots were under detention and many thousands more subject to total house curfew, forbidden to leave their houses by night or day.

Meanwhile, the British government went on with its programme of implementing the Macmillan plan. It authorised the setting up of separate Greek and Turkish Cypriot municipal councils—thereby increasing Greek fears of a de facto partition. These fears also began to prompt a reconsideration of Greek Cypriot policy. On September 7, 1958, Makarios told the Greek government privately that he was now ready to accept independence for Cyprus under United Nations auspices after a period of self-government. He repeated this proposal in a published interview with Barbara Castle, then chairman of the British Labour Party. In a letter to Grivas on September 28, Makarios gave as his reasons for this new line the state of British public opinion, especially the cooling attitude of the Labour Party, and the American support for British policy in Cyprus. He said that the only hope for success at the United Nations lay in asking for independence. Otherwise the Greek Cypriots might be faced with a fait accompli. The imposition of the Macmillan plan would either lead to partition or would give the Turks rights which it would be impossible later to remove. The answer of Grivas was that Makarios should stick to the original demand for self-determination.[5]

Makarios' new proposal for an independent Cyprus was rejected by the British Conservative government, which refused to commit itself to any final solution, but was supported by the Labour opposition. By the end of November, when the Cyprus question again came before the General Assembly's Political Committee, the outlook in the island was blacker than ever before.

Nevertheless, by Christmas Eve, only a month later, terrorism in Cyprus had ceased. Within another seven weeks, a political settlement establishing an independent Cyprus Republic had been signed in London by Britain, Greece, Turkey and the Cypriots. How did this come about?

CHAPTER TWELVE

How the Peace was Made

THE VERY DARKNESS of the prospect in Cyprus was one of the pressures working for a quick settlement. The outlook was black not only in the island but internationally. Khrushchev, flushed with the success of Russia's first sputnik, was putting pressure on the Western powers over Berlin. There was a call from Washington for a closing of the ranks in NATO to meet the new Soviet threat. Cyprus was drifting into a civil war which threatened to involve Britain, Greece and Turkey—all NATO members—in deepening conflict. All of the parties concerned found they had reasons for considering a compromise.

The British government had reviewed its strategic requirements in Cyprus after a visit to the island by the minister of Defence, Duncan Sandys, in 1957. It had come to the conclusion, on Sandys' advice, that it no longer needed the whole island. A base under its sovereign control would be enough. Moreover, it was concerned at the cost in military man-power of dealing with the EOKA rebellion; 28,000 troops were engaged in chasing two or three hundred terrorists. It was a game that could go on indefinitely. Meanwhile the whole population of the island was being alienated. The chiefs of staff at first insisted that they must have the whole of Cyprus as a base. But they changed their minds when they realised that, in this case, the cabinet would not agree to have any base at all in Cyprus, because the effort of keeping control of the whole island was turning it into a military liability instead of an asset.

This decision was a turning point in British policy. It paved the way for the eventual transfer of British sovereignty to an independent republic embracing the whole of Cyprus except for two small 'sovereign areas' retained by Britain as military bases. But there were still two political reasons for trying to hold on to British sovereignty. The first was the feeling that Britain was bound to try to hold the ring in Cyprus between Greeks and Turks to prevent a civil war which might spread to war between Greece and Turkey. The second was the desire to reassure the Nuri Said regime in Iraq that Britain was still fully committed to its support. A relinquishment of British sovereignty in Cyprus might, it was thought, sap this confidence. But this latter reason was suddenly eliminated when, in July 1958, Nuri Said and the Iraqi monarchy were overthrown by the revolution led by General Kassim and Iraq began to withdraw from the Baghdad Pact into a position of neutrality. That left only Britain's responsibility for keeping the peace between Greeks and Turks. In other words, if the Greeks and Turks could agree among themselves, there was no direct British interest which required a continuation of British sovereignty over the whole of Cyprus. Indeed, if the Greeks and Turks did not agree and the Greeks went on fighting the British, there was a strong probability that public opinion in Britain might before long demand the abandonment of a thankless task.

The fear that Britain might lose patience and either forcibly partition Cyprus or withdraw in such a way that a de facto partition took place was a powerful influence on the Greek government and Archbishop Makarios. Athens, according to Averoff, believed that the British were seriously thinking of partition along the thirty-fifth parallel, if the Macmillan plan did not work. The intercommunal killings in Cyprus strengthened the dangers of partition. Greek retaliation against Turkish attacks would be bound to prove to the world that the two communities in the island could not live together, and so would justify partition. The communal struggle also endangered the Greek community in Istanbul. Although it was improbable that the strongly anti-communist Karamanlis government in Greece would be prepared to risk war with Turkey over Cyprus at a time of severe East–West tension, if the struggle in the island were prolonged it might mean serious conflict between Greece and Turkey.

In addition, the Cyprus question was approaching a dead-end at the United Nations. This was realised by the Greek Cypriot leadership as well as by Greece. The Greek Cypriots also knew that the Greek government would not go on supporting them indefinitely if it meant worsening relations with Turkey. And, although the EOKA campaign could have been kept up for a long time, the economic repercussions of the boycott and the British counter-measures—curfews, mass detentions, dismissals of workers from military establishments—were beginning to be felt by the Greek Cypriot population.*

Turkey did not need such powerful arguments for compromise,

* This analysis is based on talks in June 1965 with Archbishop Makarios and Glafkos Clerides, president of the Cyprus House of Representatives.

because, in fact, any settlement that gave her more than an assurance against enosis and protection of the Turkish community was pure gain. Hitherto these two assurances had been provided by the British presence, and it may be that Turkey also was influenced by the belief that the British, either under the Conservatives or under a new Labour government, might withdraw and give Cyprus independence. If, in addition to barring enosis, Turkey could get recognition of the Turkish Cypriots as a separate community and acceptance of Turkish troops in Cyprus, she would be well satisfied. Ankara was no more anxious than Athens to become involved in a war that would probably have meant the exclusion of both Greece and Turkey from NATO and the loss of American military and economic aid. Turkey was in serious financial difficulties through overspending on imports for her development programme. She counted on the United States and her European creditors to keep her afloat.

The first serious peace move came on December 5, 1958, when, after the defeat of the Greek resolutions on Cyprus in the General Assembly, the British ambassador to the United Nations, Sir Pierson Dixon, arranged a meeting between the Greek and Turkish foreign ministers, Averoff and Zorlu. The two ministers agreed to try to find a solution for Cyprus by direct negotiations between Greece and Turkey.[1] After the Greek government had consulted Makarios, there was a further discussion between Averoff and Zorlu during the NATO meeting in Paris on December 18, 1958, in which it was agreed to continue talks on Cyprus through diplomatic channels. Six days later, EOKA announced a truce in Cyprus and stopped its terrorist activities. While the British army continued with its operations to clean up terrorist hide-outs in the mountains, the British government cleared the way for the Greco-Turkish talks by declaring that it was prepared to give up sovereignty over Cyprus, provided it could keep bases under British sovereignty and have full use of the facilities needed to operate them.

The Greco-Turkish talks continued throughout January 1959, and on February 5, the two prime ministers, Menderes and Karamanlis, together with Zorlu and Averoff, met for a conference in Zürich. In six days they drew up the outline of a settlement which the two foreign ministers then took to London to discuss with the British government. No Cypriot representatives were present at the Zürich talks, though the Greek government had consulted Makarios beforehand, and the Turkish government had called on the advice of Raouf Denktash, the ablest of the Turkish Cypriot leaders.* The archbishop and Dr Küchük, the political head of the Turkish Cypriot community, were brought into the discussions when the British, Greek and Turkish prime ministers and foreign ministers met in conference in London to complete the final agreement. But though the two Cypriot leaders were invited to confer, the purpose of the London meeting was, in fact, for the three governments, who had agreed beforehand on the plan to be implemented, to present the Cypriots with a fait accompli which they would be forced to accept whether they liked it or not. This was achieved in forty-eight hours. The conference opened at Lancaster House on February 17, 1959, and on February 19 the London agreements were initialled.

Menderes signed the agreement at his bedside in the London Clinic where he was recovering from an air disaster. He amazingly survived when the aircraft carrying part of the Turkish delegation to the London conference crashed near Gatwick airport. This escape was later to be exploited politically by his followers in Turkey as evidence of special protection by Divine Providence.

The settlement formed by the Zürich and London agreements had two main parts: a draft constitution for Cyprus, and three treaties. The treaties established the international status of the island and of the British sovereign bases, guaranteed this status and the constitution, and set out the terms of a military alliance between Cyprus, Greece and Turkey. These terms included the presence of Greek and Turkish troops in Cyprus. A Treaty of Establishment between Cyprus and Britain laid down that the island should become an independent sovereign republic, except for two areas round the British air base at Akrotiri and the army base at Dhekelia on the south coast. These were to remain under British sovereignty. Britain would also have the right to use sites and facilities elsewhere in the island for military purposes. A Treaty of Guarantee between Cyprus, Britain, Greece and Turkey provided that Cyprus should maintain its independence and respect for its constitution. It forbade either enosis or partition or any activity designed to bring them about. Greece, Turkey and Britain guaranteed the independence of the island as thus defined and 'the state of affairs established by the Basic Articles of its constitution'.

There followed a clause which Turkey was later to invoke to claim the right of military intervention in Cyprus. It said: 'In the event

* Denktash was chief political adviser to Dr Küchük. A brilliant lawyer, educated in England, he was also the main Turkish Cypriot link with the government in Ankara, where he now lives.

of a breach of the provisions of the present Treaty, Greece, Turkey and the United Kingdom undertake to consult together with respect to the representations or measures necessary to ensure observance of these provisions. In so far as common or concerted action may not prove possible, each of the three guaranteeing Powers reserves the right to take action with the sole aim of re-establishing the state of affairs created by the present Treaty.'

A Treaty of Alliance between Cyprus, Greece and Turkey established a tripartite headquarters in Cyprus and the presence in the island of 950 Greek and 650 Turkish troops. These forces would help to train the Cyprus army, but their unspoken purpose was to act as an additional guarantee of the status of the island and of the agreed relations between the Greek and Turkish Cypriot communities. These relations were defined in the elaborate draft Constitution.

Since the Constitution was to prove the Achilles heel of the settlement, it may be useful to set out here the gist of its most important clauses, although the final version was not completed and signed until April 1960, after a year's work by a joint constitutional commission.

The Constitution laid down that Cyprus was to be an independent republic with a presidential system of government. Greek and Turkish were to be its official languages. The executive power, over all except communal affairs, was vested in a Greek president and a Turkish vice-president, both elected by their respective communities, and assisted by a council of ministers. Seven of the ministers would be Greek and three Turkish, and one of the key portfolios of foreign affairs, defence and finance must go to a Turk. The council or cabinet would take decisions by majority vote, but the president and vice-president would have 'separately or jointly' the right of veto over foreign affairs, defence and security. They could also send back the budget to the House of Representatives, the central legislature.

The House of Representatives was to have fifty members elected on separate communal rolls in the proportion of 70 per cent Greek to 30 per cent Turkish members. The president of the House would be a Greek and the vice-president a Turk. The House was to vote by simple majority, except in the case of modifications to the electoral law or any laws relating to municipalities or imposing taxes or duties. In this case, separate majorities were required from both the Greek and Turkish members.

In addition to this joint parliament, there were also to be separate Greek and Turkish elected 'Communal Chambers' to deal with such matters as religious affairs, education and culture, personal status (e.g. marriage and divorce) and communal activities, including the control of co-operatives and credit societies (an important feature of Cypriot rural life). The House of Representatives was to allocate not less than £2 million in the annual budget to the Communal Chambers; £1,600,000 to the Greeks and £400,000 to the Turks, in proportion to population. The Chambers were also given the right to levy taxes of their own to supplement this grant in order to finance their communal responsibilities. Furthermore, the five main towns of the island—Nicosia, Limassol, Famagusta, Larnaca and Paphos—were to have separate Greek and Turkish municipalities with their own elected councils. In each town there was to be a co-ordinating body of two Greeks, two Turks and a chairman, to be agreed upon, to operate joint municipal services. But there was also a provision that within four years the president and vice-president should examine whether or not this system of separate municipalities should continue.

The civil service was to be shared between Greeks and Turks in the 70–30 ratio in all grades. The same ratio was to apply to the police and gendarmerie, fixed at a strength of two thousand. But the army, also limited to two thousand, was to be recruited on the basis of 60 per cent Greek and 40 per cent Turk. One of the heads of the army, the police or the gendarmerie must be a Turk.

One other unusual feature of the Constitution was the provision that both the Supreme Constitutional Court and the High Court should be presided over by a neutral judge who was not to be a Cypriot, or from Greece, Turkey or Britain. The Constitutional Court, composed of one Greek and one Turkish judge with a neutral president, would hear appeals concerning contested legislations or acts of government alleged to be unconstitutional. The High Court, a court of appeal, was composed of two Greek judges, one Turkish judge and a neutral president casting two votes.

Some important aspects of the Zürich and London agreements flowed naturally from the political and military situation at the time and from earlier developments and proposals. The status of independence, barring enosis and partition, was a natural compromise between the Greek and Turkish maximum claims. But the compromise was made possible only by Britain's decision that she no longer needed sovereignty over the whole island for military purposes. The idea behind the Constitutional Court had appeared in the Radcliffe Constitution in 1956. The scheme of Communal Chambers and separate municipalities was in the Macmillan plan which had also introduced the idea, though in a different form, of joint guarantees from Britain, Greece and Turkey. The main new features added by the Zürich and London agreements were the additional guarantees for both Turkey's security and the rights of the Turkish Cypriot community: the presence of Turkish troops in the island; the right of intervention; the Turkish vice-president's veto powers; the separate majority voting—amounting to another Turkish veto in the House of Representatives; and the guaranteed proportion of posts for Turks in the civil service, army and police.

These features of the agreements were the subject of dispute at the time between the Greek Cypriot leaders and the Greek government. They have since led to much controversy in Athens and Nicosia about the agreements and the way they were made. The following account is based in part on talks the author had in June 1965 in Nicosia, Ankara and Athens with Archbishop Makarios, Glafkos Clerides (now Greek president of the Cyprus House of Representatives), Averoff, Greek foreign minister at the time, and senior officials of the Turkish foreign ministry.

In the talks leading up to the Zürich conference, the Greek government consulted Archbishop Makarios—who was then in Athens—and two other leading Cypriot churchmen: the bishop of Kition and the abbot of Kykko Monastery. Averoff believed when he set off for Zürich that he had the agreement of the Greek Cypriot leaders for the basic points of the settlement, except for the clause requiring separate majorities in the House of Representatives for tax laws. This clause had not been discussed with Makarios. It was accepted by the Greek government in Zürich in response to Turkish insistence that all other guarantees would be worthless if new tax laws could be passed which might ruin the Turkish community. (A government of Turkey had itself used precisely this method of crippling the minorities in Turkey by the wartime capital levy.) The Turkish Cypriots later used this separate majority clause for the quite different purpose of blocking a non-discriminatory tax law as part of the wider struggle over the Constitution.

The three other chief points on which the Greek Cypriots claim to have disagreed with the Greek government were: the presence of Turkish troops in Cyprus; the 70–30 ratio in the civil service; and the creation of separate municipalities. According to Averoff, the division of the civil service was discussed with Makarios (who claims he did not accept it in advance). Averoff admits there may have been a difference of interpretation. There also appears to have been misunderstanding about the Turkish troops. Averoff claims that he told Makarios that Turkey had asked for a base on Cyprus and that Greece had refused. Makarios had endorsed the refusal. The archbishop's version is as follows: 'The Greek government told me, "We understand Turkey would like to have a military base on Cyprus". I said, "No, that cannot be accepted". So they said, "What if there should be an alliance?". I said, "Yes", thinking they meant not Greek and Turkish contingents but only a few officers at a headquarters—like the NATO base at Smyrna.'

The provision of sepaıate municipalities, which was later to arouse much criticism among the Greeks in Cyprus, was, Averoff claims, insisted on by the Greek Cypriot leaders themselves against his wishes. He had considered it the only really separatist measure in the agreements, in the sense that it gave the Turks administrative control of territory rather than functions. Nevertheless, the Greek Cypriots had imposed it on him. They argued that the Turkish quarters of the towns in Cyprus were in bad condition with narrow streets and poor facilities. The municipal income, they claimed, came chiefly from Greek sources. Under unified municipalities most of this money would be spent in the Turkish quarters. Yet even so the Turkish quarters would never be satisfied and there would always be friction. So it was better to have separate responsibilities.

When the Greek prime minister, Karamanlis, came back from the Zürich conference in February 1959, he saw Makarios for about two and a half hours and showed him the agreements which had been reached. They included all the main points of the later London agreements, except for the articles concerned with British military bases. The archbishop later told the press that he had congratulated and thanked the prime minister. But in private he had expressed his anxiety. He had not expected agreement to be reached in Zürich. When it came he found it difficult either to accept or reject because he did not know what the results of rejection would be. But he thought he would be able to get some changes made in the further talks to be held in London. To help him and to enable him to get an eventual agreement accepted in Cyprus, he summoned to join him in London thirty-eight leading Greek Cypriots representing all sections of the Greek community in the island. When the draft agreements were shown to them by Makarios, almost no one suggested outright rejection but they all criticised different points.

At the London conference Makarios said at first that he would accept the Zürich agreements as a *basis* for a Cyprus solution, but that he could not accept the detailed settlement without further discussion. He would accept the three principles of the independence of Cyprus, the provision of British military bases and that the Turks as a community should have certain rights. But he objected to Turkish rights being a basic principle to be embodied in the drafting of the constitution. The British and the Turks insisted that the agreement must be accepted in its entirety. In private, the Greek government was equally insistent. In often heated discussions which went on through the night, Karamanlis and Averoff threatened Makarios that Greece would have to abandon Cyprus unless the agreements were accepted. On the third day, after Makarios had tried in vain to get his formula adopted, he had to give in. In the final stages, Karamanlis is reported to have asked Queen Frederika of Greece to use her personal influence and to telephone from Athens to persuade the archbishop to agree. The course of the London negotiations is thus described by the archbishop:

> In London, I tried to get some changes made but there was not enough time to study the agreement. But at the very first reading I singled out thirteen points which were the thirteen points which I raised again in 1963. I tried hard and failed.
>
> Selwyn Lloyd said at the last meeting: 'This is an agreement, a text on which we three governments agree. You expressed your views, and expressed disagreement on certain points. We have heard your views and we don't agree with you. You have to take it or leave it. Don't try for any change.' Zorlu said: 'We don't agree with your views. We talked for a week and came to an agreement and we can't go back on it.' I said: 'I was under the impression that I had come to discuss a solution of the Cyprus question, and not to sign what you three governments had already agreed upon. You put me in a difficult situation when you say, Take it or leave it.' The answer was: 'We don't agree.'
>
> When I realised that it was impossible for me to change their minds, I asked for further time to think it over. 'The answer has to be yes or no', said Lennox-Boyd. I said: 'It can't be decided yes or no.' Lennox-Boyd said he had been invited to the Far East and that it was only one day before Mr Macmillan's trip to Moscow. 'You must answer by this afternoon.' So I said: 'If you want my answer now, my answer is, No'.
>
> The meeting was adjourned and it was agreed that I should have to

> give an answer by 10.30 the next morning. They said that if the answer were Yes, would I please contact the Foreign Office and the last meeting would be held at prime ministers' level in the afternoon to sign an agreement. If the answer is No, then, they said, 'we shall issue a communiqué saying that the conference has failed'. There was no choice for me. They told me: 'If you refuse, you will be responsible for all the repercussions in Cyprus. The world has put its hopes on the success of the conference, and you will be responsible for its failure.'
>
> I was sure that, if I did not sign the agreement, there might be partition. Cyprus would be divided as a colony and we should not be able to raise the question again. The less bad thing was to sign. The next morning I telephoned the Foreign Office.

The archbishop put the best face he could on his defeat, if defeat it was. On his return to Cyprus on March 1, 1959, he was received by huge and enthusiastic crowds and spoke of victory.

Part of the agreements was that Colonel Grivas, the EOKA leader, should be given a safe-conduct to leave the island. He and some of his EOKA followers did not conceal their disapproval of the Zürich and London agreements which ruled out enosis. But Grivas was persuaded to refrain from publicly attacking the settlement for the time being. He was given a national welcome in Greece, decorated and promoted to general with full pay for life. But, before long, Grivas' resentment burst out into attacks on Makarios and the Greek government for having accepted the settlement.

In Cyprus, the detainees were released, the British garrison was reduced and the island gradually began to return to normal. A year was spent in preparing the hand-over of power to the new Cyprus Republic, reorganising government departments, preparing for elections and completing the draft of the new Constitution. The plan was to sign the final agreements and declare the republic by February 19, 1960. A conference of the British, Greek and Turkish governments together with Makarios and Küchük—who had been elected president and vice-president of Cyprus respectively—was called in London for January 1960. It gave the archbishop an opportunity for at least partial revenge for having been hustled into agreement a year before.

His hard bargaining with the British over the size of their sovereign bases and the amount of their financial aid to Cyprus was this time supported by the Turks, and led to a postponement of the conference, initially for one month. In the event, the postponement lasted more than six months. Julian Amery, then the under-secretary for the Colonies, came out to Cyprus to continue the negotiations. He came for a week but stayed for five months. At one period there was a deadlock lasting forty-five days in which there was no meeting between Amery and Makarios. On July 1, 1960, the last day by which agreement had to be reached in order to get the Cyprus Independence Bill through the British Parliament before the summer recess, Makarios signed. He had whittled down the British base areas to just under a hundred square miles. Apparently only double and not treble figures were politically acceptable. He had also pushed up the British financial aid to £12 million over five years, together with £1,500,000 for the Turkish community, and had extracted a promise of a review of future aid requirements at the end of that period. This time the archbishop held most of the cards and got what he wanted.

CHAPTER THIRTEEN

The Cyprus Republic and its Breakdown

CYPRUS BECAME an independent republic on August 16, 1960. The next day the last British governor, Sir Hugh Foot, left the island. On September 21, 1960 the new republic was admitted to the United Nations and six months later to the Commonwealth. The treaties sealing the Cyprus settlement were signed by Britain, Greece and Turkey with profound relief. At last, it seemed, they were rid of a problem which had plagued them all for ten years past and now they could hope to rebuild their former friendly relations.

Menderes and Zorlu, the Turkish architects of the Cyprus settlement, were not there to add their signatures. Their government had been overthrown on May 27, 1960 by a military coup d'état. Turkey was now being ruled by a 'National Unity Committee' of thirty-eight army officers. The president of this committee, General Gürsel, was also head of state and prime minister. Menderes, Zorlu and Çelal Bayar, the former president, together with the former chief of the general staff and more than 400 deputies and members of the Democrat Party were being held in prison on the island of Yassi Aida, near Istanbul, awaiting trial on charges of corruption and violation of the Constitution. In September 1961, 15 of those tried were sentenced to death, 31 to life imprisonment and 418 to lesser prison terms. Menderes, Zorlu and the former finance minister, Hasan Polatkan, were hanged.

The Menderes government had lost popularity with the educated classes in Turkey because of its failure to deal with severe inflation, its exploitation of religion in politics, and its attempts to muzzle the press and the opposition parties. Additionally, resentment had arisen in the army as a result of its being used against the Republican People's Party of ex-president Inönü, for whom it had personal sympathy. The new military regime claimed that its aim was to restore freedom and democratic government in Turkey. Its leaders said they were prepared to hand over power to whichever party was elected under a new Constitution and electoral law. General elections were postponed until May 27, 1961, and a group of university professors were appointed to draft a

Constitution for consideration by a Constituent Assembly. The Democrat Party, which had ruled Turkey for ten years, was abolished. In elections held on October 15, 1961, under the new Constitution, the place of the Democrat Party was taken by the new Justice Party, led by a retired general, Ragib Gumuşpala. The Justice Party appealed discreetly to former supporters of Menderes, especially among the peasants and small traders. It won 158 out of 450 seats in the National Assembly. Inönü's Republican People's Party won 173 seats. Neither party was strong enough to form a government alone. When General Gürsel was elected president on October 26, he appointed Inönü prime minister. A coalition government of the RPP and the Justice Party was formed and the army began to withdraw into the background.

The unsettled state of Turkish politics, together with political changes in Greece, was to have some influence on developments in Cyprus especially when disputes over the Zürich constitution suddenly burst into violence at the end of 1963. By then two of the governments which signed the Cyprus treaties had been overthrown, and the breakdown of the agreements found both Greece and Turkey with unstable minority governments in the throes of political crisis.

But in 1960, the misgivings of the Greek Cypriots about the workability of the Constitution were temporarily drowned in the excitement of setting up an independent state and of ruling themselves for the first time in their history.

The new state was small, but it was not the smallest in the world. Nor is it necessarily too small to be viable. It is about the same size as the Lebanon and its population of 577,000 is four times that of Iceland, both of which manage to make a living in unpromising conditions. Nevertheless the island is very poor by European standards, though its per capita income of £139 a year in 1960 was still the highest in the Eastern Mediterranean, except for Israel.* However, the income of farmers, who form half the population, amounts per capita to only about £70 a year, or half the overall figure.[1]

Farm holdings are mostly small, and often consist of fragmented, widely separated plots. Farmers live mostly in small villages and sometimes also go to work in the towns. There is no class of large private landlords, but the Orthodox Church is the biggest landowner in the island. The level of Church rents and the use by the Church of its control of land to keep a grip on its congregations are potential sources of

* Cf. £130 for Greece and £70 for Turkey.

political friction. Makarios set up a public committee to control the lands of the archbishopric and asked other bishops and abbots to do the same with their lands, but they refused. An encouraging feature is that the Cypriot farmers, both Greek and Turkish (38 per cent of the island's land is in Turkish ownership), have a well-developed system of producers' co-operatives for credit and marketing purposes. At the end of 1961 there were 826 Greek and 293 Turkish co-operative societies with a total membership of 370,000. Agricultural products accounted in 1962 for 23 per cent of the gross national product and 37 per cent of exports. The most lucrative farm exports were carobs, cereals, citrus, potatoes and wine products.

The island's most valuable exports are minerals, especially cupreous ores. Minerals accounted for 51 per cent of the island's total exports of £17·8 million in 1961. The mining industry also provides a large part of the government revenue through taxes and royalties. The mines are in a predominantly Greek area which would undoubtedly remain Greek in any scheme of political partition, a fact which may have some political significance. Cyprus has no heavy industry but has an increasing number of light processing and consumer industries supplying local needs, operating mostly in small factories.

Two other important sources of revenue are tourism and British military expenditure. One of the ironies of the post-war history of Cyprus is that its worst years of political turmoil and tragedy were also its most prosperous period. Britain never spent more on the island than when she was trying to suppress the EOKA rebellion. The more troops she brought in and the more she expanded her bases the more the Cypriot balance of payments thrived. The gross national product also rose from £39·5 million in 1950 to £98·4 million in 1962 (in real terms corrected for price changes, from £39·5 million to £61·4 million). British military expenditure is still an important item in the Cyprus economy. After the bases agreement was settled, Makarios dropped all pressure on the British to reduce or give up their bases. Paradoxically his only complaint on this score, between 1960 and 1963, came when the British reduced the strength of their garrison and he asked them to bear in mind the effect on the Cypriot standard of living. Indeed, within a year after the British had haggled for six months to hold nearly a hundred square miles for their base areas, they were considering cutting the area down to seventy square miles, but were advised not to do so for fear of alarming the Greek Cypriots.

Military expenditure by Britain, tourism and remittances from

Cypriots abroad (about five thousand Cypriots emigrate yearly and there are about a hundred thousand in Britain) help to fill the gap in the balance of trade. The value of imports trebled between 1950 and 1960 and totalled £40,416,000 in 1961. Exports in the same year totalled £17,780,000 leaving a trade gap of £22,636,000. In 1960 Britain supplied 37 per cent of Cyprus imports and took 35 per cent of her exports.[2] In addition to military expenditure, Britain supplied most of the £14 million spent on economic development between 1956 and 1960. In August 1961, Makarios announced that £62 million would be spent on a five-year development plan. In 1962 and again in 1963 development accounted for £4·7 million each year out of a total government expenditure of £20·3 million. Britain had left behind an efficient and incorrupt administration, a good network of roads and other public services, and a successful record in water-development, afforestation and public health. Under the British, malaria, formerly widespread, was wiped out and the death rate reduced to one of the lowest in the world.

The British colonial administration also encouraged the growth of trade unions, in spite of the fact that most of them were controlled by communists or communist sympathisers. In 1962 there were about thirty trade unions with a total membership of some 71,000. Of these about 41,000 were members of the Pan-Cyprian Federation of Labour which is affiliated to the communist-controlled World Federation of Trade Unions. The Cyprus Workers Federation, affiliated to the International Confederation of Trade Unions and the Greek Federation of Labour, has about 15,000 members. The trade union movement, especially the Pan-Cyprian Federation, is vigorous and intelligently conducted. With its excellent clinics and attention to working conditions as well as wages, it is, apart from its ideological politics, one of the progressive social influences in Cyprus. The trade unions are the mainstay of AKEL, the communist-controlled political front in Cyprus.

In the island's first national elections to the new House of Representatives on July 31, 1960, AKEL, under an electoral pact with Makarios, was returned unopposed in five of the thirty-five Greek seats. The other thirty Greek seats went to the Patriotic Front which supports the archbishop, now president. Fifteen seats went to the Turkish National Party which backs Dr Küchük, the vice-president.

Among the seven Greek ministers in the first Cyprus cabinet, Makarios included two leading members of EOKA. Polycarpos Georgadjis, a former clerk, took over the Ministry of the Interior at the age of thirty, and Tassos Papadopoulos, an English-educated barrister, became minister of Labour at the age of only twenty-six. A third man associated with EOKA, Glafkos Clerides, another English-trained barrister, who had fought with the RAF in the second world war and had been shot down over Germany, became, at the age of forty-one, president of the House of Representatives. Clerides, who emerged as the ablest and calmest of Makarios's political advisers, deputised for the president during his journeys abroad. Two other English-educated lawyers in the cabinet were the twenty-eight year old foreign minister, Spyros Kyprianou, and the minister of Justice, Mrs Stella Soulioti, whose brother is the film director, Michael Cacoyiannis. Turkish ministers held the portfolios of Defence, Health and Agriculture. Apart from Küchük, the leading political figures among the Turkish Cypriots were Orek, the minister of Defence, and Raouf Denktash, the vice-president of the House of Representatives. The role of Denktash on the Turkish side matched that of Clerides among the Greeks.

Makarios and Küchük are an extraordinary contrast—almost caricatures of the national stereotypes of quick-witted Greek and slow-moving solid Turk. The archbishop is sharply alert, lightly built and physically graceful, with a ready eloquence and a mischievous sense of humour. The Turkish leader is a thick-set heavy, red-faced man; a gruff and serious talker. Both men have strong and stubborn characters. Makarios has often been described as 'Byzantine' in his political methods, which is presumably intended to be an unflattering attribution of duplicity and devious intrigue. He is certainly a shrewd tactician and a patient bargainer, but the most striking feature of his policies has been their simplicity and consistency of purpose.

Compared with a subtle strategist like Macmillan, Makarios has often appeared almost clumsily direct and inflexible. He has never essentially wavered from his conviction that the Greek Cypriots whom he represents and who form four-fifths of the population, should have the right freely to decide the kind of government they want and the kind of status the island should have, whether it be independence or enosis. He accepted a compromise in 1959 because he could not do otherwise, but the belief remained. At home, he has had to manoeuvre and choose his words carefully to maintain control of a difficult and undisciplined following. He has had to deal with nationalist extremists, communists and armed groups not under his direct control. He has not always been successful. Nor did he show great skill in handling the Turkish Cypriots after the establishment of the republic, though part of this failure may be put down to the narrow-mindedness of the Greek Cypriots as a whole, as well as to the short-sightedness of the Turkish Cypriots in overplaying their hand. Unavoidable differences of national temperament played their part.

In cabinet meetings, the Turkish ministers began to feel they were being by-passed by the Greeks who, they believed, settled every important question among themselves beforehand. The cabinet discussions were conducted in English, the common language of the two communities. Küchük, in particular, whose foreign language is French rather than English, would find it difficult to keep up with the proceedings, especially the quick Greek jokes which could have seemed, however wrongly, to be at the Turks' expense. A proud and touchy Turkish minister, remembering who had once ruled the island, might well come out of a cabinet meeting fuming and muttering that the Turks used to skin archbishops alive in the old days. It must also have been difficult for the Greek Cypriots, who had never ruled themselves before, to restrain the impulse to show off their new power and put the Turks in their place. Küchük complained that he was not consulted about important diplomatic appointments or about the general conduct of foreign policy.

But perhaps the biggest mistake the Greeks made was in their indifference to Turkish poverty. The Turkish community as a whole is poorer and socially less developed than the Greek. The average Greek Cypriot attributes this simply to Turkish laziness or lack of enterprise, and the enervating influence of Islam. But the problems of the Turkish community have complex social and historical causes. They require a heavy investment in education, welfare services and economic development if they are to be overcome. Most of the money for this would have to come from the Greeks, since, being richer, the Greeks pay more taxes. But when it came to sharing out development aid between the two communities, the majority of Greeks wanted to share it strictly according to population, giving the Turks 20 per cent, instead of the communal ratio of 30–70 used in sharing civil service jobs and seats in Parliament. Makarios himself tried to be more generous than his followers and raised the figure to 28·5 per cent, but the Turks still felt dissatisfied. Turkish poverty and Greek political imagination might have suggested a more generous offer of 40–60. A similar tight-fisted attitude on the part of the Greeks was shown in the allocation of funds for Turkish education.

The Turks complained with some justice that the Greeks never really accepted their status as a separate national community but regarded them simply as a minority in a Greek island. The Greeks felt from the start that the London agreements were artificial and transient and suspected the Turks of preparing to use them as a stepping-stone to partition. Even before independence was officially declared these suspicions had been strengthened by the capture of a Turkish caique smuggling rifle ammunition. While Makarios failed to win Turkish confidence, the Turkish Cypriots on their side showed little forbearance in the exercise of the disproportionate and potentially crippling powers they had been given under the Zürich Constitution. Conscious of Turkey's power at their back and Turkish troops on the island itself, they were intransigent in claiming their full rights as a separate community, even where these rights were likely to be unworkable in practice or to conflict with the interests of the state as a whole. Consequently, as the first flush of independence faded, friction grew between Greeks and Turks over a number of questions: foreign policy, civil service jobs, the army, the separation of municipalities, taxation by the communal chambers, and the use of the veto on central government taxation.

Cyprus was linked by an alliance with Greece and Turkey, both members of NATO, and had a military agreement with Britain. But she was not herself a member of NATO and the British bases and Greek and Turkish troops on the island were not officially part of the NATO system. Instead, Makarios, perhaps with an eye on the future diplomatic needs of the Greek Cypriots, brought her into the group of non-aligned Afro-Asian countries. At the United Nations Assembly Cyprus was an active member of the Afro-Asian group—though there could have been no one more European than the chief Cyprus delegate, M. Zenon Rossides, a meticulous Greek Cypriot lawyer. Makarios developed close relations with President Nasser, of the United Arab Republic, a neighbour and a leading figure among the non-aligned countries. The archbishop was one of the heads of state who attended the two summit conferences of non-aligned countries in Belgrade in September 1961, and in Cairo in October 1964. He also visited the United States and, in November 1962, accepted an invitation to visit Turkey. There were student demonstrations during his Turkish visit but otherwise the courtesies were maintained. But his non-aligned policy, even though the presence of British, Greek and Turkish troops on the island limited its military significance, was not popular with the Turkish Cypriots, with the Greek and Turkish governments, or with the United States.

The development of the island's own military forces was soon held up by a dispute over the way they should be organised. The Cyprus army never got far beyond a nucleus of officer-cadets. Instead, both Greek and Turkish Cypriots began to train and equip their own private armies in secret. The treaties had provided for a Cypriot army of two thousand men composed of Greeks and Turks in a 60–40 ratio. The Turkish leaders also demanded that there should be separate Greek and Turkish units. The Turkish minister of Defence, Orek, has claimed that the Greek commander of the army agreed that, for practical reasons of language and different customs, there should be separate units at platoon or company level. But Makarios decided there should be no separation at any level; this decision was vetoed by vice-president Küchük. Makarios then said that it would be better to have no army at all, because Cyprus was a non-aligned country with limited resources. The 150 Greeks—all former EOKA men—among the army cadets were used as instructors to build up the secret Greek Cypriot 'army'.[3]

In the sharing out of civil service jobs, the greatest difficulties arose because the 70–30 ratio had to be applied not simply to the total number of jobs but in every grade. There were not enough trained Turks to fill their quota of jobs in the higher grades, though Dr Küchük had plans to send a hundred young men to be trained in Ankara for this purpose. Meanwhile, fulfilling the letter of the agreement would have meant disrupting the civil service. According to the Greek Cypriot leaders it meant holding Greeks back from promotion to jobs for which they were qualified in order to find places for unqualified Turks. The Turks, however, claimed that their people were often passed over, even when qualified, especially in the agricultural services. Within three years no fewer than 2,000 civil service appointments had been contested on communal grounds and brought before the Constitutional Court. If all the appointments had been declared invalid, it would have meant the collapse of the island's administration.

One of the most serious practical problems for the conduct of government arose over the taxation rights of the two communal chambers. These institutions imposed taxes to meet community purposes but, particularly in the case of education, these funds had to be supplemented by grants from the central government. Having taxed their communities once already, through the communal chambers, the leaders of each community were reluctant to agree to the additional central government taxation required to provide for the supplementary grants.

The issue which above all others became a symbol of the political conflict between the Greeks and Turks was the separation of municipalities in the five main towns. It was this dispute which led the Turks in December 1961 to use their veto on the income tax laws in the budget and so brought about a constitutional deadlock. It will be recalled that, according to Averoff, the Greek foreign minister during the Zürich and London conferences, it was the Greek Cypriots who pressed for the creation of separate municipalities. A law establishing them had in any case already been issued by the British in 1958 as part of their attempt to implement the Macmillan plan. But, whether or not separate municipalities had been considered desirable at one time by the Greek Cypriots, they soon came to regard them not only as unworkable in practice but as a politically dangerous step towards partition. For the Turks, on the other hand, they became the main test of how far the Greeks genuinely accepted the separate identity of the Turkish community.

New laws for the separate municipalities were supposed to come into effect not more than six months after the constitution. But in the transitional period between independence there was a deadlock on the municipal question. The principle of separation had been accepted by the Greeks in the Zürich agreements, though subject to a review of how the principle worked in practice. The Turks claimed that the question of jointly operated municipal services had also been settled and that the only remaining problem was to fix the municipal boundaries. De facto boundaries existed and, pending a final agreement, the law creating separate municipalities which had existed under the British administration, was renewed annually. But at the end of 1962, just before the law was to be renewed again, Makarios announced that it could no longer be extended. Negotiations were then resumed and on Christmas Eve, 1962, after haggling lasting late into the night, it looked as if agreement had miraculously been achieved. A joint communiqué was issued announcing an agreement in principle, but within twenty-four hours it had been repudiated by the Turkish Cypriots.

This crucial meeting, which was a turning point in the gradual breakdown of the Zürich agreements, is a subject of great controversy. The Greek version, as given to the author by one of the Greek leaders who took part in the talks, is that the Turks accepted a proposal for the operation of a unified municipal system for an experimental period of one year. The Turkish members of the municipality would be elected by Turks in proportion to population and, for those areas in which Turks were in a majority, a proportionate sum of the budget would be under the Turkish members' control. Jobs in the municipal services would be allocated in proportion to population in each area. The agreement was drafted by Glafkos Clerides, Greek president of the House of Representatives, and by the Greek attorney-general, Tornaritis. These two men then went through the agreement point by point with Raouf Denktash, the Turkish leader. Denktash signified his agreement and Tornaritis then suggested that they should all initial the document. But Makarios said: 'No, we are all gentlemen here. Why do we need to initial it?' So it was not initialled. The communiqué issued after the meeting announcing a basis of agreement was drafted jointly by Clerides and Denktash who had shown himself moderate and reasonable in the negotiations, despite his later reputation for extremism. However the next day the agreement was rejected by Küchük, either because the Turks had had second thoughts or because of instructions from Ankara.

One of the Turkish ministers who took part in the meeting gave the author a different version. He said that the Turks had suggested setting up a committee to study the whole problem over a period of a year, during which time the existing municipal legislation would be renewed again, but the Greeks wanted the Turks to accept the principle of unified municipalities as prior condition of this study. The Turks said they were willing to open up and re-examine the whole question, but they never agreed in advance to the principle of unified municipalities. When the Greeks issued a communiqué suggesting that the Turks had accepted this principle, the Turks were obliged to reject it.

Whichever version is correct, there is no doubt that the sequel to the meeting was calamitous. A week later the Greek majority in the House of Representatives rejected a Turkish proposal to extend the municipal legislation for another year. On January 2, 1963, the council of ministers set up 'development boards' to run the main towns. The Greek municipalities surrendered their powers to these boards, but the Turkish municipalities refused to do so—the Turkish communal chamber declaring that the separate municipalities were still legal. The Turkish Cypriot leaders consulted the government in Ankara and referred the dispute to the Cyprus Constitutional Court. In March 1963, by the casting votes of the neutral president, Dr Fortshoff of West Germany (who later resigned), the court decided that the 'development boards' and the Turkish attempt to legalise the separate municipalities were both invalid. Since the court had already, on February 8, decided that the Turkish veto on the tax laws in 1961 meant the government had no authority to collect customs duties and income tax, both central and local government were now threatened with paralysis.

Greek Cypriot pressure for a review of the constitution began to increase. In speeches in the summer of 1963, Makarios criticised the rights of intervention given to the British, Greek and Turkish governments under the Cyprus treaties and spoke of referring the matter to the Commonwealth Prime Ministers' Conference. He was told by the British that this would be inopportune and advised to wait until a calmer mood prevailed in both Turkey and Greece. For by this time the fall of the Karamanlis government in Greece and the continued political instability in Turkey had begun to complicate the constitutional troubles in Cyprus. Both Makarios and the Turkish Cypriot leaders were under increasing pressure from extremists reviving the old demands for enosis and partition.

In Greece, Karamanlis resigned, ostensibly because of a dispute with King Paul over the royal visit to London. Karamanlis had opposed the visit because of a campaign in Britain for the release of communist and leftwing prisoners in Greece, in the course of which Queen Frederika, during a private visit to London, had been molested by a demonstrator. After eight years in office, the Karamanlis government had begun to lose its grip and its popularity. Economic difficulties, aggravated by the end of American aid, led to unrest among the industrial workers. The government was accused of being implicated through the police in the murder of a leftwing member of parliament, Gregoris Lambrakis, who was run over by a motor-cycle after leaving a political meeting in Salonika. This, and the affair of the queen and the communist prisoners, began to tarnish the government's reputation at home and abroad. Karamanlis was a symbol of the anti-communist mood of the cold war and the period after the Greek civil war. With the passage of time and the thaw in the international cold war, this image became out of date and Karamanlis began to look like a 'reactionary'—which he was not.

In their campaign against the Karamanlis government, the Greek opposition attacked the Cyprus agreements as one of the government's failures. They hinted that if they were returned to power they would help the Cypriots to achieve enosis. This both alarmed Turkey—which had hitherto counted on the Karamanlis government to enforce the Cyprus treaties—and changed the situation for Makarios. It is difficult to be sure how far Makarios himself encouraged this attitude in the Greek opposition or was encouraged by it. But in any case he would have found it politically difficult in Cyprus to take a more moderate line than those who, in Greece, looked like forming the next Greek government.

In Turkey, the coalition under Inönü continued in power during 1963 but there was growing conflict within the government over the amnesty of the former Democrat leaders who were still in prison. The release on parole of ex-president Bayar led to demonstrations of welcome by former Democrat supporters, counter-demonstrations by students, and Bayar's eventual return to prison. In May 1963, there was a second abortive military coup by the Ankara military academy students, again led by ex-Colonel Talat Aydemir who was later tried and executed. The attempted coup was a protest against the liberty given to the revival of the former Democrats under the guise of the Justice Party. The amnesty dispute was symbolic of the basic conflict in Turkey. The army leaders who had overthrown Menderes wanted both to preserve the results of their revolution and to restore constitutional democracy. But these two aims were difficult to reconcile because a majority in the country, particularly the peasants, still supported the former Democrats and would, if they had been allowed, have reversed the revolution. This became increasingly clear in the local elections in November 1963 when the Justice Party, the undeclared heirs of Menderes, pushed their share of the vote up from 35 to 45 per cent. The ensuing political crisis led to the resignation of Inönü on December 2, 1963.

It was in the middle of this crisis and when Greece, after inconclusive elections on November 3, was also struggling to form a government, that Makarios chose to make his first formal bid to change the deadlocked Cyprus constitution. He submitted to Küchük a memorandum listing thirteen proposed amendments to the Constitution and the Cyprus treaties, as a basis for negotiation. He sent copies of the memorandum to the British, Greek and Turkish governments 'for information'. The Greek Cypriot leaders claim that the memorandum and its timing were decided upon in consultation with the British high commission in Nicosia and that they consequently expected support from the British government for their move.

The effect of the archbishop's 'thirteen points' would have been to abolish many of the provisions for separate communal institutions or rights and to create an integrated unitary state with some limited guarantees for the Turkish community. It would have ended the veto embodied in the powers of the president and vice-president, and in the separate majorities required for certain laws in the House of Representatives. The Greek president and Turkish vice-president of the House would have been elected by the House as a whole instead of by separate votes of Greek and Turkish members. As some compensation for the Turks, the Turkish vice-presidents of the state and of the House of Representatives would have been permitted to deputise for the Greek presidents. This would have meant, for example, that during Makarios' absences abroad, Küchük would have been in full charge of the government, instead of Clerides. The Makarios proposals would also have put the municipalities and the administration of justice on a unified instead of a communal basis. They would have abolished the Greek communal chamber but allowed the Turks to keep their communal chamber if they wished. The police and the gendarmerie would have been united and their strength and that of the army decided by law. The ratios of Greek and Turkish participation in these forces, and in the public services laid down in the Constitution and the treaties, would have been changed to the ratio of the Greek and Turkish populations.

Makarios claims that a few days after handing over the memorandum he was told by Küchük that he was studying the proposals and hoped to give his comments on them by the end of the month. But before these comments were made, the Turkish government had on December 16, 1963, in the bluntest language categorically rejected the entire memorandum and insisted that no change whatsoever could be made in the Constitution. The crisis and rising tension in Cyprus were then overshadowed for the rest of the world by the aftermath of the assassination of President Kennedy. But within five days of the Turkish rejection of the 'thirteen points', shooting had begun in Cyprus. By Christmas the island was torn by civil war, hundreds of people lay dead and Cyprus was once again the centre of an international crisis.

CHAPTER FOURTEEN

The Christmas Crisis 1963

THE CYPRIOTS are indefatigable and uninhibited propagandists. Each community has produced its own melodramatic explanation of the Christmas crisis of 1963.

The Greeks claim that the Turkish Cypriots had planned an insurrection in order to provoke the military intervention of Turkey and produce a de facto partition of the island—though Archbishop Makarios does not seriously believe this. They base this claim on the allegation that the Turks had been smuggling arms into the island and training a secret military organisation, known as Türk Müdafaa Teşkilati (TMT).* They produce as evidence an alleged captured Turkish document revealing a plan for military action, including the intervention of Turkey, in the event of a breakdown of the Constitution. These allegations may be founded in fact—in the sense that the Turks were arming and training and that they had an emergency plan. But they do not prove that the Turkish leadership started the Christmas crisis with the deliberate purpose of bringing about partition.

The same may be said about the Turkish claim that the Greeks provoked the crisis as part of a deliberate plan to exterminate the Turkish community. A less extravagant Turkish version is that the Greeks were trying to frighten the Turks into accepting Greek political demands or leaving Cyprus. The Turkish accusation that the Greeks built up secret armed forces is factually correct. There is also no doubt that these forces were brought into action during the crisis and that part of them got out of control, resulting at one stage in a small but savage massacre.

Yet neither the suggestion of a carefully planned Turkish rebellion nor that of a systematic Greek attempt at extermination or terror will bear close examination. Despite their clandestine activities, both sides were ill-prepared militarily and politically when the clash came. Nor had either side taken the elementary precautions which should have been evident if they had been preparing for battle, such as the removal

* Turkish Defence Organisation.

of their compatriots from unsafe areas. It was not until after the fighting had begun that the Turks began to move out of some of the mixed villages and to concentrate in the Nicosia area, either voluntarily or from fear or, in some cases, under pressure from the Turkish leadership. The same is true of the Greek evacuation from some areas where they were outnumbered and in danger. There were extremists on both sides waiting for the opportunity to fish in troubled waters; but there is no reason to doubt that when Makarios put forward his thirteen points he genuinely thought he was making moderate proposals designed to make Cyprus a more workable independent state. Nor is there any reason to believe that the aims of the Turkish leadership went beyond the preservation of their rights under the Zürich Constitution. But in the disputes over the application of the Zürich and London agreements, a heavy burden of mutual suspicion and fear had been created. Each side prepared secretly for the worst without necessarily wishing it to come about.

For some months before the crisis there had been signs of a split between the Greeks and Turks in the police force. The Greek Cypriot police began to take more intensive action against suspected arms smuggling by the Turks. Greek patrols were used to check Turkish traffic on the roads and to search Turkish areas in the towns. The Turkish public and press complained that ex-EOKA men in plain clothes, as well as Greek uniformed police, were being used to search houses and keep the Turkish quarter of Nicosia under close observation. The Turks believed that this was an attempt to intimidate them and assert Greek authority, possibly as a prelude to a serious effort to disarm them. They were determined to show that they would not be dominated.

With this tense atmosphere, made worse by the accumulation of arms and the political conflicts in Greece and Turkey, only a spark was needed to set the island aflame. It came at 2 a.m. on December 21, 1963, when a Greek police patrol stopped a Turkish car on the border of the Greek and Turkish areas in the red light district of Nicosia. The Turks in the car refused to be searched. An hostile Turkish crowd gathered and the police opened fire; the shooting spread and two Turks were killed and a Greek policeman was wounded. Later that morning Turkish crowds began to gather in the Turkish quarter of Nicosia and in villages on the road north to Kyrenia. Greek policemen were stoned and Greeks passing in vehicles or on foot were shot at. In Nicosia, the Greek police, but not the Turkish police, were issued with arms. An armed Greek police patrol, sent into the Turkish quarter following a report of an attack on some Greek government employees, was stoned by Turkish schoolboys as it passed by the Turkish high school. The patrol opened fire, injuring two of the boys, whereupon the Turkish leaders went to Archbishop Makarios to protest at what they regarded as provocative behaviour by the Greek police. In order to avoid further trouble it was agreed that when the funerals of the victims of the earlier shooting were held in the Turkish quarter the next day (December 22) there should be no police patrols. The funerals, followed by big crowds, passed off without incident.

But that evening the shooting began again. The Greeks blame the Turks and the Turks say it was the Greeks. According to the Greeks, Turkish police disarmed Greek police who had been attacked with automatic weapons on the Kyrenia road, and a Turkish crowd armed with guns attacked the Paphos Gate police station in Nicosia. The Turks say that Greek police began firing on Turkish cars on the Kyrenia road and eventually the whole of the Turkish quarter of Nicosia was being fired on from all sides. The Greek police put out a general alert that night and all Turkish telephone and telegraphic communication was cut. The Greeks took control of the Nicosia airport and all the ports and took over all the rural police posts. The Turkish minister of Defence, Orek, says he tried to contact Makarios but failed. The firing stopped at 3 a.m. and four hours later the radio broadcast a statement from Makarios claiming that the government was in control of the situation and calling on civil servants to go to their offices.

However, soon afterwards the shooting was resumed. Turkish police and gendarmerie began to leave their posts and the Turks took up arms in earnest. They seized the gendarmerie post in Nicosia and launched an attack with Bren guns on flats housing the families of Greek police in a mixed suburb of Nicosia. Makarios says that this was the first tragic turning point in the crisis. The Turkish leaders thought, mistakenly, that the Greeks were about to make a planned attack on them and decided to attack first. But for this, he believes, the situation might have calmed down in a few days because, until then, there had been comparatively few casualties. At noon on December 23 Makarios met the Turkish leaders at the Paphos Gate police station and agreed to a cease-fire. But, despite the agreed truce, fighting went on during the day, and spread during the night to the town of Larnaca. The next day, Christmas Eve, the fighting grew heavier in Nicosia. The Turks set up sandbagged road-blocks and put machine-gun posts in the minarets of the two main mosques of the city. Attacks on the police flats were resumed. Another cease-fire meeting was arranged at which the British deputy high commissioner and the American ambassador were also present. Makarios suggested that there should be mixed Greek and Turkish police patrols to ensure the observance of the cease-fire. The Turkish leaders insisted that the Turkish police must have the same arms as the Greeks. Makarios agreed, but the Greek police commander later said there were not enough arms to give the same weapons to the Turks.

The second and graver turning point came at 8 p.m. on Christmas Eve, when Greek 'security forces', police and armed irregulars, mostly ex-EOKA, launched a massive counter-attack on the Turkish positions in Nicosia. Greeks in the mixed suburb of Ormophita had been surrounded and sent out an SOS for help. The Greek forces used their full strength to break the siege. They captured the Turkish positions and the irregulars ran wild, killing scores of Turks, including women and children, smashing and looting Turkish houses, and taking hundreds of hostages. Shortly before midnight Makarios and Orek again agreed to a cease-fire, but again it was broken during the night and the following morning by both sides. The Turks now feared that the Greeks were beginning an indiscriminate massacre and appealed to Ankara for help. Turkey began to act. At six o'clock on Christmas morning there were reports that Turkish invasion ships were assembling at Alexandretta. The Turkish, Greek and British governments issued a call for a cease-fire to be supervised by their troops in the island. A truce meeting was arranged at the British high commissioner's house.*

Turkey issued a warning of unilateral action if the fighting did not stop. While the peace talks were in progress on Christmas Day, Turkish jets flew low over Nicosia. At the meeting Makarios agreed to allow the British to supervise the cease-fire, and accepted the principle of a buffer zone, known later as the Green Line. At the request of the British commander, Major-General Peter Young, Makarios agreed to the withdrawal of the Greeks from positions they held in this zone and their replacement by British troops. The archbishop claims that the Greeks were then in control of the situation; he did not realise that, after the Greek withdrawal, the Turks would be allowed to stop Greeks from entering or leaving the Turkish quarter. The Turkish army contingent

* The high commissioner, Sir Arthur Clark, had flown back from sick leave in England a few hours before to find three dead Turkish peasants propped up against his front gate.

in Cyprus moved out of its camp, north of Nicosia, and took up positions controlling the road to Kyrenia. That evening (December 25), there were rumours that a Turkish invasion fleet was on its way to the island. Greece let it be known that, if Turkish troops intervened, Greek troops would do likewise. The NATO Council held an emergency meeting in Paris and the Cyprus government called for an urgent meeting of the United Nations Security Council. In the event the Turkish invasion scare proved to be a false alarm. It is doubtful whether the Turks had enough landing-craft or other material ready at that time to make good their threat.

The following day a formal agreement was reached on British peace-keeping and mediation. The Greek and Turkish army contingents on the island were put under British command as part of a joint peace force, and British troops took over positions on both sides in the buffer zone. After an urgent telephone talk with the British high commissioner in Nicosia, Duncan Sandys, the secretary for Commonwealth Relations, flew to Cyprus. His first task was to consolidate the ceasefire. His second aim was the speedy arrangement of a conference to produce a political settlement. A truce liaison committee under his chairmanship drew up an agreement on the 'Green Line', a neutral zone dividing the Turkish and Greek sectors of Nicosia—so-called because it was marked on the map with a green chinagraph pencil which happened to be on the table. It was also agreed that the Greek and Turkish contingents would play no active part in the peace-keeping operations but should leave this task to the 2,700 British troops. As a result of strong pressure from Sandys, hostages were exchanged under his personal supervision, though some had already been murdered on each side.

There were unexpected hazards to be overcome on the way to peace. Without any prior consultation, the Cyprus government announced on January 1, 1964 that Makarios had abrogated the treaties with Greece, Turkey and Britain. Hearing this on the radio, Sandys rushed round to the archbishop's palace, where a meeting of Greek Cypriot ministers was in session. The heated scene between Sandys and Makarios was described as follows (to the author) by one who was present.

Sandys protested to Makarios: 'You can't do this'. The archbishop replied: 'Well, I've done it'. Sandys said: 'If you don't retract, the Turks will be here in twenty-four hours and everyone will think they were quite within their rights. What consultations did you have with anyone before doing this?' Makarios replied: 'I've written to all the heads of government in the world'. 'All of them, including the British government?' 'Well, not quite all. I didn't send notes to the British, Turkish and Greek governments, because I thought they were all too closely involved.' 'You've got to eat your words, and there's no time to be lost.' The archbishop retorted: 'I never eat my words'. Sandys replied: 'I'm afraid you have no option and I will do my best to help you find a formula'.

Eventually a formula was worked out and the archbishop issued the following official statement:

> In my telegrams today to heads of government I stated that we have decided to abrogate the treaties of guarantee and alliance. This may have given the impression that we had abrogated these treaties.
>
> I wish to make it clear that the meaning intended to be conveyed was that it is our desire to secure the termination of these treaties by appropriate means.

At the end of the meeting, Makarios said to Sandys: 'This was all a misunderstanding. It was the fault of the translation from the Greek. You see, the Greek word doesn't mean *abrogate* but only *desire to abrogate*'. Sandys turned to Kyprianou, the Cyprus foreign minister, and asked: 'Which was the original text, the Greek or the English?' Kyprianou blushed and said: 'The English'.

Sandys' next task was to persuade Makarios to accept his plan for a conference in London of the Greek and Turkish Cypriots and the three guarantor powers, Britain, Greece and Turkey. The plan was first worked out at a secret dinner party in Nicosia which brought together Sandys and the Greek and Turkish Cypriot leaders, Clerides and Denktash. The British high commissioner, Sir Arthur Clark, and the British commander-in-chief, Air Marshal Sir Denis Barnett, were also present. Clerides arrived for the dinner with an enormous brown cardboard box which he presented to Denktash. It contained all the letters addressed to the Turkish population in the old city of Nicosia which had been held up by the Greek-controlled post office. The gesture helped to create a good atmosphere and Denktash and Clerides were soon talking like brothers in a sincere effort to find a political solution.

Küchük and the other Turkish Cypriot leaders agreed to the London conference and so eventually did all the Greek Cypriot ministers except Makarios himself. Makarios wanted to take the dispute straight to the United Nations. His intention was to declare there that the Cyprus treaties had been imposed on the Cypriots and were therefore invalid.

He wanted to ensure recognition of the unfettered sovereign status of his government and was against a conference which would include the treaty powers. He was afraid that if the conference failed, as he expected, it would raise tension in the island instead of helping to reduce it. But he was persuaded, under strong pressure from the Greek ambassador, to agree to the conference. His own ministers had pointed out that under article 33 of the UN Charter, parties to a dispute were expected to make every effort to negotiate a peaceful settlement before having recourse to the United Nations. In the archbishop's own words: 'I preferred to let the conference fail slowly rather than refuse to be represented'. The archbishop's doubts about the outcome of the conference were shared by some British officials who believed that it was unwise to try to rush the Cypriots into the political talks before the passions aroused by the Christmas massacres had been given time to subside.

In Britain there was some criticism of the dual British role of policeman and political mediator. The critics suggested that the two roles should be separated, since an active political role would make it more difficult for the British to be convincingly impartial as policemen. The Labour opposition proposed calling on the United Nations to do the job. Officially the Foreign Office at first resisted this course, though there were some senior officials who foresaw that the dispute would end up sooner or later at the United Nations and believed that the sooner it went there the better. Partly in response to these feelings and partly to put pressure on the Cypriots at the London conference, the British prime minister, Sir Alec Douglas-Home, hinted that there might be a time-limit of a month or two beyond which Britain would not be able to keep her troops on the task of peace-keeping.

The London conference got off to a bad start on January 15, 1964, with a violent tirade from Erkin, the Turkish foreign minister.* But Sandys, the chairman of the London conference, was hopeful that, if he could get the Greek and Turkish Cypriots alone, some more constructive discussion would be possible. He borrowed Chequers from the prime minister and invited the two groups of Cypriot leaders down separately for week-end talks, which were continued afterwards in London. At the start each side naturally stated its own position in an

* The Christmas crisis had put Inönü back into power in Ankara. But he had a majority of only four and his coalition leant to an uncertain degree on army support. Greece under a caretaker government was preparing for elections which, on February 16, 1964, returned Papandreou, a veteran like Inönü, to power with a substantial majority for his coalition of centre parties.

extreme form. The Greek Cypriots insisted on the ending of the treaties, with their rights of intervention. They wanted the conversion of Cyprus into a unitary state with minority rights for the Turks but otherwise enjoying 'unfettered' sovereignty. The Turkish Cypriots insisted that the treaties and their rights under the Zürich Constitution must be maintained in full. In addition, they claimed that the Christmas fighting, which had cost the Turks 200 dead and 200 missing, made it imperative that the two communities should, for security reasons, be physically separated. They proposed the conversion of Cyprus into a confederal state with a Turkish-administered canton into which the Turkish Cypriots would be concentrated. The Greek Cypriots rejected this proposal as being a disguised form of partition.

Yet as the hours went by at Chequers, the atmosphere of the English country home and its glowing log fires began to have a mellowing effect. Possible compromises were calmly examined, and in fact some headway was made in the preparation of a tentative paper which could provide the basis for joint discussion between the two sides. After the week-end Sandys continued his separate consultations with the two Cypriot delegations in London. But just when the British felt that some further progress was being made, the talks were suddenly interrupted by the recall of the Greek Cypriot leader to Nicosia followed by the summoning of Denktash to Ankara. Both delegations were then ordered to stand firm on their original positions. On their return, the whole tone of the London meetings hardened. Both sides became totally unyielding and refused to pursue the earlier discussion of possible compromises.

As the conference dragged on with no further prospect of a settlement, Sandys turned the discussion to the immediate problem of keeping the peace. Britain was in danger of being left indefinitely holding a very unruly baby and of becoming involved in a threatened Turkish invasion of Cyprus. The London negotiations turned to the creation of an enlarged international police force for Cyprus. Believing that the reference to the Security Council would involve long delays, the British were still reluctant to go to the United Nations. With American backing they proposed the immediate despatch of a force drawn from NATO countries, together with the appointment of a neutral mediator and an administrative committee of NATO ambassadors. Turkey and Greece accepted the NATO plan, the latter reluctantly. But Makarios rejected it. Any international force, he said, should be under the control of the

United Nations Security Council. The plan aroused no enthusiasm in NATO itself: France was against it and West Germany lukewarm. Russia, to whom Makarios had earlier appealed for support against the renewed Turkish threat of invasion, issued a warning that any attempt to bring Cyprus under NATO control would be a threat to world peace.

President Johnson sent George Ball of the American State Department to Cyprus to try to persuade or bully the archbishop into accepting the NATO plan. But he failed to move him. The archbishop preferred to rely on the United Nations where he could count on support from the Afro-Asian countries, so long as Cyprus remained non-aligned. Accepting a NATO police force, and what amounted to a form of NATO political supervision, would have lost him much of this support. It would also, he estimated, have left his government at the mercy of powers he suspected of being more inclined to favour a strong Turkey than a weak Greece.

During the three days in mid-February 1964 that Ball spent arguing vainly with Makarios, a battle raged between Greek and Turkish Cypriots in the port town of Limassol. There had been a number of shooting incidents in different parts of the island since the Christmas cease-fire, and in the northern mountain range the Turkish Cypriots had taken over a key position at the Crusader castle of Saint Hilarion, dominating the road from Nicosia to Kyrenia. The Limassol fighting was the worst to date. The Turks in Limassol suffered heavy losses when the Greeks broke a cease-fire agreement made with the commander of the British peace force, General Young, and bombarded the Turkish positions with mortars and bazookas. Turkey was roused by the Limassol casualties and declared that the Turkish Cypriots were no longer being adequately protected. She announced, once again, that Turkish ships were sailing for Cyprus. American diplomacy, backed by the discreet obstruction of the United States Sixth Fleet, persuaded the Turks to hold their hand. But it was clear that the NATO plan was dead. A tentative proposal for joint military and mediatory action by the Commonwealth rather than NATO similarly made no headway, though Makarios showed some interest in it. There was now nothing for it but the United Nations.

In February, Britain appealed to the Security Council, forestalling by hours an appeal from the Cyprus government. The Council met to debate Cyprus three days later. Ten days more talk and behind-the-scenes negotiation were needed before the Council agreed on a resolution authorising a United Nations peace force for Cyprus, for three months, and the appointment of a United Nations mediator to help find a political solution. The resolution also called on all states to refrain from any action or threat of action 'likely to worsen the situation in the sovereign Republic of Cyprus', or to endanger international peace. Russia, contrary to earlier gloomy forecasts in London and Washington, did not obstruct the move for a UN force, despite her known disapproval of the financial and legal aspects of previous peace-keeping operations. Moscow had, in fact, throughout the Cyprus crisis shown little desire to fan the flames; its chief concern was to prevent the formal inclusion of the island in the NATO orbit. Russia's attitude was also influenced by the fact that it was the Security Council and not the General Assembly which was being asked to authorise the UN force. Moreover the force was to be financed, not out of UN funds, but by voluntary contributions from interested and participating states. As a result, Russia voted for the Security Council resolution as a whole, but abstained on its fourth clause which authorised the peace force and put it under the control of the secretary-general, U Thant.

It was one thing to recommend a UN peace force and another thing to bring it into being. U Thant set a target of 7,000 men for the force and appointed General Giyani of India as its first commander. Britain offered 2,400 out of her existing peace force as the backbone of the UN force. U Thant looked for the rest of the force to Canada, Ireland and the Scandinavians. At first, firm offers of troops were slow in arriving, but they were speeded up by another battle in Cyprus and a new threat of Turkish intervention. The battle began at Ktima, a mixed town in western Cyprus, on March 4, the day of the Security Council resolution. Fighting started with a Turkish attack aimed at seizing Greek hostages. It ended with a violent Greek offensive and a Turkish defeat, despite a cease-fire agreement and the presence of British troops in the town. Fourteen Turks and eleven Greeks were killed and about sixty wounded. The town, especially the Turkish quarter, was heavily damaged.

The Turkish Cypriot leader, Küchük, appealed to the United Nations and accused the Greeks of 'genocide'. British public opinion was roused by the Greek Cypriots' high-handed treatment of British peace-keeping troops. After eight days had passed without another shot being fired, the Turkish government reacted. On March 13, it sent a Note to Makarios threatening unilateral intervention under the Cyprus Treaty of Guarantee unless there was an immediate cease-fire, a release of all hostages and the restoration of freedom of movement for Turkish Cypriots. The Turkish government summoned the British and American ambassadors in Ankara in the middle of the night, telling them that Turkish troops at Iskanderun (Alexandretta) would invade Cyprus within thirty-six hours unless Greek Cypriots stopped maltreating Turks. In Athens, where Archbishop Makarios had gone to attend the funeral of King Paul, the Greek government ordered military counter-measures and let it be known that, if Turkey decided to fight, Greece would fight too. In New York the Security Council held an emergency meeting and passed a resolution reaffirming its call to states to show restraint over Cyprus. It asked member states to co-operate with the secretary-general in organising the peace force. America and Britain urged Turkey to be patient.

The next day, March 14, the Canadian advance guard of the UN force flew into Cyprus. They were followed by nearly 5,000 troops from Sweden, Ireland, Denmark and Finland and a medical unit from Austria. Together with the British contingent already in the island, they eventually made up a peace force of nearly 7,000 men. On March 24, U Thant appointed, as the United Nations mediator for Cyprus, a fifty-seven year old Finnish diplomatist and former premier, Sakari Tuomioja, and three days later, the United Nations Force in Cyprus, UNFICYP, officially took over its peace-keeping duties in the island.

CHAPTER FIFTEEN

The United Nations in Cyprus

AT FIRST SIGHT, the United Nations in Cyprus looked strangely like the international force of the European Concert of Powers that had intervened in Crete sixty-five years before. But there were two important differences. The European admirals in Crete had had no scruples about enforcing their will by shot and shell. They were prepared to disarm irregulars and establish peace by force if necessary. Secondly, they represented all the European great powers of the time, including Russia —though Germany dropped out later. By contrast, the United Nations force rested on a fragile political consensus to which Russia was not fully committed. Even more important, the force was not allowed to shoot except in self-defence. Its only real sanction was international public opinion and ultimately the threat of the consequences of its own withdrawal.

The essence of the peace-keeping philosophy which had developed under Dag Hammarskjöld's secretary-generalship, in the earlier operations in the Middle East and the Congo, was that the United Nations could insulate a conflict and prevent its being aggravated by outside intervention, especially from the great powers. It could also act as a buffer between the opposed local forces. But a United Nations force could operate only with the consent of the government of the country to which it was sent. It could not be used to impose the will of one party to the dispute on another. Nor could it enforce a political settlement devised by others, or even by the United Nations itself. The purpose of the United Nations was to prevent a settlement by force and to encourage one by negotiation.

The function of the United Nations force in Cyprus was defined in the Security Council resolution of March 4, 1964, as being: 'in the interest of preserving international peace and security, to use its best efforts to prevent a recurrence of fighting and, as necessary, to contribute to the maintenance and restoration of law and order and a return to normal conditions'. An earlier clause of the resolution had referred to the 'government of Cyprus' as being responsible for the maintenance and restoration of law and order, and had called on this government to 'take all necessary measures to stop violence and bloodshed in Cyprus'. Like many Security Council resolutions, this one was a compromise worded in such a way as to evade controversial issues. Its main purpose was to get a United Nations force to Cyprus as soon as possible. The resolution by-passed, for example, the question of who constituted the 'government of Cyprus'. Was it Archbishop Makarios and his Greek ministers, who claimed to be still the legal government after the withdrawal of the Turkish Cypriots from the vice-presidency, the cabinet, parliament and the civil service? Or was there validity in the claim of the Turkish Cypriots that, without their participation, the Makarios government was unconstitutional and illegal? The Security Council resolution left this point vague but in practice the United Nations continued to deal with Makarios and his ministers as the Cyprus government, while also consulting the Turkish leaders.

There was another unresolved dilemma in the Security Council resolution. In conditions of civil war how does a government maintain and restore law and order without the use of force? The United Nations answer was that it must be done by negotiation. Pending a political settlement, each side must be persuaded to remove obstacles to peaceful conditions, such as fortifications, road blocks and irregular forces. But, in such negotiations, possession becomes nine points of the law and each side feels that its relative military strength is an important bargaining element in a future political settlement. The Greek Cypriots claimed that the Security Council resolution had upheld the legality of their government and the sovereignty of the Cyprus Republic. Consequently, they asserted, the Turkish Cypriots must be considered as rebels against the lawful government. If the Turks refused to give up their arms, dismantle their fortifications and road blocks and obey the law, then the legal government was entitled to compel them to do so and to call on the help of the United Nations for this purpose. Apart from this help the main purpose of the United Nations force, in Greek Cypriot eyes, was to prevent a Turkish invasion of the island. For the Turkish Cypriots the force's chief duty was to protect them from coercion by the Greek Cypriots backed by Greece.

In dealing with the United Nations, Archbishop Makarios showed some of the caution he had earlier displayed in his rejection of a NATO force and as he was later to demonstrate even in his dealings with Greece. He wanted protection for the Greek Cypriots but not control. He was determined to preserve his freedom of action and the ability of the

Greek Cypriots to decide their own future. He had suspected NATO of wanting to impose a kind of 'trusteeship' and a solution of its own, irrespective of Greek Cypriot wishes. His aim was to secure the endorsement by the United Nations General Assembly of his claim for 'unfettered' independence and self-determination for Cyprus. But he did not intend the United Nations to be in a position to *impose* its views if they differed from those of his government. While using the United Nations to shelter the Greek Cypriots from Turkish intervention, Makarios denounced the treaty of alliance with Greece and Turkey—by virtue of which Turkish troops were stationed in Cyprus—and began to build up Greek armed strength in the island. He thus decreased his military reliance on the United Nations without at the same time becoming totally dependent on Greece. Remembering the making of the Zürich and London agreements, he was determined there should be no repetition of the situation then, when Greece settled the fate of Cyprus with Turkey over the head of the Greek Cypriots. He aimed to increase his ability to manoeuvre, leaning now on Athens and now on the United Nations, according to the prospects he saw or the pressures to which he was subjected. In dealing with the Turkish Cypriots, Makarios' strategy was to avoid a military showdown which might provoke a Turkish intervention. His method was to nibble away at the Turkish Cypriot positions in a struggle of military, political and economic attrition. Sometimes his own military leaders or political extremists went further than he might have intended. One of the means of pressure used by the Athens government in its efforts to control Makarios was the influence of General Grivas, who returned to Cyprus in June 1964. In this curious reversal of relationships, as compared with the standpoint of the two men during the period of the EOKA rebellion, Athens relied on Grivas to ensure that Makarios, in his pursuit of independence and neutrality and communist support, did not stray too far from the Hellenic, Western and anti-communist fold.

The Turkish Cypriots' plan was to refuse to give up arms unless, at the very least, the 1960 Constitution was restored intact. Otherwise they would create and maintain a state of de facto partition in the island. They also brought in from Turkey such arms and men as they could. To counter Greek pressures, Turkey used not only the recurrent threat of invasion but also reprisals against the Greek nationals in Istanbul, through deportation and confiscation of property. Turkish diplomacy aimed at achieving a settlement through direct negotiation with Greece.

Whereas Makarios struggled, with success, to maintain his independence even of Athens, the Turkish Cypriots were totally dependent on Turkey for their political, military and economic existence.

Only a fortnight after it took over in Cyprus, the United Nations force had a foretaste of the kind of problems it had to face. Greek Cypriots tried to drive the Turkish Cypriot irregulars out of Saint Hilarion castle from which they dominated the Kyrenia road and the surrounding Greek villages. They had partially succeeded when United Nations intervention halted the fighting and brought about a local agreement. This was to be the pattern for many future incidents of varying seriousness in different parts of the island. At points where fighting occurred or was likely to take place, the United Nations tried to put its forces in between the combatants, to separate them and establish a cease-fire and a neutral zone under its control. It was quite often successful. But it was unable to prevent, in August, a battle at Kokkina in the north-west corner of the island which led to Turkish air attacks and a renewed danger of Greco-Turkish war.

The Kokkina battle was the climax of a phase of steadily increasing political and economic pressures and of intensified military preparations on both sides. At the beginning of June 1964, the introduction of military conscription in Cyprus by the Makarios government was followed by another threat of Turkish intervention. A fortnight later General Grivas arrived in Cyprus from Athens to take a hand in the organisation and training of the new Cyprus National Guard. Men and arms began to pour in from Greece and were hurried away from the ports to the mountains in secret night convoys. The Greek influx was variously estimated at between 2,000 and 5,000 men. The Greek Cypriots became more intransigent about allowing the United Nations into military areas under their control. At the same time there were reports that 500 Turkish volunteers had landed secretly, at the rate of 100 a week, on the north-west coast of Cyprus. One of the main points for these landings and for the entry of Turkish arms supplies was the area round the village of Kokkina, a small enclave on the coast held by the Turkish Cypriots.

July was a month of rising tension. A first round of talks in Geneva between Greek and Turkish representatives, with the UN mediator in the chair, ended in disagreement. The Greek Cypriot members of the House of Representatives passed laws to unify the judiciary and the municipalities and to change the taxation system. The Makarios government began an economic blockade of the Turkish-held areas in

Cyprus, stopping supplies of motor fuel and other materials which could be used for military purposes. It also restricted the deliveries of relief food supplies from the Turkish Red Crescent on which half the Turkish Cypriot population depended for their existence. The Turkish government retaliated by expelling more Greeks from Istanbul, bringing the total of expellees to about 1,000. The property of some 8,000 other Greeks in the city, valued at £80 million, was seized as security for the payment of taxes owed by those deported. The position of these Greeks, who previously numbered about 12,000, had been safeguarded in the Greco-Turkish Convention of 1930 but their expulsion had begun in March a few days after Turkey denounced the Convention. By September 1964, 6,000 Greeks had been expelled and the expulsions continued during the first half of 1965. As part of its reprisals the Turkish government also curtailed the rights guaranteed to Greek-speaking Turkish citizens to maintain their own schools in their own language. The saddest act of this kind was the sudden order closing the Greek orphanage on the island of Prinkipo, near Istanbul. Some 200 children were thrown out at forty-eight hours' notice, and had to take refuge in two neighbouring monasteries. The Greek government, to its credit, did not retaliate against Turkish citizens or the Turkish minority in Greece.

On July 17, the United Nations secretary-general, U Thant, warned the Greek, Turkish and Cyprus governments that their military build-up was increasing the risks of a serious clash. Within three weeks his warning proved justified when the Greek Cypriots decided to launch an attack to cut off the Turkish supply line at Kokkina. The attack was launched on August 6 by strong detachments of the new National Guard armed with 25-pounders, mortars and bazookas. The Turkish Cypriots were driven out of four coastal villages with heavy losses and squeezed into a small beach-head round the village of Kokkina. The Greek attack was made in breach of an agreement with the United Nations commander, General Thimayya of India, who had replaced General Giyani. It is also said to have been made against the advice of the commander of the National Guard, Lieutenant-General Karayannis, a Greek army officer who later resigned and was replaced by General Grivas. Swedish troops of the United Nations force who were watching the Kokkina area were unable to stop the fighting, and Makarios rejected General Thimayya's appeal for a cease-fire.

On August 8, Turkish jet fighter-bombers intervened to check the Greek Cypriot advance. For two days in a series of raids they attacked

Greek positions and villages with high explosives, napalm bombs, rockets and machine-gun fire. The Greek Cypriots reported 300 people killed or wounded and the destruction of several villages. The Security Council was summoned, heard a Greek Cypriot allegation that a Turkish invasion was imminent, and issued a call for an immediate cease-fire. The Greek government promised full support for Cyprus if the Turkish attacks were renewed. The Greek Cypriot leaders gave a warning, through the American embassy in Nicosia, that they would attack and seize the Turkish Cypriot areas throughout the island unless the Turkish bombing stopped. They also said that the appearance of Turkish ships within Cyprus territorial waters would be taken as an invasion signal. This, they reckoned, would give them ninety minutes in which they could complete an all-out assault on the Turkish Cypriot community before the Turkish army landed. Whether for these reasons or because thought to have achieved their objective, the Turkish air attacks were not resumed and the crisis subsided. Not, however, before Makarios had appealed to Russia for help and received a promise of Soviet support if Cyprus were invaded. President Johnson had already, on June 5, 1964, secretly warned Turkey that she could not count on American or NATO support against Russia if she unilaterally took action which led to Soviet intervention.

On August 15, representatives of the Greek and Turkish governments met again with the United Nations mediator in Geneva to resume the search for a political settlement. In Cyprus, Makarios agreed to ease the economic blockade of the Turkish Cypriots. Restrictions on food supplies were lifted and imports of petrol and oil were allowed for distribution under United Nations supervision. By the end of the month the Geneva talks had ended with the death from a heart attack of the UN mediator, Tuomioja, and the rejection by Makarios of the proposals for a political settlement put forward by the American diplomatist, Dean Acheson. Instead the archbishop secured the agreement of the Greek government to raise the Cyprus question at the United Nations General Assembly on the basis of 'unfettered' independence with minority rights for the Turkish Cypriots.

U Thant appointed an Ecuadorian diplomatist of talent and experience, Galo Plaza, to succeed Tuomioja as the United Nations mediator. A new and quieter chapter opened in the affairs of Cyprus. The Kokkina affair had been a chastening experience for all concerned. With an eye on future support in the General Assembly, both sides showed greater respect for the United Nations and tried to be on their best behaviour. The Greek Cypriots gave up what thoughts they may have had of forcing a fait accompli by military or economic means. The Turkish Cypriots abandoned, for the time being, their hopes of a Turkish invasion. While both sides set themselves to build up diplomatic support, the island settled down to wait.

The balance of forces which had been established in Cyprus by the summer of 1964 was to continue with little change for at least another year. It was a balance which varied a great deal throughout the island.

The main Turkish stronghold was an enclave comprising the Turkish quarters of the old city of Nicosia, part of the city's north-western suburbs and a bulge of countryside stretching some fifteen miles northwards on either side of the Kyrenia road across the mountains to the outskirts of Kyrenia itself. There were lesser strongholds in the Turkish quarters of the ports of Famagusta and Larnaca, in the town of Louroujina on the central plain halfway between Larnaca and Nicosia, and in a series of smaller enclaves and beach-heads on the north-west coast. In the words of a United Nations report, all these enclaves were ringed by fortified positions manned by Turkish Cypriot fighters who enforced their exclusive control by force of arms against any attempted encroachment by the Cyprus government; facing them were similar government positions. The United Nations force was present or interposed in most of these places. Inside all these areas, in which about half of their population was concentrated, the Turkish Cypriots exercised complete military and administrative control. Access to them was completely blocked to government troops, police and officials and to Greek Cypriots in general, except for travel on the Kyrenia road and across the Limnitis area on the north-west coast in convoys escorted by the United Nations. Within the main Nicosia enclave were gathered most of the 25,000 refugees from ninety-four Turkish or mixed villages in Greek-held territory. The Turkish army contingent was also stationed inside this enclave and held positions controlling the Kyrenia road. A neutral zone manned by United Nations troops separated Greek and Turkish fortified positions in Nicosia. Inside the old city of Nicosia were the headquarters of the Turkish Cypriot leadership under Küchük and of the Turkish Cypriot forces: a combination of police, gendarmes and irregulars of the TMT, stiffened by specialists recruited from Turkey. Within the Turkish quarter of the capital were also a number of important government buildings and facilities, including the Ministry of Justice which contained all the official legal records, such as wills, birth and marriage certificates and the Land Registry. The Turks refused to let these documents be taken away. The lack of them was a serious handicap to the administration of the Greek areas of the island.

The main public services, such as electricity and the postal, telephone and telegraph services were in Greek hands, made available to the Turkish enclaves only on sufferance. The Turks were receiving no employment, salaries or revenue from government sources; many of their farms had had to be left to be worked by Greeks; and 56,000 out of a Turkish population of 116,000 were living off relief supplies from Turkey. Half of the Turkish Cypriot population was still living outside the enclaves under exclusive Turkish control and, in some of the scattered areas in small towns and villages still inhabited by Turkish Cypriots, the influence of the Turkish Cypriot leadership was still felt, despite the government's overall control. Both the government and the Turkish Cypriots maintained restrictions on freedom of movement for their opponents, despite efforts by the United Nations to persuade them to restore normal conditions. The Turkish Cypriots were also restricted by their own leadership which was trying to prove that coexistence with the Greeks was no longer possible and that only geographical separation of the communities would work. Turkish Cypriots leaving the main Turkish enclaves had to have exit permits: obedience was enforced when necessary at the point of a gun.

By far the greater part of the island was in Greek Cypriot hands. Except for the absence of young men on military service, the Greek-held area showed few signs of the conflict in its everyday life. The government functioned smoothly, except for such problems as the absence of some official records. The economy had suffered less than was feared, though the new burden of military expenditure posed a serious problem for the future. There were anomalies, too, in Greco-Turkish relations. In certain areas, such as Nicosia, the separation of the two communities was complete. But in Limassol, for example, there was some freedom of movement and contact between the two sides. This was partly due to the quality of the local leadership, both Greek and Turkish. Then, even in Nicosia, the judges on both sides still met and worked together. The Greek Cypriot rump in the House of Representatives had passed a bill abolishing the separate administration of justice set up under the 1960 agreements, and created a unified legal system. The High Court and Constitutional Court were merged into a single Supreme Court and the neutral presidencies were abolished. A Turkish judge was appointed chief justice and president of the Supreme Court. The new chief justice and his Turkish colleagues continued to hear cases in the higher courts located in the Greek part of Nicosia. They had special UN escorts from their homes in the Turkish enclave to the courts.

By the summer of 1965 the local military balance had tipped heavily in favour of the Greek Cypriots. They had some 14,000 conscripts in the new National Guard, largely organised and trained by Greek army officers. In addition, there were 5,000 Greek Cypriot police together with the volunteer militia in the villages. Estimates of the number of Greek regular troops on the island varied from 3,000 to 10,000. The Greek Cypriots had also acquired considerable quantities of new arms, including heavy equipment, from Greece and from Russia as a result of an arms deal in the autumn of 1964. According to some reports, arms had also been supplied by Egypt. The new weapons were said to include tanks, anti-aircraft guns and Soviet anti-aircraft missiles, though there was no confirmation that the missiles had actually arrived in Cyprus. The Turkish army probably had about 1,000 men in Cyprus and the Turkish Cypriots some 12,000 men under arms.

But if the Greeks had local military superiority, this had to be set against Turkey's much greater overall strength in any general Greco-Turkish conflict. Turkey's position was stronger geographically. Only forty miles from the Turkish coast, Cyprus was within easy striking distance of Turkish aircraft and invasion forces. Greece was 500 miles away—too far for quick reinforcement or for jet-fighters operating from bases in Greece, or even from the nearer Crete. Turkey had a population four times that of Greece, and an army of about 500,000 men compared with the Greek armed forces' 165,000. The air forces of the two countries were more evenly balanced in numbers with each side having about 400 operational aircraft. In naval power neither side had a decisive advantage. These were facts which could not be ignored in the search for a political settlement of the Cyprus problem.

After the failure of the London conference, the next attempt at negotiation was the two rounds of talks held in Geneva in the summer of 1964 under the chairmanship of Tuomioja, the United Nations mediator. They were attended by representatives of the Greek and Turkish governments, with Dean Acheson, special envoy of President Johnson, and Lord Hood of the Foreign Office, holding watching briefs on behalf of the United States and Britain. The basis of the talks was a set of proposals put forward by Acheson. The United States had become concerned at the possibility (never very serious) that Cyprus might become a 'Mediterranean Cuba'. Washington was perturbed by the close links Makarios had built up with Nasser and the non-aligned camp, by his readiness to rely on Russian support and his rejection of NATO, and by the strength of the Greek Cypriot communists. The Americans came to the conclusion that enosis was the best answer to these fears. It would bring the Greek Cypriots under the control of Greece and so into NATO. Moreover, enosis was also what the Greek Cypriots said they really wanted. But what about Turkey? There had to be some balm for her pride, some reassurance for her security fears and some guarantees for the rights of the Turkish Cypriots. Ankara still insisted that, short of outright partition, Turkish troops must stay in Cyprus with their treaty rights of intervention, and the Turkish Cypriots must have self-governing cantons in which they could be concentrated.

The first 'Acheson plan' was an attempt to bring all these elements together. It proposed the union of Cyprus with Greece, except for an area in the north-east of the island which would become a military base area under Turkish sovereignty. Inside the Greek area of the island there would be one or two Turkish cantons with local autonomy. Those Turkish Cypriots who wished to leave Cyprus would receive compensation. In addition, Greece would cede to Turkey the small island of Castellorizon off the Turkish coast.

The Turkish government under Ismet Inönü accepted the plan as a basis for negotiation. But it wanted the sovereign base area in Cyprus to be large enough to form a sanctuary for most of the Turkish Cypriot population. In other words, it saw the plan as another variant of partition or 'double enosis' and the bargaining as centred on the size of the Turkish area. This was also the way the Greek government and the Greek Cypriots saw the plan, and for that reason found it unacceptable. The breakdown of the first round of talks was followed by the Kokkina battle and the Turkish air attacks on Cyprus.

When the talks were resumed in August, Acheson put forward a revised version of his plan. The main change, as recounted to the author by Ismet Inönü in June 1965, was that the Turkish base area would not be under Turkish sovereignty but would be leased to Turkey for a term of twenty to twenty-five years. This was rejected both by the Turks and Makarios, although the Greek government saw it as a possible basis for discussion. With Makarios determined to seek the backing of the United Nations Assembly for his claim to 'unfettered' independence, the Americans decided to leave the search for a solution in the hands of the new UN mediator, Galo Plaza, at least until the question had gone through the Assembly.

By the end of 1964, Galo Plaza had completed a series of talks with all the parties concerned but was holding back his report until the Cyprus debate at the United Nations was over. It was generally thought that the Greek Cypriots would get less clear-cut support from the Assembly than they expected; some of the Afro-Asian countries had already made their backing for Cyprus independence conditional on its not leading automatically to enosis. Turkey's hopes of doing well out of the Assembly had also been raised high, probably too high, by her rapprochement with Russia which had begun to develop in the autumn of 1964. In an exchange of visits between the Turkish and Soviet foreign ministers, Russia had assured Turkey of her friendly intentions and had signed a communiqué which appeared to support the Turkish case for two separate communities in a federal state in Cyprus. On the Russian side it was an obvious move to counter the American support for enosis and to exploit Turkish resentment of the United States. For the Turks it was the climax of Inönü's policy of improving relations with Russia and moving away from Turkey's inflexible commitment to the West. Inönü believed that this inflexibility had robbed Turkey of room for diplomatic manoeuvre over Cyprus and other matters.

These hopes of each side about the 1964–65 Assembly were not put to the test. The Assembly session never got properly under way because of the dispute over financial contributions to the cost of UN peace-keeping operations; one result of this was that Cyprus was not debated. Consequently on March 26, 1965, after a further round of talks, Galo Plaza submitted his report to the secretary-general and it was then published. In this report, the mediator recognised that there had been no progress towards a settlement and he deliberately took the risk of going beyond his strict terms of reference to suggest an outline solution of his own to replace the Zürich and London agreements. The main points of Plaza's plan were:

1. Cyprus should remain an independent state and should voluntarily renounce its right to choose union with Greece.
2. The island should be demilitarised, the question of the British sovereign bases being left aside for further consideration.
3. There should be no partition or physical separation of the Greek and Turkish communities, but Turkish Cypriot rights should be

guaranteed by the United Nations and supervised by a United Nations commissioner in the island.

4. A settlement must depend in the first place on the agreement between the people of Cyprus themselves and talks should take place between the Greek and Turkish Cypriots.

The Galo Plaza plan had a generally sympathetic reception from Greece and a rather more tepid one from the Greek Cypriots. Makarios objected to the proposed surrender of the right to choose enosis and his military advisers argued that Cyprus could be safely demilitarised only if it were united with Greece. A demilitarised, independent Cyprus would be defenceless and a dangerous temptation—'a feather floating on the waves' was how Georgadjis, Greek Cypriot minister of the Interior, described it to the author. The Turkish government of Urguplu, which had taken over from Inönü, was a caretaker administration to fill in the gap until the next election in October 1965. A weak government, conscious of the army in the background, it felt obliged to take a strong line in public over Cyprus. It not only rejected the Galo Plaza plan outright but also rejected Galo Plaza himself as a future mediator, proposing instead direct talks between Greece and Turkey.

This proposal, strongly opposed by Makarios, was taken up by the Greek government at the meeting of NATO foreign ministers in London in May 1965. The Greek and Turkish foreign ministers met in London and agreed to continue talks through diplomatic channels. The Greek government was induced to take part in the talks partly as a result of pressure from the United States and other allies, but also as a result of the increasing strain in its relations with Makarios. Greece found herself more heavily committed than ever before to defending the interests of the Greek Cypriots but without any comparable increase in her influence over or control of the policies of the Cyprus government. To the Turks it seemed inconceivable, but the fact was that, despite the presence of several thousand Greek troops in Cyprus, Archbishop Makarios was far from being a Greek puppet.

The power of the Greek government to influence Makarios was further weakened in the latter half of 1965 by a prolonged political crisis in Athens. The crisis also led to the petering out of the Greco-Turkish talks. A conflict of authority between the prime minister, Papandreou, and King Constantine over the political control of the armed forces brought about the prime minister's resignation and a split in the left-centre coalition which he led. The king's intervention, denounced by Papandreou and many of his supporters as unconstitutional, provoked repeated and large-scale riots in which leftwing organisations played a prominent part. Stefanopoulos, the former deputy prime minister, eventually succeeded in forming a government with the help of those deputies of the centre who had been alarmed by the evidence of revived leftwing militancy in the support for Papandreou. While in Greece a weak government succeeded one which had been broadly based, in Turkey a caretaker government gave way to one with a more solid mandate. In the elections of October 1965, the Justice Party was returned to power with a clear majority over its chief rival, the Republican People's Party, and its leader Süleyman Demirel, became prime minister. The new Turkish government soon faced a diplomatic set-back over Cyprus.

In December 1965 the Makarios government succeeded in securing the adoption by the United Nations Assembly of a resolution which appeared to support its claim for the 'unfettered' independence of Cyprus and to discount the Turkish claim to the right of intervention based on the Zürich and London treaties. Makarios had prepared the ground by submitting a declaration on minority rights in Cyprus which was closely in line with the proposals of the UN mediator. The Assembly's resolution, after noting this declaration, went on to take 'cognizance of the fact that Cyprus should enjoy full sovereignty and complete independence without any foreign intervention or interference', and called on 'all states to respect the sovereignty, unity, independence and territorial integrity of Cyprus'. However, the force of the resolution was weakened by the fact that, although it was carried by 47 votes against 5, there were 54 abstentions. Britain and Russia were among those who abstained. The United States voted against. Nevertheless, the passing of the resolution aroused angry protests in Turkey. The British abstention was bitterly criticised by the Turks, who felt that Britain, as one of the signatories of the Cyprus treaties, should have supported them more strongly in defending the validity of the treaties. Shortly after the resolution was passed the UN mediator, Galo Plaza, resigned, since it had become clear that Turkey would not relent in rejecting his good offices.

Thus out of the see-saw of Greek and Turkish policies during 1965, only Makarios seemed at the year's end to have gained some slight advantage.

CHAPTER SIXTEEN

Lessons and Pointers

WHATEVER THE CHARACTER of the Cyprus dispute may have been in the past, it has now become primarily a problem of Greco-Turkish relations. Britain's decision to give up her sovereignty except over the small base areas meant that she would accept any settlement of the dispute which was agreed to by Greece and Turkey. She no longer had a direct interest of her own in the status of the island—apart from the general interest of ensuring that it should not be controlled by a hostile power. She was even ready to reconsider the position of her sovereign base areas if it appeared that they were standing in the way of a general settlement.

It may be asked whether the British surrender of sovereignty was bound to bring the Greeks and Turks face to face in a dangerous confrontation, or whether the crisis which arose at the end of 1963 could have been avoided. Such questions are, of course, always easier for the historian to answer confidently in calm retrospect than for a statesman faced with complex decisions in the heat of action. Any change in the status of Cyprus which gave greater dominance to the Greek Cypriot majority, or brought closer their union with Greece, would inevitably have aroused bitter opposition from the Turkish Cypriots and deep concern on the part of the Turkish government. But, even allowing for the wisdom of hindsight, it is arguable that neither of these factors would have led to a dispute of such intensity if Britain had been able to take a broader view of her own interests and responsibilities in the Eastern Mediterranean, and if she had recognised that minimising Greco-Turkish friction was more important, even for herself, than the retention of British sovereignty over Cyprus.

At the end of both the first and second world wars, Britain had reasonable chances of making a bilateral settlement with Greece, or the Greek Cypriots, on the future of Cyprus without risking a major crisis with Turkey. After the first world war, when Turkey lay defeated, and even later when Ataturk had driven the Greeks out of Asia Minor, Britain could have ceded Cyprus to Greece in return for the use of military bases—though at that time she did not even need the bases. Or she could at least have offered Cyprus the same kind of national independence with a bilateral treaty that she conceded to Egypt and later to Iraq. Another opportunity occurred after the second world war when the Dodecanese Islands were given to Greece. Although a similar cession of Cyprus to Greece would have been bitter medicine for the Turks to swallow, it would probably have been swallowed if only because Turkey's record in the war gave her little ground for complaint. After all, Ankara accepted the Greek acquisition of the Dodecanese, which are nearer to the Turkish mainland than Cyprus—though admittedly their Turkish population was smaller than that of Cyprus. Britain's power was temporarily supreme in the Near East and Turkey herself was absorbed both in her domestic democratic revolution and in working her passage back to the Western alliance. An Anglo-Greek agreement on Cyprus would have brought a less violent reaction then than later on. Turkey at that time needed the help and alliance of the West so badly that it is unlikely that she would have renounced them because of Cyprus. It would, of course, have been incumbent on Greece to do everything in her power to convince Turkey of her good intentions by a generous treatment of the Turkish minority and the demilitarisation of the island, as in the case of the Aegean Islands.

The failure to settle the Cyprus issue, when a settlement might have been achieved without serious conflict, was part of a wider tragedy of lost British opportunities in the post-war Middle East. This is not the place to attempt a detailed analysis of recent British Middle East policy; one can only offer some broad observations. Some of the tragedy was inevitable. The dangerous times of a fast-changing and unfamiliar post-war world found successive British governments at grips with problems all round the globe, while Britain herself was struggling to recover from the war and to adapt herself psychologically to the changed pattern of world power. Governments were under conflicting political pressures at home and from allies. There was the sheer intractability of the key problem of Palestine. There were above all those difficulties of timing, with one problem overlapping another, which are the bugbear of diplomacy.

But some of the causes of the tragedy might have been avoided. In saying this one inevitably lays oneself open to the charge of being wise after the event. One can only plead that it is better to be wise afterwards than never to learn anything (and that one did make at least some of these judgements in print at the time). If 'too little, too late' must be the verdict on much of British post-war policy in the Middle East, the reason is to be found not only in the British government's limited freedom of action at vital moments, but also in one basic failure of political imagination and one serious miscalculation.

Britain was able to disengage from the Indian subcontinent and retain India and Pakistan as friends, as members of the Commonwealth (and, in the case of Pakistan, as a military ally), because the freedom she gave them was unconditional. The lesson of India was that, when a relationship can no longer be maintained by force, the only effective alternative is to abandon the attempt at coercion and to try to rebuild the relationship in terms of complete freedom on the basis of common interest. Some of those who helped to form British policy failed to see that this lesson also applied to the peoples of the Middle East. Others who may have seen it nevertheless judged the danger of a Russian military attack on the Middle East to be so great as to make imperative a British military presence there, whatever the damage done to political relationships in that area. This was proved to be a misjudgement not only of Russian policy but also of British military resources.

At the end of the second world war, Britain had the chance—a brief and difficult but real chance—to refashion her relations with the whole of her Middle East shadow-empire: a refashioning in parallel with her successful adjustment of relations with the Indian subcontinent. Quite apart from the new pressures coming from the Middle East countries themselves, the very fact that she was preparing to end her Indian empire made it also imperative that Britain should change her policy in the Middle East. The British did indeed begin a process of change through the negotiation of new bilateral treaties with the Arab states and through the withdrawal from Palestine. But, in the first case, the policy was too timid to meet the demands of the new situation created by the reduction, both relative and absolute, in British power and by the post-war surge of nationalist and anti-imperialist feeling. Instead of the bold break with the past which enabled a fresh start to be made in India, there was a slow, indignant, piecemeal retreat which stirred popular passions on both sides. In the second case, Palestine, where there were grounds for a more gradual and careful withdrawal in the interests of both Jews and Arabs, the British departure was abrupt and disruptive. The two cases, admittedly, reacted on one another in the most difficult way. The British decision to abandon the Palestine mandate was an attempt to escape from the dilemma posed, on the one hand, by the need for alliances with the Arab states and, on the other, by the pressure of the Zionist rebellion backed by influential sections of opinion in Britain and the United States. Yet the very withdrawal from Palestine increased the urgency for a radical revision of British relations with the Arab states, based on readiness to withdraw British forces if necessary. The outcome of the Palestine conflict made it all the more likely that the kind of military treaties the British were seeking—in Egypt, for example—could only be secured by force, but Britain no longer disposed of the power sufficient to ensure that the application of force would not be self-defeating. In such circumstances as Britain's, a military base in the midst of a hostile popuation becomes a liability and not an asset. Instead of contributing to the maintenance of regional peace and stability, the base becomes itself a cause of strife and instability.

Underestimating the strength of Middle East national feeling as against the strength of political pressures at home, and hagridden by the fear of Russian military intervention in the area, post-war British policy failed to give sufficient weight to such considerations: a failure which caused the eventual change of policy in Cyprus, as in the Arab states, to come too late. The misjudgement was less excusable in the case of Cyprus because the British military presence there was not seriously questioned by the Greek Cypriots or by Greece. On the contrary, Athens was ready to offer Britain bases not only in Cyprus but in Greece itself. Greek hostility was directed against Britain's claim that she needed sovereignty over the island for her strategic purposes. It is difficult to avoid the conclusion that the eventual decision to make do with small sovereign base areas instead of the whole island could just as well have been taken ten or more years earlier and that, if it had, much of the strife which led to the Greco-Turkish deadlock could have been avoided. It would have been possible for Britain to concentrate on allaying Turkish fears and building confidence between Greek and Turk before the island had been thrown into turmoil and Turkey had begun to raise the price for her alliance.

Misjudgement, however, was not confined to the British. There is no doubt that the Greek leaders both in Cyprus and in Greece itself consistently underestimated the degree of Turkish feeling about Cyprus and the later strength of Turkey's strategic and diplomatic position. The method of Makarios was to ignore the Turks and to attack the British. Certainly, the EOKA operations hastened the relinquishment of British sovereignty, but they did so in a way which left the more enduring and obdurate problem of Greco-Turkish relations unsolved, and indeed further from solution. The archbishop was slow to grasp the point that, of the two obstacles to enosis—the British and the Turks—the latter were likely to be the more difficult and the less removable. This misjudgement prevented him from perceiving that it would have been wiser to make use of the temporary umbrella of British power in order to establish Turkish confidence and promote an understanding with Ankara.

Makarios, shrewd though he was in recognising and mobilising the appeal of anticolonialism at the United Nations, only partly understood the significance of Britain's post-war colonial policy and the opportunities it offered. This miscalculation is partly explicable on the grounds of the British government's proclaimed determination not to allow Cyprus to follow the same course as other colonial territories, through self-government to independence. But it is probable that, if from the beginning Makarios had concentrated on the broadest self-government with a view to independence rather than on enosis and self-determination, it would have been more difficult for any British government to defend at home the policy of holding on indefinitely to British sovereignty. It was not until 1958, when Cyprus was seriously threatened with partition and after the British had already decided they no longer needed sovereignty, that the archbishop put forward the idea of independence. In the meantime an opportunity for a basically Anglo-Greek settlement, which would have given the Greek Cypriots a chance to consolidate their position, had been missed in the Makarios–Harding talks in 1956–57. The chance was missed partly because of the domestic political pressures on each side but also because of a misunderstanding by each party of the other's negotiating methods. The archbishop mistook the British impatience for hard bargaining; the British misinterpreted the archbishop's slow, step-by-step haggling as insincerity.

This was not the only occasion on which differences of national temperament and tradition, either real or imagined, played their part in aggravating the Cyprus problem and Greco-Turkish relations. Greeks tend to think of Turks as bullies and Turks tend to think of Greeks as cheats. Turks consider themselves as made of sterner stuff than Greeks, and Greeks see themselves as more alert and energetic than Turks. The Turks suffer from physical arrogance and the Greeks from intellectual pride. Yet there are, of course, many brave Greeks and plenty of intelligent Turks who do not conform to the national stereotypes. With the Greeks and Turks the British have had a curious mixed relation. There is something in each people, the imagination of the Greek and the solidity of the Turk, which appeals to different sides of the British character, producing philhellene liberals and poets and turcophil conservatives and men of power.

National temperaments and historical attitudes are two elements which have to be taken into account in assessing the future of Cyprus and of Greco-Turkish relations. This is particularly true of the Turks. For the future of Turkish–Greek relations it is important that a Cyprus settlement should not leave the Turks feeling that they have been duped or unfairly treated. This is important even for Turkey's relations with the West generally, for Turkish national pride is intense and the Turks are still struggling to carry through the westernisation begun or rather accelerated by Ataturk. They are still quick to suspect that the West favours the Greeks in Cyprus, not because it thinks their cause is right, but because the Greeks are more readily acceptable than the Turks as fellow-Europeans.

There are, however, three more basic elements in the Greco-Turkish equation. 1. There are four times as many Greek Cypriots as Turkish Cypriots on the island. 2. Cyprus is ten times further from Greece than it is from Turkey. 3. There are four times as many Turks as there are Greeks. As a Turkish Cypriot leader put it to me: 'Ethnographically our position is weak, geographically it is strong'. Or, as a Greek foreign minister once said: 'The problem is that Cyprus is dominated militarily by Turkey. Put Cyprus in the place of Corfu and I would solve the problem immediately.'

Neither Greece nor the Greek Cypriots alone were strong enough to impose annexation or enosis against the will of Turkey. No great power or combination of smaller powers was prepared to help them to do so. The Western powers would not offend Turkey, and Russia would not help Cyprus to be absorbed into NATO. The non-aligned countries, who are the decisive voting bloc at the United Nations, would support independence for Cyprus but not enosis, which would end Cypriot non-alignment. If the Greeks could not impose enosis, could they buy it? They probably could if they offered Turkey a good enough price. But they claimed that they could not afford the price demanded. The Greek Cypriots refused to pay the kind of territorial compensation required in Cyprus itself under proposals, such as the Acheson plan, which were really a modified form of partition. Greece herself would not or could not offer adequate compensation elsewhere. It was, for example, suggested that Greece might compensate Turkey by the cession of part of Thrace, in which most of the Turkish minority in Greece is concentrated, or by giving up a sizeable island, such as Samos or Mitylene. But many Greeks have now settled in the Turkish minority areas and, Greece points out, Thrace is internationally more sensitive than Cyprus. Any change of frontier there would at once raise demands from Bulgaria, with Russian support. The cession of Samos or Mitylene with their Greek populations would be even more difficult for a Greek government to accept. Another suggestion was that, as part of a settlement, the Turkish Cypriots might be exchanged with the Greek minority in Istanbul and that the Orthodox patriarchate should be withdrawn from that city. Although this idea had some support in Athens, it was never seriously pursued, for no Greek government would wish to be responsible for severing the last historic links with Constantinople. Moreover there would be strong international pressure, on both sentimental and political grounds, to keep the patriarchate in the city where it has been established continuously since the third century AD. There would be the fear, particularly on the part of the Americans, that the removal of the patriarch would diminish his status in the Orthodox world and relatively enhance the international influence of the Russian Orthodox Church.

But, though Turkey was strong enough to prevent enosis except at her own price and Greece would not or could not pay the kind of price expected, the Greeks could at least hope to prevent the partition of Cyprus. For the cost of a Turkish intervention in Cyprus on the scale needed to impose partition against the will of the Greek Cypriots backed by Greece would be too high to make the operation worthwhile. The Turks were not likely to try it so long as the Greeks did not attempt annexation or a large-scale massacre of the Turkish Cypriot community. In this situation, Makarios' policy was to go cautiously, to consolidate the Greek hold on most of the island, to raise the cost of a Turkish invasion by strengthening the Greek defences and to maintain diplomatic pressure at the United Nations. His hope was that in the course of time the resolution of the Turkish Cypriots under semi-siege conditions would gradually weaken and that Turkey herself would become more ready to compromise. He was prepared to wait several years if necessary in order gradually to increase his freedom of action and to establish, at least de facto, the 'unfettered' independence of Cyprus. Then the question of enosis could be looked at again in a new light.

In the island itself the Turks had no ready answer to these tactics.

They could put pressure on Greece, but they had no means of putting pressure on the Greek Cypriots, except by threats of invasion which lost force with every repetition, or by air attacks which it was difficult to repeat except under conditions of extreme provocation. There were, however, the Greeks living in Istanbul, both Greek citizens and Greek-speaking Turkish citizens. The Turks began slowly but systematically to expel the first and to harass the second. There were also the Greek off-shore islands, the Dodecanese and the Aegean Islands, some of them less than five miles from the Turkish coast. The Turks began to spread the word that, if provoked in Cyprus, they would seize some of these islands as hostages. They began to interfere with the traditional fishing rights of the Greek islanders and sent Turkish jets flying low every other day over the airport on Mitylene. The Turkish aim was to force Greece to bring pressure to bear on Makarios to accept a settlement negotiated direct between Athens and Ankara. The Turks believed that Greece could if she wished oblige the Greek Cypriots to obey her. They underestimated the strength of Makarios' position. But because Greece suffered more than the Cypriots from the prolongation of the crisis, the Turkish tactics helped to create friction between Makarios and Athens.

Because this friction centred on Makarios' rejection of proposals such as the Acheson plan, which suggested enosis in return for a Turkish base in Cyprus and other concessions to Turkey, some observers came to the conclusion that Makarios was no longer interested in enosis. This was an oversimplification. Certainly, there were strong economic arguments against enosis but these were not decisive. Some of them could have been answered by the kind of special economic regime granted by Greece to Rhodes. The undoubted aim of the Greek Cypriot leaders was union of Cyprus with Greece, in the same way that Crete had been united. However, they were not prepared to buy enosis in a hurry at a price which they considered would be ruinous to the Cypriots, namely, a thinly disguised partition or the strengthening of the Turkish military presence on the island on a permanent, unchallengeable basis. This was the most serious objection to schemes which implied some form of 'double enosis' or 'partition'.

There were other objections. The original Turkish plan for a 'confederal state' would have created a Turkish Cypriot autonomous state occupying 1,084 square miles or about 38 per cent of the island. This was later reduced to 750 square miles or 20 per cent of the island (only a little more than the 18 per cent Turkish share of the population) behind a line running from the north coast, west of Kyrenia, south-west to include the Turkish sector of Nicosia and then down to the Turkish section of Famagusta on the south-east coast. The Turkish plan would have meant an exchange of population between the Turkish and Greek areas. Some 10,000 Greek families would have had to move out of the Turkish area and would have been replaced by Turks from the Greek area. Turks and Greeks in Cyprus had in many ways remained distinct communities in their language, religion and customs and their close links with Turkey and Greece; but, except for some separate quarters in the main towns, they had not been physically separated. In most of the island, they were closely intermingled. Before the civil war, out of 619 villages, 393 were wholly or mostly Greek, 120 were Turkish and 106 were mixed. Even in the towns where they lived apart, Greeks and Turks often worked in the same places. An upheaval on the scale proposed in the Turkish plan would have had a disastrous effect on the economy and social life of a small island. It is arguable that, even so, partition would have been worthwhile if it produced a lasting stable settlement. But the United Nations mediator came to the conclusion in his report that partition, whether outright or in the disguised form of the Turkish plan, would have created a lasting source of unrest. It would have set up either a new administrative or national frontier of a dangerous and provocative kind.

If outright enosis or partition or the modified forms of them were to be ruled out, what was left? As far as the international status of the island was concerned there was the compromise of continued independence. Within the island there was the problem of satisfying the Turkish community's need for security by some means which neither involved a rigid geographical separation nor paralysed the working of the central government. Above all, there was the question of how independence and the Turkish community's rights were to be guaranteed if the rights of intervention under the 1960 treaties were no longer acceptable.

In his report, Galo Plaza noted that Archbishop Makarios was ready to promise the Turkish Cypriots a charter of individual human rights, to be embodied in the Cyprus constitution. The archbishop also offered them continued communal autonomy in matters of religion, education and personal status and a guaranteed representation in parliament and in the central government. Plaza suggested that, in addition, municipal and other forms of local government could be so organised as to give the greatest possible measure of local autonomy in areas where one community or another predominated. He proposed three forms of guarantee. 1. A demilitarised independent state which voluntarily renounced self-determination: i.e., enosis or partition. (Demilitarisation was accepted by Makarios and agreed to by the Turkish government as meeting Turkey's security requirements.) 2. A United Nations commissioner with a team of observers to watch over the rights of the Turkish Cypriot community for a transitional period. 3. The guaranteeing of the terms of the settlement by the United Nations itself.

But how was this guarantee to be implemented? The mediator did not say.

CHAPTER SEVENTEEN

An Approach to a Solution

CYPRUS IN 1965 was a stalemate between Greeks and Turks which looked as if it could be changed only by force or, in the long term, by a process of attrition. The history of the island and of Greco-Turkish relations in general suggested that, unless some new factor intervened, it would be optimistic to expect a long-term solution which did not involve some separation of Greek and Turkish Cypriots either by partition or by an exchange of populations. Yet there were strong arguments for going on trying to avoid such an outcome.

It was tempting to denounce the current state of Cyprus as another example of the harm wrought by unbridled nationalism, and to sentimentalise over the Pax Britannica, or even over that graveyard peace of the Ottoman empire in its days of decline. But one does not have to be an historical determinist to recognise that nationalism, for all its attendant disasters, was in many ways an essential part of the healthy development of the former subject peoples of the Ottoman empire and, eventually, of the Turks themselves. Equally, the conviction that the old empires were bound to disappear does not preclude recognition of the fact that they also performed some functions so useful that other means must now be found to fulfil them.

Nationalism, like imperialism, had to have its day. It poses old problems in a new form: problems which cannot be solved simply by trying to go back to old methods. Cyprus provides a good illustration of two common and recurrent causes of conflict in the post-imperial era: disputes over minorities within new states; and regional security problems raised by the break-up of old empires. The question now is how to find new ways of dealing with these disputes in their new context.

In suggesting a new approach that might be made to help bring about a compromise solution in Cyprus, short of partition, I am conscious that forecasting the course of the future—especially in regard to a situation as unstable as that of Cyprus—can be even more presumptuous than putting under judgement the events of the past. But I believe that this new approach, even if not applied to or immediately successful in

Cyprus, is one which is bound to be developed in the future to deal with international problems of the Cyprus type. Moreover, the manner in which the Cyprus dispute has evolved, coupled with the comparatively small size of the island itself, has created unusually favourable conditions for trying out a new method.

The positive role of the old imperial powers in maintaining a multiracial or multinational system, and in preserving internal peace over a wide area, has now to be performed by national states co-operating through international organisations. This does not mean that the great powers, who once acted independently, or jointly through the Concert of Europe, in the affairs of the Near East, no longer have any role to play. The United States, Russia and Britain all helped to limit the repercussions of the Cyprus civil war. Yet not only the world political climate but also their relationship with each other now make it desirable for even the greatest powers to act in such disputes, wherever possible, through the medium of international bodies. In some cases these may be regional organisations, such as NATO or the Organisation of American States, the Arab League or the Organisation for African Unity. These regional bodies may need the backing of the United Nations to carry out their tasks. In cases where they are unacceptable as arbiters or peace-keepers—as with NATO in Cyprus—the obligation falls entirely on the United Nations.

The appointment of a United Nations commissioner and a staff of observers to keep a watch on Turkish community rights, as proposed by the UN mediator, Plaza, would be in itself a valuable innovation in dealing with minority problems. But it would be easier to achieve, and also be more effective in practice, if the United Nations had more clearly visible means of supporting the authority of the commissioner and his staff in an emergency, such as a threatened massacre. The same is true of a United Nations guarantee of the demilitarisation and independence of Cyprus.

Might not these visible guarantees formerly provided by Greek, Turkish and British troops on the island now be ensured by the continued presence of a United Nations force? Such a guarantee could be the new factor needed to produce a compromise. A force established on the island on the same kind of semi-permanent basis as UNEF—the United Nations force in the Gaza Strip—could also have a value extending beyond Cyprus itself. It could supplement the role of the Gaza force as a base, and could become a manpower pool and training centre for other United Nations peace-keeping operations, particularly in the

Middle East. The existence of UNEF was of great help in mounting the UN operations in the Congo and the Yemen.

Cyprus could also open up another new possibility for the United Nations. If the United Nations force were to take over one or both of the British sovereign areas in the island by agreement with both Britain and Cyprus, it would acquire a base for international peace-keeping operations from which it could not be removed at the demand of a single national government.

It may fairly be objected, first, that there is no such thing as United Nations sovereignty which could be exercised over these areas and, secondly, that Britain still needs the bases. As to the first point, the United Nations tenure of the base areas could be simply an extended form of the extraterritoriality already enjoyed by the United Nations headquarters in New York. As for the second, the Cyprus bases are losing their importance for Britain; a British government looking desperately for ways of cutting overseas defence expenditure would soon regard them as expensive luxuries. The army base at Dhekelia is intended to provide troops and supplies for intervention in support of British treaty obligations in the Persian Gulf. It is also intended theoretically to back up the tripartite declaration of 1950, guaranteeing the Arab–Israel armistice lines. But the base is no longer needed for these purposes. In so far as support is still needed in the Persian Gulf since Kuwait became independent, it has recently been provided from Aden and in future will probably be given directly on the spot from Bahrein.

Since the British intervention in Jordan in 1958, Britain has let it be known that she considers keeping the peace between Israel and the Arab states and between Jordan and her Arab neighbours to be primarily a job for the United Nations. If the United Nations kept a force in the Dhekelia base it would strengthen its capacity to keep the peace both round Israel's borders and in the Persian Gulf. A final British withdrawal from anachronistic and expensive military commitments round the Arabian peninsula would be made easier.

The other British sovereign area, the air base at Akrotiri, is also obsolescent. Its purpose was to provide a nuclear air strike in support of CENTO (Central Treaty Organisation) in the event of a Russian attack on Persia, and supply a supplementary angle of nuclear attack on southern Russia as part of the general Western deterrent. By the end of the 'sixties Britain will either have ceased to be a nuclear power, or her nuclear bombers will have been replaced by Polaris submarines which can do the same job without the Akrotiri base. Already by 1965 the main nuclear support for CENTO was coming from the American deterrent.

Neither of the two British bases in Cyprus is vital any longer. Dhekelia at least could fairly quickly be made available to the United Nations if necessary. Possibly the biggest obstacle would be money. The financial crisis in the United Nations has left most of the cost of the Cyprus peace-keeping operation to be provided on the precarious basis of voluntary contributions every three months. But the sums involved are still minute compared with the defence budgets of Britain and other powers interested in maintaining peace and stability in the Middle East.

Under the protection of the United Nations, Cyprus might become a bridge between Greeks and Turks instead of hastening their final separation. It could be one of a pattern of mixed states which are needed in the Near and Middle East to overcome the ravages of nationalism. As the Lebanon provides an example of co-operation between Christians and Moslems and Latin and Orthodox, so Cyprus might bring Greek Orthodox and Turkish Moslem together. Perhaps it might in time be joined by another mixed state bringing Jews together with Arabs in a union of Israel and Jordan—though it must be admitted that at present such a prospect is extremely remote.

In the history of Cyprus there were three quiet periods under three empires: the Byzantine Greek, the Ottoman Turkish and, except for its last few years, the British. At those times Cyprus was not in the world's story. Its most lively periods in world politics, though not necessarily its most happy times, have been when it was independent—first in the middle ages under the Lusignan kings and since 1960 as a republic.

The island seems designed for an historic role as a link between the civilisations of West and East and as a 'place of arms' for the Near East. Would it not be wiser for the Cypriots to recognise this destiny by transforming their divided island into a centre for bringing Greek and Turk, Christian and Moslem, democrat and communist together, and by offering it as a place of arms for the new international keeper of the peace, the United Nations? Cyprus would thus have an opportunity to play a role more glorious than that offered through political union with Greece or Turkey, with whom in any case every Greek and Turkish Cypriot will always feel spiritually linked.

Thomas Aquinas wrote for King Hugh II of Cyprus an unfinished treatise on government entitled *De Regno*. Of this, Sir George Hill writes in his *History of Cyprus*: 'It is interesting to find the King of

Cyprus in the thirteenth century singled out as a mark for exhortation by the most distinguished Christian philosopher of his time. . . . It was fondly hoped that the throne of Cyprus was an experimental station in which principles which commended themselves to the active thinkers of their times could be treated with a chance of favourable results.'

The actual results may be a warning to optimists of today, but it would be sad to admit to greater despair than the men of the thirteenth century. Who knows? Perhaps where the Kingdom of Cyprus failed, the Cyprus Republic may surprise us all.

References

INTRODUCTION

1. W. Miller, *History of the Greek People 1821–1921*, p. 96

CHAPTER 1: THE IMPERIAL SANCTUARY

1. Sir Harry Luke, *Cyprus: An Appreciation*, p. 50
2. Ibid., p. 106
3. Doros Alastos, *Cyprus in History*, pp. 61–71
4. Miller, op. cit., p. 2
5. Alastos, op. cit., p. 129
6. Luke, op. cit., p. 39
7. Alastos, op. cit., pp. 154–5
8. Ibid., p. 156

CHAPTER 2: OLD GREEKS AND NEW TURKS

1. Arnold J. Toynbee, *The Western Question in Greece and Turkey*, pp. 111–16
2. J. A. R. Marriott, *The Eastern Question*, p. 99
3. Arnold J. Toynbee, *A Study of History*, Abridgement of Vols. I–IV by D. C. Somervell, pp. 173–4. See also Toynbee, op. cit., pp. 10–11
4. Sir George Hill, *History of Cyprus*, Vol. IV, pp. 2, 18–20
5. Ibid., p. 48
6. Ibid., p. 61
7. Alastos, op. cit., p. 275
8. Hill, op. cit., Vol. IV, p. 319
9. H. A. R. Gibb and Harold Bowen, *Islamic Society in the West*, Vol. I, p. 37 n.
10. Bernard Lewis, *The Emergence of Modern Turkey*, pp. 28, 36
11. Gibb and Bowen, op. cit., Vol. I, p. 159
12. B. Lewis, op. cit., pp. 27–31

CHAPTER 3: GREEK INDEPENDENCE AND TURKISH REFORM

1. Toynbee, *Western Question . . .*, p. 17
2. B. Lewis, op. cit., p. 327
3. George Finlay, *History of Greece*, Vol. VI, p. 16, quoted in C. M. Woodhouse, *The Greek War of Independence*, p. 31
4. Toynbee, *Study of History*, Somervell abridgement, pp. 131–2
5. Woodhouse, op. cit., p. 26
6. Ibid., p. 113
7. Edward S. Forster, *A Short History of Greece 1821–1940*, p. 12
8. B. Lewis, op. cit., pp. 104–9
9. Hill, op. cit., Vol. IV, pp. 122–3
10. Ibid., p. 184

References

CHAPTER 4: BRITAIN'S NEW EMPIRE

1. Marriott, op. cit., p. 214
2. Ibid., p. 214
3. Layard Memoirs, Vol. I, f. 294, quoted in Dwight E. Lee, *Great Britain and the Cyprus Convention Policy of 1878*, p. 75
4. Luke, op. cit., p. 83
5. Hill, op. cit., Vol. IV., p. 295
6. Dwight E. Lee, "A Memorandum Concerning Cyprus" in *Journal of Modern History*, June 1931, pp. 236–41; quoted in R. W. Seton-Watson, *Disraeli, Gladstone and the Eastern Question*, p. 325
7. Lee, . . . *Cyprus Convention*, pp. 110–24

CHAPTER 5: GREEK REVOLT AND TURKISH REVOLUTION

1. Forster, op. cit., p. 27
2. Miller, op. cit., p. 90
3. Ibid., pp. 106–7
4. S. B. Chester, *Life of Venizelos*, p. 71
5. B. Lewis, op. cit., p. 174 et seq.
6. Ibid., p. 192, Lord Kinross, *Ataturk*, pp. 24, 28
7. B. Lewis, op. cit., pp. 201–2

CHAPTER 6: OTTOMAN IMPERIALISM AND HELLENISM: DEATH THROES AND DISASTER

1. B. Lewis, op. cit., pp. 198–200
2. Ibid., pp. 209–15
3. Forster, op. cit., pp. 81–2
4. Chester, op. cit., p. 230; see also Forster, op. cit., pp. 81–2
5. Lord Hankey, *The Supreme Command 1914–1918*, Vol. I, p. 286
6. Ibid., Vol. I, p. 431
7. Asquith Papers, Box IV, f. 78; quoted in Roy Jenkins, *Asquith*, p. 376 and n.
8. Kinross, op. cit., p. 134
9. Ibid., p. 117
10. Frangoulis, *La Grèce et la Crise Mondiale*, Vol. II, p. 190; quoted in A. A. Pallis, *Greece's Anatolian Venture—And After*, p. 108
11. Toynbee, *Western Question . . .*, p. 133
12. Winston Churchill, *The World Crisis*, "The Aftermath", p. 397
13. Kinross, op. cit., p. 277
14. Ibid., p. 314
15. Ibid., p. 339
16. Pallis, op. cit., p. 168
17. Toynbee, *Western Question . . .*, pp. 108–9
18. B. Lewis, op. cit., p. 348
19. Pallis, op. cit., p. 170

CHAPTER 7: COLONIAL INTERLUDE

1. Alastos, op. cit., p. 321
2. Ibid., p. 334
3. Hill, op. cit., Vol. IV, pp. 515–6
4. Sir Ronald Storrs, *Orientations*, pp. 469–70
5. Hill, op. cit., Vol. IV, p. 520

6. Pallis, op. cit., p. 149
7. Forster, op. cit., p. 172
8. Kinross, op. cit., p. 459
9. Pallis, op. cit., p. 152
10. B. Lewis, op. cit., pp. 326–7
11. Ibid., p. 350
12. Geoffrey Lewis, *Turkey*, p. 107
13. Kinross, op. cit., p. 481

CHAPTER 8: WORLD WAR, CIVIL WAR AND AFTERMATH

1. Field-Marshal Lord Wilson of Libya, *Eight Years Overseas 1939–47*, p. 73
2. Ibid., pp. 69 and 74

CHAPTER 9: ENTER—AND EXIT—THE ARCHBISHOP

1. Elizabeth Monroe, *Britain's Moment in the Middle East 1914–56*, p. 209
2. Charles Foley, ed., *Memoirs of General Grivas*, pp. 13–17
3. Ibid., pp. 19–20
4. Ibid., p. 23 et seq.
5. HMSO, Cmd. 9300, p. 12
6. Anthony Eden (Earl of Avon), *Full Circle*, p. 414
7. Ibid., p. 396
8. Foley, op. cit., p. 29
9. Ibid., p. 32
10. Eden, op. cit., p. 400 et seq.
11. Ibid., p. 400
12. Ibid., p. 403
13. Ibid., p. 409
14. Ibid., p. 412
15. Ibid., p. 411

CHAPTER 10: SUEZ, RADCLIFFE AND 'PARTITION'

1. Chatham House Memorandum, *Cyprus: The Dispute and the Settlement*, p. 31

CHAPTER 11: TURKEY TAKES A HAND

1. Foley, op. cit., pp. 121–2
2. Hugh Foot (Lord Caradon), *A Start in Freedom*, p. 159
3. Ibid., p. 150
4. Ibid., p. 168
5. Foley, op. cit., pp. 162–3

CHAPTER 12: HOW THE PEACE WAS MADE

1. Foot, op. cit., pp. 176–7

CHAPTER 13: THE CYPRUS REPUBLIC AND ITS BREAKDOWN

1. A. J. Meyer, *The Economy of Cyprus*, p. 36
2. Ibid., pp. 31–2
3. Charles Foley, *Legacy of Strife*, p. 166

Bibliography

Official Documents, Pamphlets and Other sources

BRITISH

Constitutional Proposals for Cyprus (Radcliffe Report), Cmd 42, HMSO 1956
Cyprus: Correspondence between the Governor and Archbishop Makarios Cmd, 9708, HMSO, London 1956
Cyprus: the London and Zürich Agreements and Report on the Implementation, Cmd 1093, HMSO, London 1960
Parliamentary Debates: Official Report (Hansard)
Proceedings of the Lausanne Conference 1922–23: Turkey N.1 (1923), HMSO, London 1923
Terrorism in Cyprus: The Captured Documents of George Grivas, HMSO, London 1956
Treaty of Lausanne, Treaty Series N.16, Cmd 1929, HMSO, London 1923
Tripartite Conference on the Eastern Mediterranean and Cyprus, Cmd 9594, HMSO, London 1955

GREEK AND GREEK CYPRIOT

Cyprus: A Handbook on the Island's Past and Present, Greek Communal Chamber, Nicosia 1964
Greek Minority in Turkey and Turkish Minority in Greece, Greek Information Services, Athens 1965
Rossides, Zenon, *The Problem of Cyprus,* Athens 1957

TURKISH AND TURKISH CYPRIOT

Federation and the Cyprus Economy, Turkish Communal Chamber, Nicosia 1964
History Speaks: A Documentary Survey of Greek Atrocities against Turks in Cyprus, Nicosia 1964
Looking Back: An Official Briefing, Turkish Communal Chamber, Nicosia 1963
Riza, Halit Ali, *The House of Representatives: the Separate Majority Right,* Nicosia 1963
The Turkish Case, 70–30, and the Greek Tactics, Turkish Communal Chamber, Nicosia 1963
Turkey and Cyprus: A Survey of the Cyprus Question, Turkish Embassy, London 1956
Turks in Cyprus, Nicosia 1964

UNITED NATIONS

Proceedings of the General Assembly and the Security Council, 1954–65
Reports on Cyprus of the Secretary General and the Mediator, 1964–65

OTHER SOURCES

Other sources consulted include the *Annual Register* (London), the bulletins of the BBC Radio Monitoring Service, and various newspapers and journals, in particular *The Times*, *Observer*, *Guardian* and *New York Times*.

GENERAL AND SPECIAL STUDIES

Alastos, Doros, *Cyprus in History*, Zeno Publishers, London 1955
Armstrong, H. C., *Grey Wolf: Mustafa Kemal, An Intimate Study of a Dictator*, Barker, London 1932
Bilge, A. Suat, *Le Conflit de Chypre et les Cypriotes Turcs*, Political Science Faculty, Ankara University, Ankara 1961
Cecil, Lady Gwendolen, *Life of Robert, Third Marquis of Salisbury*, 2 vols., Hodder and Stoughton, London 1921
Chester, S. B., *Life of Venizelos*, Constable, London 1921
Churchill, Winston S., *The World Crisis: The Aftermath*, Macmillan, London 1941; Scribner, New York 1941. *The Second World War*, 6 vols., Cassell, London 1948–52; Houghton Mifflin, New York 1948–53.
Cromer, Lord, *Modern Egypt*, 2 vols., Macmillan, London 1908
Dobell, William M., *A Respite for Cyprus*, Canadian Institute of International Affairs, Toronto 1965
Durrell, Lawrence, *Bitter Lemons*, Faber and Faber, London 1957; Dutton, New York 1959
Eden, Anthony (Earl of Avon), *Full Circle*, Cassell, London 1960; Houghton Mifflin, Boston 1960
Foley, Charles, *Island in Revolt*, Longmans, London 1962. *Legacy of Strife: Cyprus from Rebellion to Civil War*, Penguin, Harmondsworth and Baltimore, Md., 1964
Foot, Hugh (Lord Caradon), *A Start in Freedom*, Hodder and Stoughton, London 1964; Harper and Row, New York 1964
Forster, Edward S., *A Short History of Modern Greece*, Methuen, London 1941; 3rd rev. edn, Praeger, New York 1957
George, David Lloyd, *The Truth About the Peace Treaties*, 2 vols., Gollancz, London 1938
Gibb, H. A. R. and Bowen, Harold, *Islamic Society and the West*, Vol. I, Oxford University Press, London and New York: Part I, 1950; Part II, 1957
Gibbons, H. A., *The Foundations of the Ottoman Empire*, Oxford University Press, Oxford 1916
Grivas, George, *Memoirs*, ed. Charles Foley, Longmans, London 1964; published in the United States under the title, *Memoirs of General Grivas*, Praeger, New York 1965
Hankey, Lord, *The Supreme Command 1914–18*, 2 vols., Allen and Unwin, London 1961; Macmillan, New York 1961
Heyd, U., *Foundations of Turkish Nationalism*. Luzac, London 1950

Hill, Sir George, *History of Cyprus*, 4 vols., Cambridge University Press, Cambridge 1940–52

Hoskins, H. C., *British Routes to India*, Longmans, London 1928

Hurewitz, J. C., *Diplomacy in the Near and Middle East: Documentary Record*, 2 vols., Van Nostrand, Princeton, N.J., 1956

Jenkins, Roy, *Asquith*, Collins, London 1964; Chilmark Press, New York 1965

Jones, Thomas, *Lloyd George*, Oxford University Press, London 1951

Kinross, Lord, *Ataturk*, Weidenfeld and Nicolson, London 1964; Morrow, New York 1964

Kirk, George, *The Middle East in the War 1939–1946*, and *The Middle East 1945–1950*, Oxford University Press for the Royal Institute of International Affairs, London and New York 1952 and 1954

Lanitis, N. C., *Rural Indebtedness and Agricultural Co-operation in Cyprus*, Nicolaou, Nicosia 1944

Lee, Dwight E., *Great Britain and the Cyprus Convention Policy of 1878*, Harvard University Press, Cambridge, Mass., 1934

Lenczowski, George, *The Middle East in World Affairs*, Cornell University Press, Ithaca, N.Y., 1952

Lewis, Bernard, *The Emergence of Modern Turkey*, Oxford University Press for the Royal Institute of International Affairs, London and New York 1961

Lewis, Geoffrey, *Turkey*, 3rd rev. edn, Benn, London 1965; Praeger, New York 1965

Luke, Sir Harry, *Cyprus under the Turks 1571–1878*, Oxford University Press, Oxford 1921. *Cyprus: An Appreciation*, Harrap, London 1957; Roy, New York 1957

Marriott, J. A. R., *The Eastern Question: An Historical Study in European Diplomacy*, 4th edn, Oxford University Press, Oxford and New York 1940

Meyer, A. J., with Vassiliou, Simos, *The Economy of Cyprus*, Harvard University Press, Cambridge, Mass. 1962

Miller, William, *The Ottoman Empire and its Successors 1801–1927*, 4th edn, Cambridge University Press, Cambridge 1936. *A History of the Greek People 1821–1921*, Methuen, London 1922

Monroe, Elizabeth, *The Mediterranean in Politics*, Oxford University Press, Oxford, 1938. *Britain's Moment in the Middle East 1914–56*, Chatto and Windus, London 1963

Pallis, A. A., *Greece's Anatolian Venture—And After*, Methuen, London 1937

Royal Institute of International Affairs, memoranda and briefings published by the Oxford University Press, London: *The Middle East—A Political and Economic Survey*, 3rd edn, 1958; *British Interests in the Middle East—Report by a Study Group*, 1958; *Cyprus—The Dispute and the Settlement*, 1959

Runciman, Steven, *Byzantine Civilization*, Edward Arnold, London 1936; St Martin's, New York 1936. *A History of the Crusades*, 3 vols, Cambridge University Press, London and New York 1952–54

Seton-Watson, R. W., *Disraeli, Gladstone and the Eastern Question*, Macmillan, London 1935

Storrs, Sir Ronald, *Orientations*, Nicholson and Watson, London 1949

Sweet-Escott, Bickham, *Greece: A Political and Economic Survey 1939–53*, Oxford University Press for the Royal Institute of International Affairs, London 1954

Temperley, H. W. V., ed., *A History of the Peace Conference in Paris*, 6 vols., Frowde with Hodder and Stoughton, for the Institute of International Affairs, London 1920–24

Toynbee, Arnold J., *The Western Question in Greece and Turkey*, Constable, London 1922. *A Study of History*, abridgement of Vols. I-IV by D. C. Somervell, Oxford University Press, London and New York 1947. Ed. of *Survey of International Affairs*, Oxford University Press for the Royal Institute of International Affairs, London: editions of 1925 and 1931

Wilson of Libya, Field Marshal Lord, *Eight Years Overseas 1939–47*, Hutchinson, London 1950

Windsor, Philip, *NATO and the Cyprus Crisis*, Adelphi Papers No. 14, Institute of Strategic Studies, London 1964

Woodhouse, C. M., *Apple of Discord*, Hutchinson, London 1948. *The Greek War of Independence: Its Historical Setting*, Hutchinson, London 1952

Index

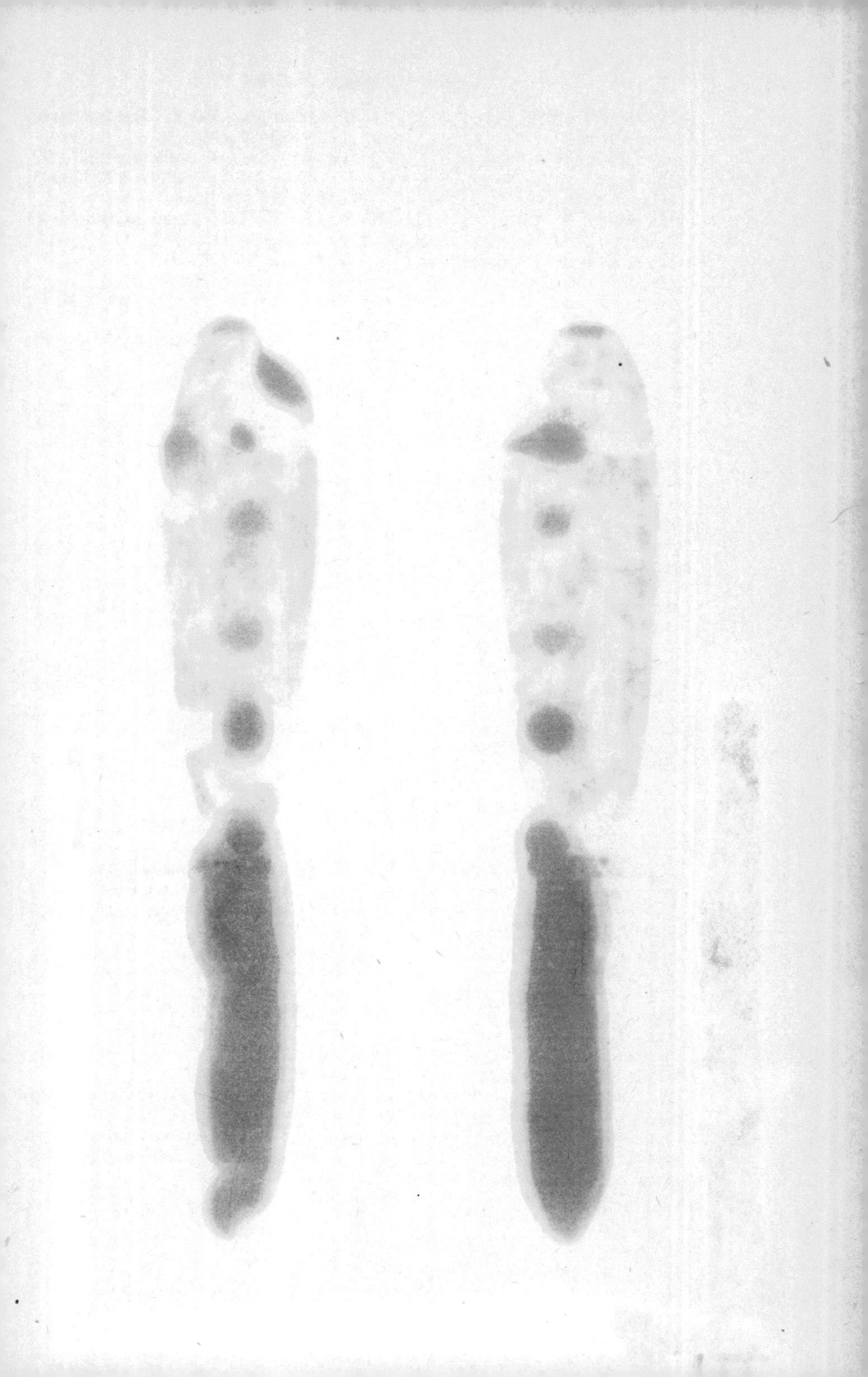